# VIETNAM TODAY AND INDO-VIETNAM RELATIONS

# VIETNAM TODAY AND INDO-VIETNAM RELATIONS

V.D. CHOPRA

GYAN

*on behalf of*
INTERNATIONAL INSTITUTE FOR
ASIA-PACIFIC STUDIES
NEW DELHI

*Published by*

Gyan Publishing House
5, Ansari Road
Daryaganj, New Delhi-110002
Phone: 011-47034999, 9811692060
E-mail: books@gyanbooks.com

*Distribution Network*
gyanbooks.com
India, USA, Canada, UK, Australia, France



ISBN: 978-93-6280-467-9 (PB)

First Published, 2024

*Printed at:* Gyan Press, Delhi.



**Vietnam Today and IndoVietnam Relations**
Author: V.D. Chopra

# CONTENTS

# PREFACE

This book is the product of a collective mind of the outstanding scholars of India and diplomats of the embassy of Socialist Republic of Vietnam in India. The International Institute of Asia Pacific Studies organised a two-day national seminar on "Vietnam Today and Indo-Vietnamese Relations" on December 13 and 14, 1998. The objective of this seminar was to exchange ideas, experiences and assessments with each other with a view to give a fresh look to this theme on the basis of changing realities, both within Vietnam and at the international level in the post— Cold War period including globalisation of economy.

India has traditional, historical, cultural, economic and political ties with Vietnam. These relations were temporarily snapped during the colonial rule, but they were too strong and deep rooted to be eliminated entirely . It was, therefore, natural that with India becoming independent earlier and the defeat of imperialism in Vietnam in 1973, these relations were revived, renewed and reinforced. However, after the disintegration of the Soviet Union and ushering in of the era of globalisation of economy, these relations were not upgraded. The moral of the situation is that it is both in the national interests of India and Vietnam that a new thrust should be given to strengthen the economic relations between the two countries. There is a big lag between strengthening of the mutual economic relations of the two countries and the centuries old ties between these two ancient nations, notwithstanding the fact that both private and public sector enterprises have begun to take keen interest in raising the level of co-operation between the two countries to a higher level.

Economic development is indivisible particularly an era of globalisation of economy and the technical revolution. If there is an element of truth in this assessment, you cannot build a new world economic order in which rich nations are becoming richer and richer and backward nations remain steeped in poverty and backwardness.

This contradiction has to be resolved, because sooner or later, mounting discontent in the poverty stricken nation-states will burst through seams and threaten the world peace. These trends have already begun to unfold themselves. That is why economic relations should be strengthened to eliminate poverty. This factor underlines that the most developed among the developing nations and the most backward developing nations need to evolve new parameters for economic cooperation. It is herein that the new historic significance of elevating Indo-Vietnamese relations lies.

Vietnam is not only geo-politically important counry, it is the second biggest socialist country of the world after China. It has exhibited a remarkable capacity to rise above rigid dogmas and is experimenting with its concept of "socialist oriented market economy" with a free market economy without diluting its basic policy of building a really welfare state. Indo-Vietnamese relations, therefore, have assumed a new historic significance. We hope that this book will stimulate discussion on this aspect both in India and Vietnam.

The Institute is thankful to all the scholars, young and old who have contributed papers to this book after making modifications in light of the discussions in the Seminar. We are also grateful to Prof. V.P. Dutt, former pro-Vice-Chancellor of Delhi University for writing an introduction to this book. The Institute also thanks senior members of the Gyan Publishing House for their co-operation in bringing out this book.

**V.D. Chopra**

Nov. 1999
New Delhi

# PRIMARY DATA ON VIETNAM

Vietnam has the shape of the letter S, is located on the east side of the IndoChinese peninsula in South-East Asia, looking onto the Pacific Ocean and East-Sea (also called South China Sea).

| | |
|---|---|
| Official name | : Socialist Republic of Vietnam |
| Capital city | : Hanoi |
| Land area | : 331,700.00 sq. km² with coastline of 3,260 km mostly sand beached. |
| Two biggest rivers | : Red river and Mekong |
| Population | : 80 millions (Rural : 79%, Urban : 21%) |
| Literacy | : 93% (1998) |
| Administration | : 61 provinces and cities under Central Government; |
| Metropolitan cities | : Ho Chi Minh City : 4.8 mil<br>Hanoi : 3.5 mil<br>Haiphong : 1.5 mil<br>Danang : 0.8 mil |
| Language | : Vietnamese is the only official language. English, French, Russian, Chinese, Khmer and tribal languages are also spoken here. |
| Time difference | : GMT plus 7 hrs; 1.5 hrs ahead of IST |
| Climate | : tropical monsoon-warm weather, high humidity and abundant seasonal rainfall. |
| Weather | : Hottest in June (from 26°C to 30°C);<br>Coldest in January (from 12°C to 20°C);<br>Wettest in August (343 mm average rainfall);<br>Driest in February (18 mm average rainfall). |

| | |
|---|---|
| Religion | : many Vietnamese privately practise Buddhism (85%), Christianity (12%), Confucianism (3%) and other religions. |
| Ethnic groupings | : Vietnamese (90%) and other 52 national minorities. |
| Legal system | : based on people's democratic republic socialist legal theory and state civil law system |
| Weight and measures | : metric system |
| Public holidays | : January 1, National New Year (- Tet- usually in February); April 4 (Emperor-Founder Hung Vuong's Day); April 30 (Liberation Day); May 1 (Labour Day); September 2 (Independence Day). |
| Foreign relations | : Vietnam has diplomatic relations and Ambassadorial level with 167 countries, is a full member of UNO, ASEAN, APEC, IBRD, WB, IMF, ADB, ECOSOC, UNESCO, UNIDO, UNFPA, UNDP, IFC, ISO, ICAO, UNCTAD, WCO, WIPO...; |
| Fiscal year | : January 1 - December 31. Currency : Dong; GDP : about USD 28 billions. Annual GDP growth rate : 1995:9.54, 1996: 9.5, 1997: 9.01, 1998: 6.0. Main industries: cement, chemical, engineering, leather, oil, natural gas, plastics, pulp and paper, textiles. Oil and gas : resources of 4-6 billion barrels, annual export of crude oil : 14.00 million tonnes in 1999. Foreign investors: Leading investors: Singapore, Taiwan, South Korea, Japan, Hong Kong, France, USA. |

**Political System:** Internal : people's democracy, socialist with the vision to build Vietnam into a country of wealthy people, strong nation, just and civilized society; external: independent, self-mastership, international solidarity with progressive mankind, open-door, to befriend with all nations in the world for peace, independence and development.

**Government :** Vietnam is administratively divided into 61 provinces and cities under the direct control of the central authority. Provinces are divided into districts, provincial capitals and towns. The districts are subdivided into communes (that consist of villages) or wards. Municipalities remain under central authority and are branched into precincts and townships, which in turn are mapped into wards.

Local People's Councils are elected by the local population in each area. The Councils have duty to maintain respect of the law and order, to carry out state policies and tasks assigned from above and plans from local decisions. The Local People's Committees are the executive bodies to the Local People's Councils at the same level. Chairman, Vice-Chairman and members of the People's Committees are elected by the People's Councils. General elections are held every five years to elect the National Assembly. National Assembly themselves elects President and elected Premier upon President's proposal; and then elects Deputy Premiers and ministers upon the Premiers proposals.

**Economy :** From Doi Moi in 1986, our country moved from a command economy to market socialist oriented framework. Towards this aim, the state took a number of incremental steps including liberalisation of price control, relaxation of foreign exchange control, adoption of a Foreign Investment Code, etc.

# LIST OF CONTRIBUTORS

| | |
|---|---|
| 1. **V.D. Chopra** | Former Head of Economics Department in West Punjab (now in Pakistan), Former Chief Editor, *Patriot* Daily and *Link* Weekly; Vice-President for International Institute for Asia Pacific Studies. |
| 2. **Dr. V.P. Dutt** | Former Pro-Vice Chancellor, Delhi University, Former Member Rajya Sabha, Leading Expert on International Affairs. |
| 3. **Pham Sy Tam** | Ambassador of Vietnam to India. |
| 4. **Prof. B.D. Arora** | Former Professor, School of International Studies, Jawaharlal Nehru University, New Delhi. Expert on International Affairs. |
| 5. **Dr. Udai Bhanu Singh** | Research Fellow at Institute for Defence Studies and Analyses, New Delhi. |
| 6. **Dr. Ganganath Jha** | Associate Professor in South-East Asian and South-West Pacific Studies of the School of International Studies, Jawaharlal Nehru University, New Delhi. |
| 7. **Nguyen Si Xung** | Minister Counsellor, Embassy of Vietnam in India. |
| 8. **(Ms.) Shankari Sundararaman** | Researcher at Institute for Defence Studies and Analyses, New Delhi. |

| | |
|---|---|
| 9. **Col. Do Tat Thi** | Military, Naval and Air Attache, Embassy of Vietnam in India. |
| 10. **Dr. Parmanand** | Reader in Political Science, SCC & CE, University of Delhi and Hon. Director, South Asian Studies Foundation, New Delhi. |
| 11. **Puja Khattar** | Researcher, Educationist, and Lawyer. |
| 12. **Dr. G.V.C. Naidu** | Fellow at Institute for Defence Studies and Analyses, New Delhi. |
| 13. **Prof. R.L. Varshney** | Former Director, Indian Institute of Foreign Trade. |
| 14. **R.K. Wadhwa** | Associate Professor, Indian Institute of Foreign Trade. |
| 15. **Prof. Shri Prakash** | Director, Academy of Third World Studies, Jamia Millia Islamia, New Delhi. One of the leading experts on economic history and economic development. |
| 16. **Dang Ngoc Hung** | Counsellor, Embassy of Vietnam in India |

# INTRODUCTION

Indo-Vietnam relations is a classic case of India's failure to seize to opportunities. This analyst does not share the views of those who have never seen any virtue in India's foreign policy from the fifties to the eighties. The general course of India's foreign policy was on the right track during this period. But certainly mistakes can be made. Our failure to utilise our opportunity in regard to relations with Vietnam was certainly one such mistake.

We did not appropriately appreciate the importance of India-Vietnam relations for us. There was a time (in the 70s to 80s) when it was entirely feasible to develop a unique and special relationship with it serving their interests, our interests, and the interests of a better balance of forces in the vital South-East Asian region. It was not the lack of goodwill for Vietnam but the inability to muster the determination, even if it meant making some financial and other sacrifices, to translate our strategic vision into reality. Vietnam also needed strategic help from us. They were in urgent need of substantial assistance from India despite the massive flow of funds from the Soviet Union (Present Russia). Undoubtedly the Vietnamese would have welcomed large-scale assistance from India.

A very special relationship could have been forged which would have provided us, as well as Vietnam with new strategic advantages in meeting the pressures of our neighbours, in establishing a friendly presence in the region and in enabling India to function in close concert with one of the important countries of the region. It would have helped both countries to meet the problems and challenges in their neighbourhood.

It should be clear that one is not talking about friendly relations between the two countries, but a special strategic partnership, like the one that has existed between China and Pakistan. It perhaps required a streak of ruthlessness which we have lacked with both its advantages and disadvantages. So far as friendly relations are concerned, they have existed and will exist for a long time.

India could have given the kind of support to Vietnam that China gave to Pakistan. Even as early as the time of the Bandung Conference, China had realized the potential for its own policy in the India-Pakistan conflict. When I was in Beijing in 1956-58, I learnt that the late Prime Minister Zhou Enlai had reported on his return from Bandung to Beijing (the report was also duly circulated in Beijing University where I was an Indian scholar under the exchange of research scholars programme) that the then Pakistan Prime Minister had told him that all the anti-communist noises that he was making at Bandung were really directed against India and that it should not worry China. Gradually the understanding deepened in the ruling circles in China, especially as the relations with India slipped downwards, that Pakistan could be a useful second front against India. From making-up for the weapons and equipment losses in 1965 and 1971 wars, China gave more military assistance to Pakistan than the U.S. did, and went on to provide critical aid to Islamabad in acquiring nuclear and ballistic missiles capability.

We need not have thought of Vietnam as a second front against China, but building up of Vietnam's economic, political and military strength would have provided both countries with counter-balancing relationships in Asia. Let us not forget that for a very considerable period in history Vietnam had to contend with Chinese dominance. History, of course is not static and continues to evolve, but the lessons of history are not easily forgotten and live long in the consciousness of the people. Vietnam too needed balancing relationships to meet its geographically limiting realities. Both countries would have gained in extending each other's leverage in the regional situation.

But then this may be the difference between a dictatorship (even if of the proletariat) and a democracy. A dictatorship can impose sacrifices without having to explain very much, but in a democracy it is not so easy. The costs cannot be transferred on the people without full explanation, which can be sometimes self-stultifying, and without considerable demurring and resistance. Be that as if may, India failed to establish a special relationship with Vietnam, even though their ties remained friendly and cordial.

The Vietnam connection was not a divisive political issue in India. No party opposed it, most had a positive attitude about it. Even though there was change of government in India in December 1989, there was no diminution in the policy of friendship with Vietnam and the level of contacts with Hanoi and Phnom Penh. The new External Affairs Minister, I.K. Gujral, went to Hanoi in April 1990, to participate in the 4th meeting of the Indo-Vietnamese Joint Ministrial Commission and to hold consultation with the Vietnamese leaders. During his visit, India and Vietnam agreed to establish a credit-line of 100 million rupees in 1991, to be mainly used for railways and telecommunications as well as to increase the trade quotas between the two countries.

Gujral also offered the Vietnamese cooperation in whatever field they wanted or "whatever we know about technology and science that is required is always at the disposal of Vietnam, because we want Vietnam to develop fast, to consolidate its economy and for that India will always be willing partner and willing cooperator to try to help Vietnam advance".

The political affinities were also evident from the Vietnamese Foreign Minister's replies to newsmen on the Kashmir issue. Nguyen Co Thatch said that they (Gujral and he) did not discuss much about Kashmir for the sole reason that both sides did not hold differing views. As Thatch put it, in 1980, during his visit to Kashmir, former Prime Minister Pham Van Dong had made it clear that Kashmir was a sacred part of India. "Our stand is clear and unchanged. We support the view that Kashmir belongs to India because this is a just cause".

India had also already established very considerable cooperation in the area of railway construction since 1977, including supply of rolling stock for Vietnam National Railways and training of their technical personnel. This cooperation was reiterated and further expanded during the nineties.

Yet another step forward was taken when the then Commerce Minister, Arun Nehru, visited Vietnam and signed a three year trade protocol which envisaged lifting the trade level from a meagre Rs. 200 million to a target of $100 million annually as soon as possible. India undertook to achieve an import turnover of goods worth $50 million during the first year of the operation of the protocol, gradually stepping up its imports from Vietnam, while Hanoi too decided to strive for an import turnover of a similar volume. In continuation of the spirit of this agreement, India undertook to supply cotton worth $17 million to Hanoi.

India also spudded its first well in oil exploration in Vietnam in mid 1990. Of the total foreign investment in oil exploration in mid 1990, the U.K. contributed a share of 20.8 per cent, France 18.8, Holland 14.3, Japan 14.2 and India 8.4 per cent. It may also be noted that between 1978-90, India had opened a credit-line of some Rs. 850 million in addition to the Rs. 450 million credit offered by the Exim Bank.

Relations continued to be cemented through exchange of visits of dignitaries of both sides. The legendary hero of the Vietnam War of Independence, General Vo Nguyen Giap and Madam Giap, who was a political and social worker in her own right, visited India in January 1991 and equally notably, then President R. Venkataraman went to Vietnam in April 1991.

The change of Government in New Delhi made no difference so far as continuity of ties with Vietnam was concerned. If anything the return of a Congress Government headed by P.V. Narasimha Rao brought greater stability to this relationship. Both economic and political cooperation were further expanded.

In the economic sphere, Vietnam expressed keenness to have an oil refinery with Indian assistance and was ready to supply crude oil to India by adding a four per cent depressant in Vietnamese crude. India too conveyed its interest in the gas project in Vietnam and its capabilities in the field of providing services from preparation of commissioning of the pipe-line system.

The fifth meeting of the Indo-Vietnam Joint Commission took place in New Delhi on 24 March, 1992, identified new areas for cooperation including mining, rock phosphate, rubber plantation and related industries, cotton development, cashew and tea plantation and processing of the transport sector, exploration for natural gas, maritime transport, remote sensing, sugar mills and many others. India also urged Vietnam to examine possibilities for assisting it with restoration of the Cham monuments in central and southern Vietnam that were the symbols of India's cultural interaction with Vietnam. The two sides also expressed satisfaction at the fact that a number of Indian business delegations had visited Vietnam for expansion of economic relations.

Another highlight in the leadership exchanges was new Secretary General of the Vietnam Communist Party Du Muoi's visit from 8-13 September, 1992, accompanied by a large delegation. He was the highest-ranking dignitary to come to India from Vietnam since Ho Chi Minh's visit in 1957. The visit provided the leaders of the two countries an opportunity to exchange views on the international situation, where very considerable propinquity was reflected in the joint statement. The visit pushed the process of cooperation to achieve a new depth as the two sides decided to further strengthen their ties both in political terms and in the economic sphere. The two sides agreed to implement more effectively the existing agreements and to identify more areas and forms of cooperation, with emphasis on joint ventures in the fields of oil exploration, exploiting and processing of minerals, small industry, agriculture and agro-based industries, hotel industry and marine products. They also decided to finalize as soon as possible an air services agreement and an agreement to avoid double taxation.

The relationship remained strong and contacts were maintained at ministrial and other levels. The then Vice-President, K.R. Narayanan, visited Vietnam a year later. He was no stranger to Vietnam, having served there as a diplomat some thirty years earlier. The Indian Vice-President extended full support to the economic reforms programme now underway in Vietnam, or "creative renovation", as it was often described in Vietnam, and endorsed its foreign policy of independence, openness and diversified relations, as also Vietnam's efforts to strengthen relations with South-East Asian nations. General Secretary Du Muoi in his meeting with Narayanan affirmed Vietnam's support to India's quest for a permanent seat in the UN Security Council. He also reiterated the Vietnamese position that Kashmir was an integral part of India.

The Vietnamese desired the shifting of the focus in their ties to the economic dimension. This was reportedly indicated to the visiting Vice-President by the Vietnamese Prime Minister, Vo Van Kiet. The Vietnamese, while welcoming joint ventures with India, were keen to obtain not just technical and technological assistance, but investment of Indian capital too. They were greatly in need of capital investment, since it was extremely difficult for them to raise their own funds for joint ventures. India's trade with Vietnam by the end of that year was constituted by exports worth $22 million and imports worth $52 million. Exports jumped to Rs. 184 crore in 1994-95 and Rs. 412 crores in 1995-96, while imports remained marginal.

India-Vietnam ties received a further boost when Prime Minister Narasimha Rao made a call at Hanoi a year later, pledging to lift India's friendly relations with Vietnam to a new level by giving them a strong and meaningful economic content. He told his Vietnamese counterpart at a banquet hosted by the latter that India was "fully ready to be a partner in Vietnam's development". On his part the Vietnamese Premier Van Kiet extended Hanoi's support to India to expand its activities and enhance its role at the United Nations and welcomed India's efforts at participating in the activities of the nations in the Asia-Pacific region in particular and in the world as a whole. This was significant in view of the fact that Vietnam was a candidate for ASEAN membership and India was striving to forge a closer relationship with ASEAN and with other Asia-Pacific forums.

By this time even the business community had woken up to the business possibilities in Vietnam whose economy had begun to take a turn towards a thriving development. A large representative business delegation accompanied the Prime Minister to Vietnam (of course they were also going to Singapore, which was the Prime Minister's next port of call). The business delegation led by R.P. Goenka, signed six joint venture agreements worth $158 million with Vietnam. The agreements included transmission tower manufacturing and turnkey transmission line, assembly of railway coaches, generation of power and fertilizer from municipal wastes, a sugar mill and truck tyres.

It should, however, be mentioned that for all the goodwill, India had by the end of 1995, just one joint venture with Vietnam under implementation with an equity participation of Rs. 5.5 crore; but altogether six had come up by now.

Summing up, it would be appropriate for India to put a high value on relations with Vietnam, both for their own sake and for the sake of a healthier balance in East Asia. Vietnam has been passing through a transitional phase. Vietnam was equally subject to the winds of change that blew over and shook socialist countries, the stagnation of a highly centralized economy and the demand for political change. Vietnam had to launch upon its own version of reforms, with its buzz word *doi moi,* often translated as transformation, new way or radical change.

Even while the economy showed a rapid recovery, reforms ran into heavy political weather for both political and economic reasons. There were divisions within the Communist Party over the nature and pace of reforms. Hanoi's excruciating dilemma was strongly reminiscent of the debates in Beijing, both leaderships finally deciding to curtail political change, hoping to contain the problems through economic liberalization and the attendant improvement of living conditions.

As in China, cadre corruption, inflation and inefficiency have plagued the system. The strong link between political and economic change cannot be severed so easily. Furthermore, economic transformation requires a structural change which is inevitably agonizing and an agonizingly prolonged process.

In any case in this transitional phase Vietnam requires large doses of foreign assistance both in terms of capital and technology for the construction and modernization of its infrastructure. India could not have met all its needs but could have done better than it has done. It can still play a useful role in Hanoi's economic development and in balancing its dependence on other countries.

Vietnam is an important balancing force in East and South-East Asia. It resisted the American efforts to dominate the region and subsequently frustrated the Chinese attempt to establish their hegemony. A strong Vietnam complements India's interest in the region. Earlier the ASEAN countries were wary of Vietnam because of the presence of Vietnamese troops in Cambodia and its bid to form an Indo-China federation. With the withdrawal of troops and abandonment of any plans to bring together organizationally the countries of the peninsula, the way was cleared for closer relations with other South-East Asian countries.

Not only has Vietnam become a full member of ASEAN, but the economic opportunities there are attracting worldwide attention. Thailand and Indonesia were making serious efforts at a substantial presence, Japan has moved in a big way, and even the United States, shedding its inhibitions, is eyeing Hanoi's economic potentialities. It was clearly in India's interests to keep expanding extensive relations with Hanoi, secure as much coordination as possible and not be marginalized in the emerging situation.

**V. P. Dutt**

# 1

# PHYSIOGRAPHY AND ECONOMIC RESOURCES

**V.D. CHOPRA**

The Socialist Republic of Vietnam stretches along the eastward limits of the Indochinese peninsula, acting as a border to the continent. Its uninterrupted range of mountains and hills in the west form its spine, from which the land falls away to the Eastern Sea and the vast Pacific. The coastal area is over 3,260 km long, and there is about 3,750 km of land border— 1150 km with China, 1650 km with Laos, and 950 km with Cambodia, a very long border compared to the country's surface area. This geographical feature of Vietnam and its long history had its own impact on country's geopolitics and pace of economic development. This continues to play an important role, particularly its long border with China and its geopolitical location. In this sense, both geography and rich economic resources continue to be important factors. It is a strange paradox that Vietnam is a rich country inhabited by poor but proud people.

However, Vietnam's borders can hardly be described as natural borders, since the mountains and rivers cross in and out of the various national territories. On the one hand, this has facilitated trade and cultural exchanges with other Asian countries, as well as with the rest of the world. On the other hand, defence and national security are made more complex.

Vietnam is in the intertropical zone, situated in the centre of South-East Asia. Its territory lies closer to the Tropic of Cancer. The furthest point north in Vietnam is 23°22N, and south 8°30N, while its easternmost and westernmost points are 102°10 and

109°21E. Thus, the land territory excluding the Hoang Sa or Paracels at 113°30E, the Truong Sa or Spartleys at 117°E, and the islands lying south of Ca Mau Cape, all of which are far-flung islands, come under Vietnamese sovereignty, according to official documents of Vietnam. The total area of the country is about 331,700 sq. km, three quarters of which is mountains and hills, and the rest coastal plain.

Vietnam is the fourth largest south-east Asian country after Indonesia, Myanmar, and Thailand. It is also the second largest of the world socialist country after China. Before the disintegration of the USSR, it was the fourth largest socialist country of the world.

Vietnam's subsoil contains all the minerals necessary for industrialization: oil, coal, iron, tin, bauxite, copper, chrome, apatite, and other rare, non-ferrous metals.

There are 16 million hectares of forest land, comprising thousands of plant, animal and bird species, with many rare species.

Valuable commercial crops are grown mostly in the hilly and high plateau regions, which include coffee, tea and rubber. There are nine million hectares of arable land, the largest expanse being the vast fertile plains of Nam Bo (6 million hectares) and Bac Bo (15 million hectares), which include the Makong and Red river deltas respectively, and are admirably suited to growing cereal and orchard crops. The country's myriad rivers, streams, channels and the East Sea abound with fish and other marine products.

The span and the complexity of Vietnam's geological history, its pattern of orogenesis, and magnetic effects have endowed the country with a rare concentration of mineral wealth for a country of its size. There is much first-bearing carbonaceous rock, and metals of all kinds including rare deposits. The survey and evaluation work on these reserves is as yet incomplete.

The coal fields are concentrated in the North, where the formation of the geosynclines was gradual and where the movements of the Mesozoic era were especially strongly felt. The north-eastern region is richest in minerals. The following deposits have been known and exploited for some time:

(i) Wolfram, tin and the granite in the mountainous Phia Uac while other sedimentary seams are buried in muds 40 meter thick;

(ii) Lead, zinc and silver are found in the region of Cho Dien, Ngan Son, Lang Hit and Thanh Moi, most in sedimentary, schistous and calcareous strata;

(iii) Antimony in Ha Tuyen and Cao Lang provinces;

(iv) Mercury in Ha Tuyen province;

(v) Gold in Cao Lang and Bac Thai provinces;

(vi) Magnetite in Bac Thai and Cao Lang provinces;

(vii) Pyrite in Cho Dien and Cho Don;

(viii) Nickel and asbetos in Cao Bang;

(ix) Sedimentary manganese, bauxite and lignite in Cao Lang province;

(x) Apatite in Lao Kai;

(xi) Coal in Thai Bguyen and Quang Ninh.

Oil and natural gas have been also found.

The Northwest is no less rich in minerals than the Northeast, but the survey work there is only at its initial stage. The most important mining area in the region is located in the Da river syncline between the Song Ma mountain ridge and the Hoang Lien Son range; here Mesozoic orogenesis was powerful resulting in numerous deposits of acid and basic magma. In the Da river syncline, silver, lead, copper, nickel, iron, antimony and rare metals bituminous coal and bauxite are to be found. The Dien Bien-Lai Chau belt is also rich in mineral polymetals, copper, cassiterite, nickel, gold etc.

The Moung Lat Thanh Hoa and Ca river belts, the magma massifs of Bai Thuong and Cua Rao, and the Hong Linh, Thanh Hoa and Nghe Tinh hills also contain precious minerals, chromium, manganese, cassiterite, gold, coal, and lignite deposits.

It shows that Vietnam is not a very large country, but her natural surroundings are remarkably varied: high mountains, deep bays, fertile plains. Her vast mineral, forest, agricultural and maritime wealth underline Vietnam's economic potential.

Different regions of the country complement each other in natural resources, making a unified entity in the intertropical zone with a hot and humid monsoon climate. From Dong Van to Can Mau, and from the coastline to the summit of the Fan Si Pan, trees are green, and flowers and fruits abound all the year round. The short winter in the North, or the cold that prevails in the high mountain zone whose altitude is rarely over 1000 metre, corresponds to the summer and autumn of temperate countries. Thus, the cold does not hinder plant growth; on the contrary, it enriches Vietnam's national wealth with a whole series of products of the equatorial, tropical, subtropical, and temperate zones. The apparent variety of the relief, nevertheless, masks the close connections between the different elements of its infrastructure. The plains are but continuations of the mountains and hills, and the deltas at the estuaries are the prolongations of river valleys. The river alluviums encroach upon the sea steadily, pushing the coastline farther and farther out into sea. What is today the sea coast will tomorrow become the plain, just as the plains of today were formerly shallow bays. The coastal plains which run from Mong Cai south to Ha Tien provide easy communication between the regions. The overland route, the railway, and the sea route run parallel north to south. From the sea coast to the mountain hinterland, the network of river valleys has always served as both penetration and communication routes. A dense road network is stretching its tendrils over the territory, reaching the remotest districts and villages of the mountain regions and allowing the transport of the riches from the uplands to the plain and the deployment of massive contingents to planned new economic zones.

The historic Ho Chi Minh trail is being enlarged and asphalted. This is becoming a road artery connecting the different mountainous regions of the country, as Highway No. 1. The trans-Vietnam railway links the regions of plain together. It now takes only a couple of hours to fly from Hanoi to the furthest points of the country. Vietnam is building its infrastructure rapidly, though, it faces serious financial constraints. Building and expanding infrastructure has become top priority for industrialisation and modernisation of its economy.

The backwardness of the economy is due to the feudal and colonialist regimes and to the immense destruction. It contrasts sharply with the rich economic potential of the country, as well as with the talents, abilities and energy of Vietnamese people. Now that Vietnam has been totally liberated, reunified, has evolved its own model of development, it may become a pace setter in Asia, south-east Asia in particular.

## References


1. R.S. Chavan, *Vietnam trial and triumph*, p. 4.
2. Vu Tu Lap, *Vietnam Geographical Data Foreign Languages Publishing House*, Hanoi, 1979.

# 2

# VIETNAM : A PROUD NATION

**V.D. CHOPRA**

The Vietnamese are proud of their past. They claim that their country was inhabited by them in the Stone Age about a million years ago. This perhaps refers to the Palaeolithic period which denotes the earliest stage of human culture. Reportedly that crude chipped stone tools had been found in Tonkin[1]. In the Neolithic period, more than 5,000 years ago, the inhabitants made implements by grinding and polishing stones and even made pottery and cloth.

Although in the history of Vietnam, a reference is made to the legendary period of the Van-Lang kingdom corresponding to the Bronze Age which has been taken to be the first millennium BC, the real history of Vietnam begins from 258 B.C., when King Thuc Phan invaded the Van-Lang state, and founded Au Lac comprising three main clans— the Viet, the Muong and the Tay. King Thuc Phan declared himself King An Duong Vuong. Half a century later in 208 B.C Au Lac was occupied by Trieu Da Vassal of the Chin dynasty in China who annexed these his territory (now Kwantung), and named the two states as Nam Viet[2].

In 111 B.C. Nam Viet was conquered by the Han dynasty of China and incorporated into the Chinese Empire, as a province (Chou) and named Giao Chi.

For about one thousand years the Vietnamese struggled for their independence from Chinese domination. The insurrections of the Trung Sisters (AD 40-43)-- Lady Trieu (AD 248), Ly Bon (AD 544-602), Mai Thuc Loan (AD 722), and others are well-known in the history of Vietnam. These struggles ended in AD 939 when the Vietnamese won their independence from the Chines Empire[3].

However, Vietnamese did not get respite from foreign aggression. From the 10th to the 16th century, the Vietnamese had to struggle hard to fight back foreign aggression again to defend their hard won independence and sovereignty. They had to face fresh aggression from China by the Mongolian forces in 1280 AD, 1285 AD and 1288 AD during the 13th century; attacks from the Champ kingdom during the 14th century and invasions by the Chinese Ming troops of Emperor Young Lo during the 15th century which the Vietnamese resisted for ten years before they could get peace. Thus, for centuries the Vietnamese had to wage war against alien rulers. Perhaps no other country in the world had to face such an ordeal.

During peace time, the kings of the Le dynasty promoted agriculture, developed handicrafts and encouraged education and literature on the basis of Confucian teachings. But the feudal economy created a crisis in the 17th century. Landlords and mandarins started quarrelling for grabbing land of the peasants. For more than three centuries, internal wars continued. The feudalism hindered the progress of the Vietnamese society. From the 16th to the first half of the 19th cantury, there were civil wars between the Mac and the Trinh, and between the Trinh and the Nguyen families. There were wars between the northern and southern kingdoms which made the position of peasants very miserable. The result was an uprising by peasants led by Tay Son in the 18th century. They overthrew the Nguyen and the Trinh kings and ruled for seventeen years and repelled the invasions of Siamese troops and the Chinese Tsing forces several times. The Tay Son rebellion was finally crushed by King Nguyen Anh with the collusion of the French. Thus started the intervention by Western powers in the internal affairs of Vietnam. In 1802, Nguyen Anh ascended the throne with French help and assumed the name of Emperor Gia Long. He founded the Nguyen dynasty in Vietnam[4].

Vietnamese history highlights how struggle against foreign domination is in the genes of the Vietnamese. This psyche of the Vietnamese has become part of the consciousness of the present generation. This is their biggest asset.

They have proved themselves to be great fighters of domitable courage, who are prepared to sacrifice their lives for the independence of their fatherland. They are not only patriotic but also a determined and devoted people who pursue their cause to the end. That is why their small and materially weak nation could fight the Chinese domination for a thousand years, and later the Japanese invaders, French colonialists and American aggressors, and achieve independence for their country. President Ho Chi Minh had told Bernard Fall in 1962, in Hanoi that the Americans had greatly underestimated the character of the Vietnamese. He said that the Vietnamese had always shown great determination when faced with a foreign invasion.

When the American bombing of North Vietnam had started in 1965, the Hanoi authorities, determined to resist the aggression, shifted their capital to a safer place so that the Vietnamese could give a protracted fight for "ten or twenty years" in the words of President Ho Chi Minh. This reveals their determination and strong character. Even the sudden and unexpected 1979, invasion of Vietnam by a large number of Chinese troops "to teach Vietnam a lesson" was couragiously repelled by the Vietnamese[5].

The Vietnamese are hard working and industrious people, and so even after the large-scale devastation of their country by American bombings, they lost no time in reconstructing a new Vietnam with courage and persistence. This aspect of their character may better be expressed in the words of a member of the Japanese Trade Union delegation :

"We have seen with our own eyes evidence of the terrible devastation wrought by the US imperialism in the land of Vietnam against the heroic and valiant people. Now we feel ever greater admiration for the Vietnamese labouring people and working class who, with their revolutionary heroism, faithfully following the teachings of President Ho Chi Minh, 'nothing is more precious than independence and freedom' have valiantly fought and defeated the US imperialism's outrageous war of aggression, and are now embarking on new struggles overcoming great difficulties with enthusiasm and perseverence. After 30 years of unremitting war, they are now turning the former revolutionary heroism which won them the fight against French colonialism and US imperialism into zeal in production and the spirit of self-reliance in national construction to make their country prosperous and powerful[6].

Vietnam has developed its own culture, the base of which was firmly laid after it won independence from China in the tenth century.

During six hundred years thereafter, many works covering literature, history, law and military were produced, and persons like Han Thuyen, Ly Thong Kiet, and Tran Cuoc Than contributed a great deal to the field of culture. The creation of the Vietnamese script called 'Nom' as distinguished from 'Han' the Chinese script, became the basis of the Vietnamese language in the course of time. Between 16th and 19th centuries many literary works were written in the nom script by authors like Nguyen Binh Khiem and Le Duy Don. Vietnam produced great poets like Ho Xuan Huong, who wrote many satirical poems and Doan This Diem, the author of the *Lament of the Soldier's Wife* who spoke of her ardent desire for peace and hatred for war. There were authors who criticised the feudal society as wars amongst the feudal lords had caused great suffering to the people[7]. In the 17th century, Western missionaries worked out a phonetic transcription using the Latin alphabet. This Romanised script known as Quoc Ngu is now common in Vietnam.

To understand the specific feature of Vietnam's contemporary political and social superstructure, another factor needs to be recapitulated. After the annexation of Nam Viet to the Chinese, it was first governed according to its old customs and through native chiefs. No new taxes were imposed on the annexed territory at least for some time. But, the colonisation of the south by the Chinese was encouraged. Gradually, the oppression of the people of Nam Viet by the Chinese started. The Chinese rulers applied a stringent policy of systematic assimilation of the Vietnamese with the Chinese population. They imposed on the Vietnamese the Confucian doctrine and enforced Chinese regulations and rites so as to Sinicise the people even in the field of language and dress[8]. For instance, some Chinese governors tried to force the Vietnamese to speak Chinese language and wear Chinese dress. But the Vietnamese saw to it that their national language and dress survived in spite of the long Chinese rule. They used their mother tongue in the family and in community activities. They did not abandon their traditional dress which they wore on festivals and other occasions. In the 14th century, the Chinese Governor, Chang Fu, made a concerted effort to destroy Vietnames culture. Literary and scientific books were seized, talented men were deported to China and women were forced to wear the Chinese dress. This caused deep resentment among the Vietnamese, as it aroused not only the aesthetic sensibility but it also deeply hurt their national pride[9]. The Chinese attempts to "civilise the barbarians" were strongly resented. This led to repeated revolts against the Chinese rule.

One of such Vietnamese uprisings against the imperial Chinese rule, the most famous and the first great and well organised revolt, was by the Trung Sisters from AD 39 to 43. In AD 34 Giao Chou, which is the ancient name of the Red River Delta, was invaded by the Hans. To Dinh, the Chinese Governor, had been pursuing a policy of exploitation and oppression of the Vietnamese.

During his rule, the daughter of a military governor, Trung Trac, and her husband, Thi Sach, planned an uprising against the Chinese rulers, but because of treachery the plot was revealed too soon and Thi Sach was killed by Governor To Dinh. Fired by patriotism and to avenge her husband's death, Trung Trac and her younger sister, Trung Nha called on the people to rise and drive the Hans out of their land. In a short time, the revolt spread, and by AD 40 they defeated the Chinese armies and recaptured 65 posts of political and military importance, and thus secured independence from the Chinese rule of 150 years. Trung Trac was declared queen with Me Linh as her capital. But this freedom lasted only for about four years. After three years of hard preparation, the Chinese, in AD 43, sent a strong military force to Nam Viet under Ma Vien, a high ranking military mandarin. In the fierce fighting, the two Trung sisters being unable to defeat the stronger invading Chinese army, jumped into the Hat river to avoid falling into the hands of the enemy. Sinçe then, the Vietnamese have honoured these two sisters as their national heroines. In their memory, they built in Hanoi the Hai Ba Temple (Temple of two Sisters). A boulevard was also named after them.

Because of forced Sincisation of the Vietnamese people and forced army recruitment from amongst them, it was the common people and not the feudal lords who were afftected by the Chinese policies in Nam Viet. The widespread discontent and the desperate people needed only courageous and trustworthy leaders like the Trung Sisters to overthrow the foreign despots.

The word "nationality" denotes a group of people who speak the same language, who have common historical traditions, and who regard themselves as a distinct cultural society. Nationality in this sense need not be a political entity, but as soon as it acquires political unity and sovereign independence, it becomes a "national" or a national state[10]. In this sense Vietnam was certainly a nation as the Vietnamese people had a distinct race, language, literature, customs, and cultural unity.

At least after the establishment of the Vietnamese sovereign kingdom of Au Lao in 258 B.C., the process of emergence of Vietnamese people began to surface clearly. To restore the independence of their nation, the Vietnamese fought the Chinese for about a thousand years.

The second great revolt in Vietnam against Chinese imperialism took place in AD 248 under the leadership of another brave young woman, Trieu Thi Trinh. This revolt was against Emperor Wu whose kingdom in the south included Vietnam. She was determined to drive away the Wu's henchmen from her country and regain independence. Trieu Thi Trinh gathered patriots around her, trained them to fight, and liberated Cuu Chan, now known as the province of Nghe Tinh. After six months of independence of this province, Emperor Wu launched another expedition and reccaptured the area because of his superior forces and weapons. Trieu Thi Trinh took her own life on Mount Tung in Thanh Hoa province where a temple has been erected to honour her heroism and sacrifice for the country[11].

The third great revolt was in AD 541. Those were the days of incessant warfare and civil strife. The sufferings of the masses had been intense and the non-Chinese were subjected to the process of assimilation by the Chinese authorities, particularly by Governor Siao Tsen. The Vietnamese revolted under the leadership of Ly Bon and liberated their country in AD 544. Ly Bon installed himself as the Emperor of Vietnam under the name of Ly Nam De.

The Ly Dynasty ruled over Tonking and northern Annam. This kingdom, named by By Bon as Van Xuan (Eastern Spring) lasted for 58 years up to AD 602.

When the Chinese thought that they had restored a blissful peace in the southern region in AD 679, they named that region Annm or Annam which means "Pacified South". But for the Vietnamese, there was not to be any peace until their country was liberated from Chinese rule. They continued their struggle for independence, and offered opposition to their assimilation by the Chinese. There were insurrections led by Mai Thuo Loan in AD 722 and by Phung Hung in AD 791. However, these uprisings were shortlived. These revolts were followed by another round of struggles.

The Vietnamese were ultimately able to throw off the Chinese yoke in AD 939 after the defeat of the Chinese forces at the historic battle of the Bac Dang River under the leadership of their national leader Ngo Quyen who then founded the famous Vietnamese dynasty of Ngo (AD 939 to AD 968), and established in AD 939 an independent Vietnamese state of Dai Viet[12].

It is relevant to mention here that the Chinese rulers encouraged the people of various faiths to follow their religion including Taoism, Confucianism, and Buddhism. This had a far-reaching effect on Vietnamese intellectual life.

Some Chinese governors imposed Confucianism, Chinese rites and practices on the Vietnamese through edicts. But the Vietnamese continued to resist them. However, bacause of the Chinese domination, the Vietnamese ultimately had to accept the Chinese culture. They had to imitate to some extent Chinese social manners, dress, and food habits.

The Chinese domination unleashed a widespread nationalism giving them courage and inspiration to revolt repeatedly and ultimately overthrow Chinese imperialism, and establish their own Annamite state. The second advantage was that during the many centuries of Chinese domination, the Vietnamese learnt improved methods of cultivation and irrigation including building of dams and canals. They adopted technical skills in mining and pottery, and in building of roads, waterways and ports. In the economic field, the Vietnamese adopted new trade and commerce practices. In political administration, they gained good experience of the Chinese system of government. They found it so useful that when the independent state of the Vietnamese was founded in, AD 939, they set up their government on the Chinese model. They had found this system useful in maintaining prosperity, self-sufficency, political and cultural unity. The ablast of monarchs of the Han, Sui, Tang and Sung dynasties were assisted by hierarchy of civil officials recruited through elaborate system of civil services examinations. The adoption of Confucianism as the guiding doctrine was also another reason for the success of the Chinese system of government. Confucianism preaches that human society could prosper only when men maintained right relations with each other and the universe around them. It also preaches that education must build up the moral character which is the chief purpose of the state. Much emphasis was laid on selecting and training of suitable officials who could measure up to this deal[13]. This phase of evolution of Vietnamese Nation-State entered a new period after French colonialism was imposed on Vietnam.

French colonialists estabilshed their administration over Vietnam with a view to use this country as a launching pad to establish their domination over Asia. Cambodia always threatened by its neighbours, accepted French protection in 1863. In 1887, France joined the three protectorates of Tonkin, Annam, and Cambodia with Cochin-China to establish an administrative union of these regions called "Indo-china". When in 1893, France acquired the protectorate over Laos, it also was included in the union of "Indo-China".

The Indo-China union was administrated by a Governor-General with an advisory council to help him. The laws for Indo-china were framed by the French Parliament. The Governor-General had to follow the policies framed in Paris. All key appointments were made by the French Government in Paris on the model of British colonial rulers.

The French had thus acquired absolute power in Vietnam, and the Vietnamese control over Annam and Tonkin was only in name. Significantly even local officials were appointed only to secondary or inferior posts. All the key posts in administration were held by French officers.

French colonial rulers worked out a clear policy to keep Vietnam a backward country. After the occupation of Saigon in February 1859 Admiral Rigault de Genouilly, for instance, adopted a policy of exploitation by reducing customs duty by 50 per cent, opening the port of foreign merchant-ships, and issuing export licences for rice. His successor, Admiral Bonard restored all the royal taxes and duties, including poll-tax, reopened gambling houses and opium dens, and took drastic measures against those who opposed French colonial rule. All land, including that of the absentees, was declared as the property of the French administration. Some industrial development on Western lines too took place, mostly in consumer goods, such as, husking mills, sugar refineries, tobacco, match, soap, coconut oil, and canned food factories. This in turn led to extinction of traditional industries like handicrafts. Rice export had increased about threefold during the decade beginning 1867. The economic exploitation of Vietnam assumed a new dimension, when the concept of making Indo-China "a profitable enterprise" of France was evolved by Governor General Paul Doumer.

Measures were introduced to make this region an agrarian appendage of France. French investments in this region increased. The Bank of Indo-China developed into a real financial and political nerve-centre controlling the economic and industrial policy in Indo-China. The bank provided the colony with monetary exchange and a channel for investment of the metropolitan capital on highly profitable rates in the mining of coal, tin and zinc rubber and other industries. With a view to creating French monopoly, the products of common use like salt and alcohol were put under state monoply with high tariff. The Vietnamese exports to France stepped up from 15 per cent in 1920 to 50 per cent in 1950, and imports of consumer goods from France into Vietnam rose from 25 per cent in 1920 to 55 per cent in 1939, thereby making it difficult for the local small-scale industries to compete with the foreign goods.

The Chinese community controlled the rice trade and the Vietnamese largely confined themselves to farming and labour. Some landlords derived profit from renting their lands to poor farmers. However, some of these landlords were replaced by the French settlers who purchased lands forfeited for non-payment of loans advanced to them at exorbitant interest. This policy led to concentration of land in French hands to the extent of 80 per cent of rice fields with 2,00,000 Vietnamese families employed on them[14]. The number of French settlers who had immigrated to Vietnam before the beginning of the Second World War was about 37,000. Some Chinese and Indians also had immigrated into Vietnam for the purpose of trade.

Though, peasant constituted 85 to 90 per cent of the total population, their condition of life did not improve. In Tonkin and Annam, a large proportion of land-owners cultivated their own lands, because of population pressure, the holdings were small. In Tonkin, 62 per cent of the peasants owned less than 0.9 acres and 30 per cent less than 0.4 acres. It was under rice or rubber cultivation owned by Vietnamese and French landlords or under French-owned plantations on which a large number of Vietnamese labourers were employed. The absentee landlords rented their land on higher rents making the condition of the peasants miserable. The feudal practice of renting thousands of parcels of land and rent collection through a hierarchy of local tyrants was encouraged by the colonialists who did not bother about the improvement of techniques and means of production, the peasants continued to work with tools like those used by their ancestors. The conditions were so inhuman that instead of animals, women were used to pull the ploughs. This led to very low yield. The poor harvest meant almost starvation as after the payment of rent, taxes and debts very little was left for the peasant family.

The French rule thus contributed to the lowering of the standard of living of the people. About 95 per cent of land-owners owned about 29 per cent of the rice paddies and about 5 per cent owned above 60 per cent of rice paddies. About 95 per cent peasants owned on an average 1.73 acres per head. Poor and small peasants had to sell their land and become share croppers. The position of share croppers was no better. They worked for the French landlords who loaned them cattle, seeds, manure, tools, and sometimes money, and charged on all this more than 50 per cent of interest. The cultivators had to pay about 40 per cent of the crop to the landlord in addition to gifts and services. In Cochin-China the landlords took 50 to 80 per cent of the crop as land rent. In Tonkin and Annam it was 40 to 50 per cent. The Indo-China budget was funded mainly from taxes which had swelled from about 38 million piasters in 1912 to 109 million piasters in 1930. East inhabitants had to contribute about 8 piasters yearly and a peasant family had to pay three-fourths of its annual income towards taxes, the collection of which regarded as a calamity by the villagers. Such was the miserable plight of the people.

To consolidate their rule the French had built 3,000 km of railways, 32,000 km of roads and highways, 300 km of canals, 16,000 kms of telephone lines and invested 2 billion dollars of capital to develop agricultural lands and the industrial wealth of the country. As a result rice production increased from 3,00,000 tons in 1865 to 3,180,000 tons in 1945; rubber from 200 tons in 1911 to 2,500,000 tons in 1940.

Naturally, hatred grew against the French colonial rule. This created the objective conditions for popular movement against French colonialists.

In 1931, the Indo-Chinese Communist Party organised strikes, meetings and demonstrations of peasants and workers, but the French Colonial Government crushed these revolutionary manifestations. The Indo-Chinese Communist Party, therefore, changed its tactics. Under the leadership of Ho Chi Minh, the Indo-Chinese Communist Party rallied around it other political parties and patriotic organisations to form a Democratic Front for the Independence of Vietnam which was called in brief "Viet Minh". Ho Chi Minh became its chairman. The Viet Minh demanded a popular assembly to draft a national democratic constitution of Indo-China, the organisation of a national army, national economy, social security and several other reforms which were rejected by the French Colonical Government. The Viet Minh, therefore, launched a strong and country-wide revolutionary struggle for the liberation of Indo-China from French rule.

During the Second World War when France surrendered to Germany, Japanese overran Indo-China in 1940. Japan occupied the colony easily as in French Indo-China there was litttle loyalty to France. The reaction of the Viet Minh was promptly to start an anti-Japanese struggle along with their anti-French struggle. Indo-China was the only country in South East Asia from which the Japanese invaders had not displaced authority of the Colonial Government. For, on the fall of France, Governor Decoux in Indo-China accepted the authority of the French Vichy Government and attempted to maintain French positions by co-operating with and accepting the demands of the Japanese invaders in the light of the agreement made between the Vichy Government and Japan. The agreement of August 30, 1940, between them not only gave Japan a right of passage through French Indo-China and the use of bases in the colony, but also recognised the predominant economic and political interests of Japan in the Far East. But, because of no faith in the Vichy Government, Japan took over the colony from the French on 9th March, 1945, and before the end of the war in August, 1945, Japan proclaimed that the colonical status of Indo-China had ended. Thereupon, the kings of Laos and Cambodia and Emperor Bao Dai of Vietnam declared their country's independence.

On, September 2,1945, President Ho Chi Minh on behalf of the Provisional Government of Vietnam informed to the world of the independence of Vietnam by issuing a Declaration of Independence, thus heralding the end of eighty years of French rule.

When their independence was threatened by the French and the American aggressions, the Vietnamese courageously fought against them for about three decades, sacrificed thousands of lives, suffered terrible destruction of property caused by American bombing to preserve their hard won national independence.

The August Revolution was unique in the history of the world as it was for the first time that the colonial people fought bloody battles against a powerful Western colonial power and successfully defeated it and won their independence. It was unique also because it was the peasant and working class under the leadership of the Communist Party that defeated the French colonial power and subsequently the most powerful American aggression.

After the defeat of Fascism, after the Second World War, a new period of decolonisation had begun. Out of the biggest colonial possession of the biggest empire of the time — "the brightest jewel of the British crown", as school text books of those days used to describe it— in Asia, India emerged as an independent democratic republic. Almost simultaneously Vietnamese who had fought against Japanese fascists in Indo-china, declared themselves as an independent and sovereign state on September 2, 1945. In case of India, various plans of Balkanisation of the country were conceived and finally two sovereign states, India and Pakistan emerged. However, a different model of division of Vietnam was not only conceived but with the military might, attempts were made to impose these plans. This led to a prolonged and bitter struggle by the Vietnamese for the unification of their country. However, both the Indian and Vietnamese, through their valiant struggles, wrote a new chapter in the world history. Their struggles marked the beginning of the disintegration of the imperialist system. India becoming independent marked the ushering in of a new era which, in the course of the last 50 years, has seen country after country in the continents of Asia and Africa throwing off the shackles of imperialist bondage. Emergence of Vietnam, on the other hand, became a pace setter for struggles against imperialist intrigues in South-East Asia.

According to the directive issued to the Supreme Commander for the Allied Forces by the President of the United States, the Japanese forces to the north of the 16th parallel in Indo-China were to surrender to General Chiang Kai-Shek, and the Japanese forces to the south of the 16th parallel were to surrender either to Lord Mountbatten or to the Australian Commander. But before the Allied troops could arrive, the Democratic Republic of Vietnam had already proclaimed its independence on September 2, 1945, and in fairness and justice to the Vietnamese who had fought against Japanese fascists in Indc-china, the Democratic Republic of Vietnam should have been asked to accept the surrender of the Japanese troops in the South. But, the Allies had their own plans of helping France to reimpose its colonial rule over Vietnam[15].

When the British troops landed in Saigon on September 12, 1945, the British Commander General Gracy, not only accepted the surrender of the Japanese troops but in his own authority he also restored Vietnam, south of the 16th parallel, to the French Authorities. The British troops were supposed to restore order. But, they released the French from the Japanese internment camps and rearmed them. The French troops started fighting with the Vietnamese to re-establish their colonial rule over Vietnam. The Vietnamese, seeing their newly-gained independence in danger, fought back with all the strength at their command.

The Viet Minh were expelled from Saigon and the administration was resumed by the French authorities. The Vietnamese had once again to embark on the path of struggle. In the North chinese troops of General Chiang Kai-Shek arrived, and occupied the area north of the 16th parallel. But, for historical reasons, the Vietnamese were suspicious about the intentions of the Chinese troops. President Ho Chi Minh, therefore, persuaded the French to ask the Chinese troops to leave Vietnam as he was confident that thereafter he could effectively deal with the French.

In view of the continued resistance by the Vietnamese to the return of French rule, the French offered to negotiate on the basis of their Declaration of March 24, 1945, which offered to transform Indo-china into a Federation within the French Union after the war to give it a broader economic and administrative autonomy.

But the Vietnamese Government which was functioning in the north in Hanoi, rejected the offer and continued guerrilla warfare. On March 6, 1946, however, an agreement was signed by Jean Sainteny on behalf of the French Government and President Ho Chi Minh on behalf of the Democratic Republic of Vietnam, under which the French recognised the independence of Vietnam as a free state having its government, parliament, army and finances, and forming a part of the Indo-chinese Federation and the French Union. The people of Cochin-China, Tonkin and Annam were to have a referendum to decide what kind of government they wanted. The Vietnamese Government agreed to receive 5,000 French troops on friendly terms to relieve the Chinese troops but they were to be withdrawn within five years. Each of the contracting parties agreed to end hostilities to create an atmosphere favourable for negotiations, particularly for establishing diplomatic relations. However, at the time of the impending negotiations, to defend the country's independence, it was felt necessary to strengthen the national united front. Towards this end, on May 29, 1946, the Vietnam National United League (Lien Viet) was set up with the aim of uniting all political parties, organisations and patriotic people without distinction of class, religion, nationality or political tendencies. The Viet Minh thus formed a part of the League[16].

However, French colonialists wanted to revert to their previous position and reoccupy Indo-China. On the other hand, President Ho Chi Minh resisted the French return as the Vietnamese people had declared their independence on the Japanese surrender and the defeated France had no *locus standi* to resume its colonial rule in Indo-China.

France considered it to be its sacred mission to remove the communist influence from Indo-china, and therefore, France refused to grant the Viet Minh demands, in spite of the March 6 agreement. On the pretext of checking the spread of communism, France wanted to re-establish its old colonial rule.

During the period following this development, negotiations continued between France and Vietnam for a peaceful solution of the conflict. However, both sides increased their military activities as tension and distrust had begun to grow. The French bombarded Haiphong in November, 1946, killing thousands of Vietnamese. The Vietnamese retaliated with an attack on the French in Hanoi on December 19, 1946. Thus, a war flared up in both North and South Vietnam. President Ho Chi Minh, in his appeal to his compatriots on December 20, 1946, said: "As we desire peace, we made concessions. Yet, the more we made concessions, the more the French colonialists demanded, because they are resolved to invade our country once again. But, we would rather sacrifice all than lose our country. We are determined not to be enslaved." He gave a stirring call to his people to rise and fight French colonialists, with whatever weapons they have, to save the Fatherland. Although, the French troops had modern weapons, the Vietnamese troops had the strength of their conviction, their nationalism, and their strong determination to save their sacred Fatherland. Equipped with such inner strength the Vietnamese troops fought by adopting guerrilla tactics until the enemy was worn out and confused.

The French Government envisaged Emperor Bao Dai as a key figure who could compete with Ho Chi Minh in gathering non-communist nationalists' support in Vietnam, and at the same time who would be friendly to the French Government and pliable to their wishes. The French invited Bao Dai to head the Vietnamese Government. On May 20, 1948, Bao Dai set up a Provisional Government of Vietnam, with the support of the pro-Bao Dai nationalist group under the chairmanship of General Nguyen Van Xuan. Then followed prolonged negotiations between the French and Bao Dai, ignoring President Ho Chi Minh. The French were thus successful, though temporarily, in dividing the Vietnamese people. But this independence was not real and complete. The gist of the agreements showed that Vietnam was granted only internal autonomy, it could not have an independent foreign policy. It was further clear from the presence of French troops still fighting in Vietnam that Vietnam was not yet an independent sovereign state. Other instances of such truncated independence were that French citizens in Indo-China were not subject to local justice; the state's export-import policies and foreign policy were to be guided by French interests rather than by Vietnam's national interests. That explains why Emperor Bao Dai's Premier, Tran Van Huu, openly attacked France for its continued domination over Vietnam and demanded complete independence which alone could stop fighting in Vietnam.

American anxiety and efforts to "contain" communism in Vietnam and Asia led it along with Britain to recognise the Bao Dai Government on, February 7, 1950. Thailand, which too was afraid of communism close to its borders, also recognised that government. The US Secretary of State, Dean Acheson, announced that the US would grant military and economic aid not only to France but to the Indo-China associated states also.

While these prolonged French-Vietnamese negotiations were going on, the Democratic Republic of Vietnam troops were offering a strong resistance to the French troops. Besides a few ruined and deserted towns, they had taken control of almost all the countryside. In the battles, the French lost about 20,000 French soldiers and suffered a loss of more than 3,000 million piasters, all the French plantations, coal mines, business firms and factories were in ruins.

While the Indo-China war was dragging on without any end in sight, it suddenly acquired international significance after the Chinese communists proclaimed the establishment of the People's Republic of China on September 21, 1949. The Central People's Government was formally inaugurated on October 1. The new Chinese Communist Government and the Soviet Union recognised the Democratic Republic of Vietnam in January, 1950 and established diplomatic relations with it. This was followed by other countries in the communist bloc. It was reported in May 1950 that Communist China had secretly agreed with President Ho Chi Minh to give military aid to the Democratic Republic of Vietnam. It was after this development that direct American intervention in Vietnam began.

On May 8, 1950, the French Foreign Minister and the US Secretary of State, Dean Acheson, discussed the Indo-China situation in Paris, and the US decided to give military and economic aid to France and Indo-China Associated States in the French Union "to enable them to restore stability, and to pursue their peaceful and democratic development". President Truman announced on June 27, 1950, that he had ordered a speed up of military assistance to the French forces in Indo-China. On, January 11, 1952, a military conference involving the US, Britain and France was held in Washington to discuss the situation in Indo-China. It was reported that the United States had sent 70 shiploads of military equipment to Indo-China since July, 1950. With this began open military intervention by the United States in Vietnam.

The US administration under President Truman got itself involved in the French-Vietnamese conflict. The US administration by associating itself with French colonialism led the Vietnamese to believe that the Americans were not sincere about their declaration of national self-determination. The American imperialists gave arms and ammunitions to their stooges to massacre the Indo-Chinese.

President Ho Chi Minh expressed the Vietnamese feelings against the Americans when he said that in order to wrest back independence, the Indo-Chinese must be resolute in smashing the French colonialists who are our enemy No.1. At the same time, we must fight against the American interventionists.

Just as the US gave military aid to the French to fight their colonial war in Vietnam, Communist China gave aid to the Viet Minh which had launched a series of attacks on the French forces which were forced to retreat from the North to the South. Even in 1953, there seemed to be no hope of a French victory, as the Viet Minh army was controlling vast territories in Vietnam, while the French troops were on the defensive. Walter Lippman, the American columnist, had correctly assessed the situation when he stated that the determining factor was not guns, tanks or air planes. These, the French had in large numbers from America, far more than Ho Chi Minh had received in aid from the Chinese. The determining factor was that the French did not have popular support.

The US, which was paying for about 80 per cent of the French military expenditure in Vietnam, was growing impatient at the defensive nature of French strategy. General Navarre was sent to Vietnam as the Commander-in-Chief to start a new offensive. In a desperate bid to win the war, the French launched an attack on the fortress of Dien Bien Phu to implement the new Navarre plan of war. On, November 20,1953, French troops occupied Dien Bien Phu. From there, General Navarre had aimed at annihilating the greater part of the Vietnamese forces within 18 months, and occupying the whole of the Viet Minh territory. He concentrated most of his troops and arms at Dien Bien Phu which had become the main theatre of war in Indo-China. At the end of March, 1954, General Vo Nguyen Giap, Commander-in-Chief of the Vietnamese People's Army, planned his strategy. He staged an attack on Dien Bien Phu and encircled the French forces.

In this critical situation, US Secretary of State, John Foster Dulles, expresed his anxiety that a Viet Minh victory would lead to communist domination of all south-east Asia. The US administration therefore planned a massive use of American air and naval power to save the French forces from being massacred at Dien Bien Phu. But the American Congressional leaders would not approve the plan unless Dulles gathered the support of the Allies to take united action in Vietnam. Dulles went to London to persuade Prime Minister Churchill and Foreign Secretary Anthony Eden to accept his plan. After an emergency Cabinet meeting, Eden informed Dulles of Britain's opposition to military intervention before the impending Geneva Conference called to discuss the Korean and Indo-China problems.

Since the French troops could not get direct involvement of other western countries in Indo-China conflict, they had no other option but to surrender after a bitter fight in which a large number of their forces were wiped out by the Vietnamese freedom fighters. It was on May 7, 1954, General De Castries surrendered to Vietnamese People's Army. This great victory instilled a new sense of confidence among all the oppressed people in the world. Vietnam came to symbolise the determination of all the freedom fighters in the world. This indeed was a historic event in the post Second World War period.

The Dien Bien Phu victory was, therefore, enthusiastically welcomed by the Vietnamese. It was a victory over colonialism, its arrogant attitude towards the agreement of March 6, 1946 and President Ho Chi Minh's subsequent offers of negotiations for the solution of the Vietnam problem.

This stunning victory proved how a small but determined and dedicated people could defeat a well equipped and powerful great power. This victory was also a triumph of Asian nationalism over Western colonialism. It was after this victory that course of development in Vietnam began to change and later American ruling elite had to eat a humble pie.

If one goes by concrete evidence, it becomes clear that US foreign policy towards colonial powers is determined by its own national interests. Where American commercial, economic, political or military interests are benefited or at least not affected by the colonial rule over a people, the US does not get itself involved in the internal affairs of the colonial power. This explains why the US, in spite of its sympathy for the colonial people, did not intervene in the case of Indo-China to force France to grant independence to them.

But after Japan's conquest of Indo-China and the Pearl Harbour incident in World War II, the US suddenly recognised the strategic importance of Indo-China to Japan in view of its geographical location and natural resources. It was realised that Indo-China could be a source of military strength and a springboard for Japan's domination of South-East Asia and the Pacific region. The US wanted to deprive Japan of this politial opportunity. It therefore preferred France's rule in Indo-China to Japan's. The US, therefore, felt that it was in its national interest to assist France in regaining its lost power and influence in Indo-China.

However, there was another dimension of American policy. It wanted to stem the tide of radical nationalism in the newly liberated countries of Asia, India, China and Vietnam in particular. It is this perception which became the basis of the US policy in Indo-China countries.

In May 1950, the French Foreign Minister and the US Secretary of State had discussions in Paris over the Indo-China war in which the French Government had lost 18,00 million dollars and more than 20,000 lives since 1945, and yet the end of war was not insight. They had agreed that as there was a threat to the security of Vietnam, Laos and Cambodia, which had been granted independence within the French Union, and though the responsibility of meeting such a threat was primarily of French and of the government in Indo-China, the US had recognised that the solution to the Indo-China problem was dependent on the preservation of Indo-China's security and on the development of "genuine" nationalism in those countries. The US was convinced that its assitance was necessary to contribute to the fulfilment of this objective.

The establishment of the communist regime in China, the recognition of the Hanoi Government of Ho Chi Minh by Beijing and Moscow in January 1950 and the reported military aid agreement between the Beijing regime and Ho Chi Minh's government had created the fear of, expansion of "communism" in South-East Asia. This also posed a danger to the "Nationalist" Chinese regime in Taiwan supported by the United States.

The beginning of the Korean war in June 1950, further compounded the situation. As a counter measure, on June 27, 1950. President Truman announced that he had ordered the US air and naval forces in the Far East to go to the aid of South Korea and had directed the Seventh Fleet to prevent an attack on Taiwan. He also speeded up military aid to the French forces in Indo-China. Thus, a period of direct American involvement in this region began.

But, the granting of military aid to France to fight against the Vietnamese national liberation, to help restore French colonialism in Indo-Chine, and suppress the freedom and independence declared by the Vietnamese on 2nd.September, 1946 clearly established the new American designs in this region.

It was clear that the intention of the US in giving aid to the French was to fight radical nationalism and not to assist the French to restore their colonialism in Indo-China. But the US administration failed to understand the nature of the national liberation movement in Vietnam which had declared its independence from French rule.

Secretary of State Dulles proposed in April 1954 that its allies join in warning communist China against further aggression in Indo-China. In a speech to the Overseas Press in New York, he declared that if communist forces in Indo-China won an uncontested control over Indo-China they would resume the same pattern of aggression against other free people in the area. The US, he asserted, felt that possibility should not be accepted and met by united action. Vice President Richard Nixon stated at the American Society of Newspaper Editors meeting that the US might have to send troops to Indo-China if the only alternative were communist domination. He said that the French defeat at Dien Bien Phu would mean the French withdrawal and the fall of Indo-China, and in that case, the US would not allow further retreat in South-East Asia. It was in this context that SEATO came into being and a period of direct American involvement began. One need not recapitulate the subsequent developments in Vietnam and open American involvement, use of chemical and biological weapons against the innocent people. But finally, the Vietnamese emerged victorious and foiled the American plans. It is in the furnace of these struggles spread over the centuries, and against the most powerful imperial countries that Vietnamese nation-state has emerged. This is a unique feature of Vietnam, which has instilled in them a sense of national pride.

### References

1. *The democratic republic of Vietnam,* Hanoi, 1960, p. 15.
2. Nam Viet is the same as Viet Nam, Viet means to the South of China. The Chinese term for it is Yeuh Nan which means South of Yeuh, the ancient

name of the Chinese province of Kwantung, see Engar Snow, *The Other Side of River Red China*, New York, 1962, p. 682.

A quote by R.S. Chavan in his book : *Vietnam Trial and Triumph*, New Delhi, 1987.

3. *The Democratic Republic of Vietnam*, p.16.
4. R.S. Chavan, *Vietnam Trial and Triumph*, New Delhi, 1987, p.7.
5. *Ibid*, p. 8.
6. *Vietnam*, Hanoi NO. 229/1-1978, p. 27
7. *The Democratic Republic of Vietnam*, p. 16
8. *The Women in Vietnam*, Hanoi, 1978, pp. 74-75.
9. *Ibid.*
10. R.S. Chavan, *Nationalism in Asia*, *op. cit.*, p. 4.
11. *Women in Vietnam*, p. 313.
12. The *Democratic Republic of Vietnam*, Hanoi, 1975, p. 23.
13. R.S. Chavan, *VietnamTrial and Triumph*, New Delhi, p. 16-17.
14. J.L. Mehta, *Political and Cultural History of Vietnam*, New Delhi, p. 132.
15. *T.N. Kaul, India, China, and Indo-China*, New Delhi, 1980, pp. 45-46.
16. *Democratic Republic of Vietnam*, 1960, p. 28.

# 3

## HO CHI MINH— THE ARCHITECT OF A NATION-STATE

**V.D. CHOPRA**

Ho Chi Minh, who is the architect of Vietnamese nation-state, was born on 19th May,1890, in a village, Hoang True, NgheTinh province. He was born and grew up at the time when Vietnam was invaded by the French imperialists. From an independent, united and sovereign country,Vietnam became a colonial, semi-feudal and divided country. Under the oppression and exploitation by the French imperialists and feudal agents, the Vietnamese suffered from hunger and virtually became slaves of foreign colonial rulers and landlords. In Vietnamese society, besides the basic contradictions between the Vietnamese, chiefly between the peasants and the feudal class, there appeared another basic contradiction between the Vietnamese nation and the French imperialists. These two basic contradictions became fiercer.

Vietnam is a heroic nation. The Vietnamese have a glorious tradition of patriotism and valiant struggle against foreign aggressions. Therefore, when the French colonialists invaded Vietnam, struggle against the French imperialists and feudal henchmen broke out everywhere in various forms, and with great valour. But, these patriotiotic and anti-French movements failed one after another, chiefly for want of a correct policy. Until the 20s of the 20th century, the cause of national salvation of Vietnamese was passing through a serious crisis.

In Nghe Tinh, for many generations, the people had faced natural disasters with determination, and had rich tradition of fighting against foreign invaders. This region was one of the leading centers for national liberation.

Ho Chi Minh was born into a family of patriotic scholars. His father's name was Nguyen Sinh Huy, alias Nguyen Sinh Sac (1863-1929). Having lost both his parents when a child, Nguyen Sinh Huy had to work for a living while carrying on his studies.Because of his love for study, his intelligence, and and the solicitous teaching of the scholar Hoang Xuan Duong,who gave him his daughter in marriage and he became a Pho Bang (doctor of literature) and lived a simple life as a teacher. He instilled into his children's minds the love of labour and urged them to study in order to understand "human ethics". He became an official but displayed a negative, non-cooperative attitude. He often said, "The officials are slaves among slaves, and therefore, even more slavish".[1] A patriot and a proud man, he refused to submit to the French colonialists, and so was dismissed from office. He then went to Nam Bo where he practised traditional medicine and lived a simple life until his death.

Ho Chi Minh's mother was Hoang Thi Loan (1868-1901), a gentle and hard-working woman who devoted her life to tilling the fields and educating her children. He had an elder sister, Nguyen Thi Thanh, alias Bach Lien and an elder brother Nguyen Sinh Khiem, alias Nguyen Tat Dat. Both participated in the struggle against French colonialism. Ho Chi Minh was the third child in the family. As a child, his name was Nguyen Sinh Cung and then changed to Nguyen Tat Thanh. He was an intelligent and studious pupil, eager to learn new things. Besides school books, he loved to read patriotic novels and poems. Reading stories about heroes and listening to conversations between his father and his patriotic friends infused in him, even as a young boy, love for his country and people.

Night and day I dream of having my actions recorded in history, the most dishonourable way to win a name for oneself is through literary compositions ( in official examinations leading to high office, Tr.1)

He witnessed their daily miseries : beatings because of failure to pay rents and taxes, this suffering of the people left a deep imprint on his sensitive and indecisive mind in the formative years of his life. When he was 15, he engaged himself in underground work, and served as messenger for scholar patriots; Can Vuong movement typified by the Huong Khe uprising under the leadership of Phan Dinh Phung; Dang Du movement of Phan Boi Chau; Dong Kinh Nghia Thuc movement and Yen. The insurrections under the leadership of Hoang Hoa Tham, the drive for reforms led by Phan Chu Trinh, and the refusal by Trung Bo peasants to pay taxes —all had a profound influence on Ho Chi Minh, especially when he was studying in Quoc Hoc College in Hue. These movements not only roused his patriotic emotions but instilled a new determination to fight for the liberation of his country.

These movements took place in quick succession with great valour, but they all failed for want of a correct political policy. Owing to restrictions from historical conditions their leaders made no distinction between the French colonialists on the one hand and the French working class and labouring people on the other. They were not aware that the tasks of the Vietnamese revolution were to overthrow the French imperialists and win national independence, and to topple the feudal landlords and give land to the peasants. They were not conscious of the fact that the basic revolutionary forces among Vietnamese were the workers and the peasantry.

The Can Vuong movement failed because it could not rally the broad masses of the people, chiefly the peasants, and because the feudal landlord class had sunk into decay, and for the most part, had surrendered to the French colonialists while subjecting the people to ruthless oppression and exploitation.

The peasant insurrections led by Hoang Hoa Tham failed for want of clearly defined policies.Thus, it could neither organise the people nor it could generate a national upsurge.

Phan Boi Chau was an activist in the movement for national salvation but relied on the Japanese to topple the French, something which was tantamount to "getting a tiger out of the front door while inviting a panther in by the back door".

Although he was a patriot, Phan Chu Trinh only demanded reforms but did not advocate the overthrow of the French colonialists. He only demanded the abolition of the mandarinate, but did not advocate the overthrow of the feudal regime as a whole.

Ho Chi Minh had deep regard for Phan Dinh Phung, Hoang Hoa Tham, Phan Boi Chau and Phan Chu Trinh, but did not follow the courses charted by them. Refusing to "go east" to Japan, as advocated by the Dong Du movement, he turned to the Western countries, to which he was attracted by ideals of freedom, democracy, modern science and technology. Later, Ho Chi Minh, related, "At about the age of 13, for the first time, I heard such French terms as 'liberty', 'equality' and 'fraternity'. So I developed a desire to acquaint myself with French civilization so as to find out what exactly was meant by these terms."

In summer 1908, Ho Chi Minh gave up his studies and left Hüe for the south to find a way to go abroad. He stopped at Phan Thiet, and taught for a short time at a private school name Duc Thanh. This school was founded by some patriotic scholars. While teaching there, he not only imparted knowledge to his pupil but also taught them how to love the country.

Sometime later, Ho Chi Minh went to Saigon only to find that Nam Ky under the colonial regime was in no way different from Trung Ky under the "protectorate", and Bac Ky under the "semi-protectorate". Everywhere the people were subjected to the same oppression, exploitation, miseries and humiliations. This contributed all the more to Ho Chi Minh's urge to go to the countries of the West to see how their people had managed to become independent and strong so that at his return he could help fellow-countrymen drive out the French colonialists. This is how he turned to modern socio-economic outlook.

In search of national liberation, he went to France, Europe, Africa, the United States, Spain, Great Britain and many other countries. During these tours, though he earned his living as a manual worker, he established contacts with the Vietnamese patriots. What struck him the most was the international character of the working peoples struggle against capitalism. This was indeed a turning point in Ho Chi Minh's thinking. The Great October Revolution left a deep imprint on his mind.

The outbreak of the Russian October Socialist Revolution shook the world. It awakened the working class, working people and oppressed nations in the world in the colonies and semi-colonies in particular and roused them to struggle. It opened up a new era in the history of mankind, the era of disintegration of colonial empires. It set in motion world-wide movement for building an alternative socio-economic system based on welfare of the people based on equality.

The Russian October Revolution had a decisive influence on Ho Chi Minh's world outlook. He started evolving Vietnam's road to new order for liquidating feudalism and colonialism. As a first step, he united all patriotic forces of Vietnam and set up Communist Party of Vietnam. After setting up this party, Ho Chi Minh arrived in Siam in March, and in Malay in late April 1930. Just after its founding, the Communist Party of Vietnam organized and led a revolutionary movement which had no precedent in Vietnam. Based on worker-peasant alliance, the Soviet Power was set up in many areas in Nghe Tinh province.

As early as in 1924, he made an analysis of the objective reality. He predicted that Indo-China and the Pacific area would be a "fiery furnace". He came to the conclusion that World War II would break out because of the contradictions among the major colonial powers. He indeed could make this prediction on the basis of concrete knowledge.

In 1939, when the Second World War broke out, Communist Party of Vietnam had made a timely withdrawal and went underground. In November, 1939, the Party Central Committee held its sixth plenum, and decided on a change in strategy, concentrating forces on the task of national liberation and set up the Indo-Chinese anti-Imperialist National United Front.

As early as 1940, Ho Chi Minh (then bearing the name of Ho, Quang Comrades Tran, and Vuong) had returned to Kunming (China) to get in touch with the Party Central Committee.

In June 1940, the German fascists attacked France. The French government surrendered, the French colonialists in Indo-China were utterly confounded. Ho Chi Minh held that the time was becoming favourable for the Vietnamese revolution. In August, though he was then working in Kweilin (China), he contemplated setting up base areas in Cao Bang, where there existed a firm popular infrastructure, and from where the movement could spread to the delta region while maintaining links with the international communist movement. He gave instructions for a number of party cadres then working in China to go home and gather forces, waiting for an opportunity to seize power.

As early as 1939, Ho Chi Minh and the Party Central Committee had foreseen that the Japanese imperialists would invade Vietnam. The Japanese fascists invaded Indo-China. The French colonialists surrendered, and offered Indo-China to the Japanese. Put under a double yoke, Vietnamese were determined to rise against the

Japanese and French fascists. In November 1940, the Party Central Committee held its seventh plenum and pointed out that the Japanese fascists and French imperialists were "Two direct enemies". It decided to organise armed uprising to seize power.

In the face of new situations and tasks, Ho Chi Minh realized the importance of uniting the entire people for national salvation. He formed a broad based front called *Mat Tran Viet Nam Doc Lap Dong minh* (Vietnam Independence League). In late December 1940, Ho Chi Minh arrived at the Vietnam-China border, opened a training course for cadres based on the document, *The Road to Liberation*.

On 8th February, 1941, after 30 years of activity abroad, Ho Chi Minh returned to homeland. He started training cadres to unite all Vietnamese. The Vietnamese Communist Party decided that the slogan confiscating land and distributing it to the peasants should be temporarily shelved. Instead of this it decided to confiscate land of the imperialists and the traitors and distributed to the poor peasants, reduce land rents, and debt interests. This gave a new direction to the libaıation struggle. The liberation movement started spreading, and on 25th December, 1944, the tide turned.

After winning power, with no time to organise and consolidate forces, Vietnam had to face an extremely difficult and complicated situation. The terrible famine caused by the French colonialists and Japanese fascists was still a threat to the people. The country's economy and finance were exhausted. Meanwhile, in the North 2,00,000 troops of Chiang-Kai-Shek, on American orders poured into Vietnam under the pretext of disarming the Japanese, but in fact with the aim of attempting to destroy the Communist Party, shatter the Viet Minh, help the reactionary government to topple the people's power, and set up a reactionary government under US-Chiang control. Counter revolutionary elements such as men of the "Vietnam Quoc Dan Dang", "Phuc Quoc", "Vietnam Cach Mang Dong Chi Hoi", etc., demanded a change in the composition of the government, a new national flag and Ho Chi Minh's resignation, etc. In the South, taking cover behind British troops, the French colonialists staged a comeback. Vietnamese reactionaries reared their heads and prepared to collaborate with the French colonialists to oppose people's resistance in the South.

While the fate of the new State was hung by a thread, Ho Chi Minh assumed his heavy responsibility before the people : "My duty is like that of a helmsman who must steer the boat of the Fatherland safely through the storms, and take the people to the shore of happiness."[2]

On September 3, 1945 presiding over the first meeting of the council of Government of the Democratic Republic of Vietnam, after the August Revolution, he pointed out six urgent tasks: launching the campaign to increase production; liquidate famine and collection of rice to relieve the poor; launching the anti-illiteracy campaign; organizing, as soon as possible, the general elections with universal suffrage system, preparing the democratic constitution; launching the movement for industrial growth, thrift, integrity; and uprightness to eliminate the bad habits left by colonialism, abolishing poll tax, market taxes, and ferry-crossing toll; forbidding opium smoking; and promulgating the law of freedom of belief and unity between Catholicism and Buddhism.

When the army entered the northwest, on 1st October, 1952, he made public the following 8 orders of the Government of the Democratic Republic of Vietnam:

1. Guarantee of the property and lives of the people;
2. Protect the professions of the people;
3. Confiscate the property of the French colonialists and reactionaries;
4. Protect pagodas, churches, schools, hospitals and cultural establishments;
5. Reward those who do good and punish those who do wrong;
6. Keep order and security;
7. Gather the inhabitants, particularly the peasants, in organisations;
8. and Protect the lives and property of foreign residents.

Grasping his instructions, Vietnamese army and people fought bravely and secured victory in this campaign. Thus, Vietnam liberated eight-tenth of the enemy occupied zones in the Northwest and 250,000 people, and thwarted the enemy scheme to set up a Thai, autonomous region.

In the course of the resistance, Ho Chi Minh and the Party Central Committee advocated the policy of reduction of land rents, interests and other policies, especially that of agricultural taxes, aimed at limiting exploitaiton by the landlords, developing the forces of the peasants and building and consolidating a firm rear base for the resistance.

The victory of the anti-French war resistance ushered a new era in the history of the Vietnamese revolution. Peace was restored in Indo-China, and North Vietnam was freed from the yoke of imperialism.

In the South, the US imperialists tried their utmost to oust the French colonialists, with the aim of turning it into a new-type US colony and military base, re-kindling the war and attacking the Democratic Republic of Vietnam. The US imperialists and their henchmen became the most dangerous and wicked enemy of Vietnamese people.

In face of the new situation, Ho Chi Minh and the Party Central Committee set forth two strategic tasks to be carried out simultaneously: to build up the North, take it to socialism; to achieve the reunification of the country, and complete the people's national democratic revolution in the whole country. Both tasks had the same aim: to have peace, reunify the country on the basis of independence and democracy, and the safeguarding of peace in South-East Asia and the world.

In an atmosphere filled with joy of victory in the liberated North, Ho Chi Minh returned to the capital city together with the Party Central Committee and the Government. They proceeded from Tuyen Quang to Thai Nguyen, and arrived in Ha Noi via Phu Tho and Son Tay.

On September 19, 1954, on his way to Hanoi, Ho Chi Minh paid a visit to the Hung Kings Temple and had a meeting with officers and men from the Vanguard Division who were regrouping at Phu Tho and preparing to take over the capital city. He talked to the division's officers and men: "...Our meeting here is accidental but full of meaning. In the days of yore the Hung Kings were credited with building the nationa, today you --my nephews and I. We have to defend it." He stressed: "Vietnam's army should not indulge in relaxation because of peace. So long as the imperialists still stay in the South, so long as they still live in the world; we should keep on building a strong army".[3]

Stirred and encouraged by Ho Chi Minh's words, the Vanguard Division as well as other army units from the Viet Bac highland, from the midland and the plains enthusiastically converged towards Hanoi. In the morning of 10th October, 1954 Vietnam's infantry, artillery and motorized troops entered Hanoi. The capital city was totally liberated.

On October 11, 1954 Ho Chi Minh reached Hanoi. On the same day, he issued an Appeal calling on Vietnam's compatriots in Hanoi to preserve law and order, and to quickly stabilize production and the people's living conditions.

On October 12, 1954 he presided over the first meeting of the Government Council in Hanoi, eight years after leaving the capital city to carry out the war of resistance.

In July 1955, a Conference on protection and prevention of famine was convened. Ho Chi Minh analysed in depth the causes of famine, namely, the policy of exploitation and domination by the imperialists and feudalists directed against people. Although, they had been removed from North, they still left behind them serious consequences of their policy.

After long struggle and trials, the North slowly came back to normal, and the people's living conditions were stabilized. Ho Chi Minh and the Communist Party directed the entire efforts to increase agricultural production. Ho Chi Minh said "This is a key problem in economic restoration, a basic condition for the improvement of the people's living standards, in conformity with the actual conditions in the North of our country. Parallel to the restoration of agricultural production, we have to restore industrial production, communications and transports and private capitalists industry and trade, and step by step strengthen the State economic sector, build up cooperative economy and rebuild war-damaged cities and countryside."[4] This was his vision as early as mid-50s.

Ho Chi Minh and the Party Central Committee considered that to improve the work in cultural and social affairs was one of the most urgent tasks to be carried out simultaneously with the other ones in the restoration of economy. The improvement of general and higher education, and the training of a teaching staff with a solid political fund and a high professional qualification should be done as quickly as possible so as to respond in time to the need of developing socialist educational work in the country. Appropriate care should also be given to artistic work. Writers and artists were urged by the Party to take an active part in economic restoration, and to strive to reflect in their creations realities of the new life and the new man. Thus, alongwith increasing production, raising cultural life of the people, their educational level and political consciousness were given a very high priority, and this paid rich dividends to nation-state building of Vietnam.

In his visits to factories and construction sites and his meetings and talks with workers, Ho Chi Minh always reminded the later of their consciousness of being masters of the country. In his opinion to be conscious of being masters of the country, it was instrumental to be ideologically convinced and to have a strict organization and discipline. He pointed out that "to raise labour productivity, we should first of all heighten our sense of responsibility, have a good management, resolve to surmount all difficulties, and to do everything very punctually."[5] This was a new cultural orientation.

He repeatedly underlined the glorious role of labour. He said, "Formerly, we worked for the capitalists, feudalists and imperialists.... But now we work for ourselves. Any profession profitable to the country, the people, the class is a glorious one. Labour is the criterion for evaluating the level of political consciousness of revolutionaries".[6]

Ho Chi Minh's exemplary virtues and working style inspired the whole people to overcome all difficulties and to fight valiantly for construction in the North and to carry out the struggle to liberate the South and reunify the country.

Economic restoration in the North which started in 1955, was successful in 1957. Ho Chi Minh gave the following assessment: "Old production units have been restored, many new factories have been set up, production in many branches has reached the pre-war level, and food production has even surpassed it. Economic activites in the country have returned to normal, cultural activities have experienced an initial development, thus the people's living conditions have begun to improve".[7]

Early in 1960, in an atmosphere of ardent emulation by Vietnamese people to greet the 30th founding anniversary of the Communist Party, Ho Chi Minh wrote an article entitled "Thirty Years of Activities by the Party". This was a historic survey of the Communist Party's activities during 30 years of valiant struggle and glorious victories. In this important article, he outlined the fundamentals of the strategy and tactics of the Communists through the various stages of the revolution, which showed a creative application of Marxism-Leninism to the concrete conditions in Vietnam. Analysing the causes of the past successes of the Vietnamese revolution, he pointed out the decisive factors accounting for the victory of the people's national democratic revolution.

In the last years of his life, he evinced keen interest in the nation-building process of his nation, though unification of the country had yet to take place. He kept close touch with many cadres from South, and always exhibited confidence that Vietnam will achieve its national objective of unification of both parts of Vietnam. In 1969, his health rapidly declined. On May 10, 1969, Ho Chi Minh wrote a testament to leave for posterity. He passed away on 3rd September, 1969 at 9.47 a.m. He was 79.

Any study of the contemporary politics and ecoromy of Vietnam will be incomplete without a critical examination of thoughts and practical work of Ho Chi Minh, the architect of Vietnam's nation-state.

## References

1. *The man who made a nation — Ho Chi Minh,* Foreign Languages Publishing House, Hanoi — 1988, p. 6.
2. *Ibid.*, p. 98.
3. *Ibid.*, p. 131.
4. *Ibid.*, p. 135.
5. *Ibid.*, p. 137.
6. *Ibid.*, p. 137.
7. *Ibid.*, p. 143.

# 4

# VIETNAM: COMMITMENT TO RENEWAL, ENHANCEMENT OF INTERNAL POWER AND BROADENING INTERNATIONAL COOPERATION

**PHAM SY TAM**

According to the archaeological studies, from the days of Hung Kings, the Vietnamese nation has more than 4500 years of history. The Vietnamese people founded their first state under the name "Van Lang" in 2879 B.C. The history of Vietnam is best characterized as a long continuous struggle for nation building and safeguarding of their freedom and independence. From 111 B.C., Vietnam had undergone nearly ten centuries under domination of Chinese feudalism. With patriotic tradition and her cultural power, Vietnam won back independence in 939. From 939 to 1858, many wars of resistance still broke in Vietnam against the aggressions waged by the Chinese feudalist regimes. The 17th and 18th centuries witnessed the first technical revolution in Europe. Many European states turned into capitalism with better instruments, machines and weapons, and some of them run to conquer and establish their colony. In 19th century when the feudalist regime in Vietnam weakened, it was attacked in 1858 and later dominated by the French colonialists for nearly a century. From the first day of foreign domination, many Vietnamese generations rose up to liberate their country but they were defeated by the *colonialists* who obtained more modern weapons, technology, and severe colonial policy.

In 1930, the Vietnam Communist Party was founded by Ho Chi Minh, a follower of Marx and Lenin. The Vietnam Communist Party led the workers, peasantry, and other revolutionary forces in the movement against the French domination for the liberation of their Homeland. From 1941 to 1945, Vietnam was occupied by the Japanese. Nearly at the end of the Second World War when the Ally troops were on the way to come to Vietnam, the Vietnamese people led by the Communist Party of Vietnam with President Ho Chi Minh at its Head succeded in having overthrown the Japanese regime, culminated by the August Revolution (August 19, 1945) and had won back the power into the hands of the people; So that the Democratic Republic of Vietnam from North to South was declared independent on September 2, 1945, with great ceremony in Hanoi (the Declaration of Independence was written and read by President Ho Chi Minh). After that, President Ho Chi Minh paid his first official visit to France in September 1946, showing the hands and heart of peace and friendship of the Vietnamese people; the two governments signed their first agreements in Paris. But, with the tolerance and support of some western powers, the French colonialists decided to reoccupy Vietnam; on December 19 1946 the French Army command sent the Ultimatum to the Government of Vietnam demanding it to hand over all the rights of controlling security and order of Capital Hanoi to the French troops. Later, on the same day the First War of Resistance of the Vietnamese began spreading from South to North. The French command wanted to launch offensives which would rapidly end with the destruction of the poorly armed and inexperienced Vietnamese armed forces. But, the war lasted 9 years and ended in May 1954, with the resounded victory won by the Vietnamese at Dien Bien Fu, and the signing of the Geneva agreements on Vietnam resulted in liberation of northern part of Vietnam but dividing Vietnam into two parts: the North and the South (Vietnam). The US intervention into Vietnam escalated into a full-fledged war in March 1965, and the war continued until April 30, 1975, when the South was liberated and Vietnam was reunified, the country was called the Socialist Republic of Vietnam in January 1976. However, the legacy of war ended only in 1979, and from that day, the people engaged themselves in the economic construction in Vietnam. The days passed, but the results of economic reconstruction did not show much for the better. In 1986, at the 6th Congress, the Communist Party of Vietnam took the decision to begin with the renovation policy called Renewal. It is 12 years now. Though, the renewal is rather short compared with the nation's history, its implementation has brought about significant achievements in various fields of society's life, from economic to politics, and from security and national defence to diplomatic activities. The successes of Vietnam Renewal have been widely recognised within and outside the country.

**Main Characteristics and underlying causes of Vietnam's Renewal**

Vietnam has been pursuing a policy of Renewal mainly due to outside pressure, especially due to the collapse of the former Soviet Union and Eastern Europe and the loss of aid from them. It is completely not the case. One of the Vietnam's experiences is to be timely apt to conditions and be independent in setting forth its internal and external guidelines and policies. Conservatism and slackness are equivalent to the loss of the nation due to backwardness. In the country's history, there are not few examples of people advocating to reform the country, as they were aware of the threats to the matter of life and death of the nation, and had desire that the national independence and sovereignty would be regained and the country would develop and be ever-lasting. In the country, there were many examples like King Ho Quy Ly in the 15th century, Nguyen Truong To and Nguyen Lo Trach in the 19th century, later there were Phan Boi Chau, Phan Chu Trinh and other revolutionary personalities in the early 20th century. All of them had a desperate aspiration that Vietnam could march shoulder to shoulder with other countries in the world. However, the enthusiasm of all of them did not result in success due to the lack of scientific policy, narrow-minded views and lack of necessary conditions. These historical experiences continue to be invaluable lessons for Vietnamese today.

After the national liberation of South Vietnam and the reunification of the country, excited by great victories, subjectivism, voluntarism, disregard of objective rules made the country's economy and society engulfed in stagnancy and crisis. The pressing need of the nation was to get out of this state of matters. Various audacious initiatives emerged from different parts of the country. The conceptions of Vietnamese leaders and theorist circles were met with practical experiences of the people in different parts of Vietnam, thus creating a basis and an impetus for the drafting of the renovation line in the preparation of the 6th Congress of the Communist Party of Vietnam in 1986. The Congress asserted that "Renewal is a pressing need of the revolutionary cause, and a matter of vital significance" to Vietnam. That was Vietnamese leading party's conclusion approved five years before the fall of the Soviet Union.

The correctness of the assessment has been justified by the time. It was the experience and creativeness of the masses and the realities and needs of the country and not the outside pressure that were attributed to Vietnam's adoption of Renewal (or Renovation-Doi Moi in Vietnam). The policy of Renewal that proceeded first of all in the way of theory and economic thinking, and the achievements brought about by economic reforms in Vietnam have laid grounds of the morality, theoretical and material preconditions for subsequent major changes in policies, thus helping to stabilize the economy, the society and to firmly maintain the progressive regime when the Eastern Europe and the Soviet Union rapidly collapsed and when the country was still in great isolation created by the West and other powers.

Of course, it is undeniable that the collapse of the Eastern Europe and the former Soviet Union had affected to some extent on our renewal. First of all, it made Vietnam more determined in carrying out the renewal policy and proved the correctness of the early and timely implementation of the Renewal policy.

Therefore, the renewal in Vietnam has not been spontaneous and passive at all. On the contrary, this is a policy experimentalized with the Party's political sensitiveness and a convergence of the country's objective necessity and the tendency of our time. It is the tendency of reform and internationalization of economics and social life in the world and the considerable impact of the revolution of modern technology and science that have also constituted important factors of Vietnam's renewal. Accordingly, the country's internal needs together with the tendencies of our time have given impetus to the advocating of renewal that have rapidly changed the country.

The renewal in Vietnam is comprehensive and not limited to the economic field. Renewal has been taking place in both economics and social matters and politics, infrastructure and superstructure, culture and external policy and relations.

Vietnam's renewal is aimed at nothing but the interests, happiness and bright future of the people. These goals could only be realised together with economic growth and the development and socio-political stability of the country. Life shows that political stability is precondition ensuring economic development. Economic development with good GDP growth rate could not be achieved if there was no socio-political stability, not to say about chaos. This is the reason why while advocating renovation, the Party and Government in Vietnam has attached much importance to political stability and hold that it is necessary to ensure political stability and to implement economic reforms first and then to proceed renovation in the system and administration.

Renewal will be, however, far from perfect if it is limited to economic reforms. This is the reason why to widen democracy and broadly implement democracy are considered as one of the important driving factors of the renovation of the social life, especially in economics and has encouraged and mustered valuable initiatives and recommendations. Democratization in economics included measures to encourage and allow all sectors in the economy to do business freely in accordance with laws and to be equal before laws, price liberalization, the Government's guarantee of ownership rights and legal income, direct access to consumption markets and trading with national and international partners, right to decide good items to produce and trade and to select production yield, etc. It is well recognized that this process has resulted in a new energy and driving force for the economy. Inflation was controlled from 747.7% in 1986 to: 67.1% in 1991, 12.7% in 1995, 7% in 1996, 4.8% in 1997, and around 9.3% in 1998. The average GDP growth rates between 1991 and 1995 was 8.2%: in 1995 was 9.5%, in 1996 was 9.34%, in 1997 was 9%. Industry growth rate remain around 13% yearly, agriculture grew at the rate of 4.8% yearly. Vietnam has become a good exporter of coal, crude oil, electronics, rubber, non-ferous metals, rice, coffee, textile, sea food products, other agricultural products, garments, etc. Export increases 20% yearly. Export-import turnover was nearly USD 9 billion in 1994 which increased to nearly USD 20 billion in 1997. Vietnam gradually becomes an attractive market for trade and direct investment. Up to December 1998, total capital from FDI reaches higher than USD 34 billion, total capital from ODA is more than USD 132 billion.

The most remarkable achievement of the renewal process during its early years was that in agriculture. Within a few years of implementation of renewal, Vietnam was transformed from a rice importer to the World's Third and then Second largest rice exporter. The price liberalization and democratization in economics managed to encourage the untapped material and moral potentials of the people. Any success gained in economics is a result of the new way of thinking and new concepts. Therefore, the Vietnamese Government's policy advocating a market-oriented commodity economy under State control while recognizing the existence of other economic sectors and modes of ownership has indeed attracted both domestic and foreign investors. The approval of series of new laws, including the Law on Foreign Investment, has brought into the economy important sources of capital for the future achievements.

One of the outstanding features or characteristics of the renewal process in Vietnam is the focus on the social aspects while working out plans and policies for economic renewal. This focus also concentrates on the settlement of social problems and the protection of man's habitat. The strategy for socio-ecnomic stability and development until the year 2,000 set out by the Government emphasizes that "economic growth should be closely attached to social justice and progress, cultural development and the protection of environment". In the present renewal policy, the improvement of infrastructure, economic strength, and material welfare etc., are the bases to satisfy better human needs. They are the conditions to care for people, helping them live better and develop their abilities. As such, economic growth must go hand in hand with social safeguarding. It is necessary to recognize the close attachment between economic and social policies; economic, ecological and social targets. As a matter of course, it is not possible to settle social problems without economic growth, or to say, out of the reach of the present economic development. However, it doen not also mean that economic growth would automatically resolve all social problems. To make light on the social policies will definitely create difficulties for economic development. That is so since social problems strongly affect the economy, not only in its growth but also in its achievements. As such, the Vietnamese Communist Party and Government consider "economic development as the basis and premise for the implementation of social policies, a fine implementation of which would create a momentum for economic development". Vietnam is not to sacrifice its social and environmental targets just to reach a high economic growth. This is yet another feature of our cause of renewal.

The renewal cause in Vietnam is indeed the policy of openness and integration into the world, selecting and adapting the world's essence with due regards to the trends and spirit of the present time. It is also a process in which whatever attained by modern science and technology is useful for the people and country will be taken in. The previous state stagnation was partly due to the close-door policy. We are never allowed to pay again that high cost when international cooperation has become a common trend of the time and an important condition for development as well. As it integrates itself into the world, Vietnam has reaped quite a number of political, economic, scientific and technological benefits. It has also learned good experiences in environment protection. The openness and integration policies stemmed from a platform that previously contributed to the victory of this nation in the struggle for national liberation and independence. That platform is the policy of combination of national strength and that of the present age. The concept of nation is not separated from the concept of time. Independence does not mean isolation. Vietnam is renovating in the spirit of "to befriend with all nations for peace, independence and development". Under such a policy, Vietnam has been able to break blockade and isolation imposed upon it for many years after the war. It has also been able to actively participate in and contribute to various international activities. The full memberships that Vietnam obtains frorn ASEAN, APEC as well as many other international organizations, and the establishment of full Diplomatic relations with over 160 countries including the USA are vivid examples of the renewal made in the field of foreign relations and are significant achievements of the policy of "Doi Moi".

Apart from remarkable achievements made that have brought the country out of the socio-economic crisis, the renewal process needs to further carry out a number of important tasks. Reforms in the fields of law and administration are some among them. The development of a market economy has created the gap between the rich and the poor, bringing along a number of social vices and corruption. Stagnation in administrative procedure reform and the lack of laws are joining corruption to let many foreign investors down. Further achievements could not be reached without resolving these problems.

It is important, however, to note that with all the invaluable achievements made in the process of renewal, it is now possible to confirm the correctness as well as the bright prospects for the policy of "DOI MOI" in Vietnam. Without a clear and scientific policy with firm targets, it is hard to avoid going to the extremes or staggering. The cause of renewal in Vietnam will not face such a situation. The initial worries and distrust in some people have now been replaced by a legitimate pride and a firm confidence. The dynamics as well as the newly created momentum have changed the country's face, bringing the country nearer to the targets set for this period with the long process of industrialization-modernization in the next nearly 25 years. It is important to understand that to industrialize and modernize the country, apart from the internal power, international co-operation and foreign investment are not less significant. As such, Vietnam's wide cooperation with all nations in the world on the basis of mutual benefit and respect within the framework of the common trend of globalization is one of the reasons bringing the country nearer to its target of building Vietnam into a country of "Wealthy people, strong nation, and just and civilized society", so that its people could live in peace, freedom and happiness at last after decades of hardships and sacrifice.

The renewal policy of Vietnam is based on dialectic materialist and anti-metaphysical thinking which means a continuous process of realisation not only in internal affairs but also in the external affairs. Analysing the domestic and international experiense, the Government and people have decided to mobilise the internal potentials of the country to do their best to enhance inner strength that is to do better in building economy, developing society and culture, improving management and fighting bureaucracy and all phenomena of corruption, more effectively and rationally using natural, material and human resources. Only on the basis of enhanced inner strength, people can preserve the long-fought-for independence and broaden international co-operation. Because of that, the foreign policy of new Vietnam is the policy of national independence, sovereignty, openness, diversification, and multilateralisation of external relations, in the spirit that Vietnam wishes to be a friend of all nations in the world community who is striving for peace, independence and development. That means they are developing and strengthening multifaceted, bilateral and multilateral co-operation with all countries, international and regional organisations on the principles of respect for one another's independence, sovereignty, territorial integrity, non-interference in each other's internal affairs, equality, mutual benefit, and settlement of remaining disputes and problems by peaceful means, through dialogues and negotiations in the atmoshphere of goodwill, and taking in mind the interests of parties concerned respecting international laws.

As in the past history, at present on the road of struggle to build Vietnam into a basically industrialized modern country in the year 2,000, it has to face many hardships and challenges and can overcome not only by its own efforts but also with the international co-operation and assistance.

# 5

# VIETNAM'S MODEL OF INDUSTRIALISATION AND MODERNISATION

V.D. CHOPRA

Any objective analysis of Vietnam's model of industrialisation and modernisation has to take into account three basic factors. This alone will enable any study to grasp the specific characteristics of the Vietnamese road to industrialisation and modernisation of its socio-economic structures and their unique features.

The geopolitical location of Vietnam led to repeated occupation of Vietnam from the ancient period to the contemporary era. It is within the crucible of these bitter struggles that Vietnamese nation state has emerged, though this process is still in the formative stage like many other developing nations. That is why, its nation-state building process is throwing up problems which are of similar nature as other developing nation-states are witnessing. The only difference is that Vietnamese, their political elite, and the Vietnamese Communist Party have been and continue to show realism with their feet well entrenched in their history, past experience, and above all, among their people. This in itself has a far reaching impact on the policy making process of this country.

Secondly, political elite of Vietnam for about 70 years, since the formation of the Vietnamese Communist Party in 1930, has exhibited a remarkable capacity of bringing about synthesis between pragmatism and scientific world outlook. In a backward feudal ridden society, emergence of the Communist Party as a driving force in all the struggle for national liberation and national state building, indeed, are specific features of Vietnam's political culture. That is the main reason that it has defeated the most powerful imperial forces with sheer human determination. To quote one example, when Vietnam was engaged in a decisive struggle for national liberation in early 1940, Ho Chi Minh realised the importance of uniting the entire people for national salvation. He formed a broad based front called *mat tran viet nam doc lap dong minh* Vietnam Independence League or Viet Minh. Vietnam's political elite drew a distinction between those feudal elements who had become stooges of French imperialists and other fuedal elements. This is how Vietnam's political leadeship worked out policy on concrete realities and did not follow doctrinaire approach. In a period of globalisation of economy, through a trial and error method, it continue to follow the same policy as we shall discuss later in this study.

Thirdly, in the end of the 70s, when Vietnam began grappling with a socio-economic crisis, on the basis of the practical experience, it evolved a number of measures, which were of a "partial renewal nature". However, these measures did not go far enough. Vietnam at that stage was subjected to blockade and embargo. While implementing renewal measures, new mistakes were committed. As a result of this, socio-economic crisis persisted acutely. The inflation rate reached 774.7 per cent in 1986. Triple digit inflation for three consecutive years; a sharp decline in the living standards of wage earners and people became a harsh reality. There was a steep decline in social welfare activities. Many state enterprises and small industries and handicrafts, co-operatives slipped into stagnation. These units experienced losses. They barely maintained old production level and some of them were forced to close down. Hundreds and thousands of workers were forced to leave their enterprises. Tens of thousands of teachers gave up teaching. Credit funds collapsed. Complex international developments, particularly American policy towards Vietnam further deepened the economic crisis.

In early 1988, famine struck several parts of the country and inflation still stood at 393.8 per cent. However, from 1989, onward Vietnam exported each year from 1 to 1.5 million tons of rice. Inflation slowed down to 67.4 per cent in 1990. This was the result of implementation of economic reforms—multi-sector commodity economy operating along market mechanism with state management. Along with this living conditions of people were improved and a series of measures were taken to promote democratic institutions. Above all new thrust was given to improving relations with other countries. This helped Vietnam to break its isolation and blockade. This shows that long before other socialist countries started the process of economic reforms, Vietnam had already begun to move in this direction. It is relevant to mention here that it was precisely in this period that India under the leadership of Rajiv Gandhi too had begun the policy of economic reforms, though this model was different from that of Vietnam.

After the disintegration of the Soviet Union and collapse of the socialist system in USSR and other east European countries, Vietnam is the second largest country after China, which is struggling to build a socialist society, though the concept of building such a society itself is undergoing changes.

Nonetheless, its objective of building such a society needs an objective study because its experience and lessons will have a direct bearing on the entire developing world, particularly for those countries which are still backward both in the agrarian and industrial sectors. Above all Vietnam is the fourth largest South Asian country, after Indonesia, Myanmar and Thailand.

This shows that from whatever angle you look at the present currents and cross-currents in Vietnam, in its economy, political structures and geo-political strategy, it will have far reaching impact on the developing countries, in general and on the Southeast Asian countries in particular. This implies that India will have to pay more attention to building economic and political relations with Vietnam, both in its own interests and in the interest of peace and stability in the region in a period when the era of bipolar world has ended and new political, economic and military equations have begun to shape.

The profound crises in the socialist countries in the early 90s, created serious problems for Vietnam. Even a section of communists began to doubt the Vietnamese path of socio-economic development chosen by President Ho Chi Minh. However, political leadership of Vietnam did not deflect from this course, though, it introduced a series of new measures.

The problem was further compounded by the fact that Vietnam's trade was dislocated and embargo continued.

In the past, for instance, in guiding the revolution in relations of production, Vietnam stood for early abolition of the mixed economy and early establishment of the pre-eminence of public ownership in the national economy. But, this policy was changed and bureaucratic control on public sectors was removed and subsidies were reduced. The concept of socialist oriented mixed economy was evolved. This concept was given concrete shape and this pocess is still going on with an open mind. Vietnam's political leadership, its scholars and researchers are using tools of analysis on the basis of ground realities and international economic relations to evolve their own model. This is neither western model of market economy, nor the old Soviet model. This is perhaps the middle course with its specific Vietnamese characteristics. Vietnam's concept is to develop a socialist oriented mixed commodity economy operating according to the market system with the State control. The State and collective sectors continue to be the foundation of the national economy. Various forms of distribution, with distribution according to labour productivity and economic efficiency have become the main basis of these reforms.

Thus, the principle of "each according to his capacity to each according to his work" began to be implemented and the old utopian understanding of socialism was changed. During the last two decades, on the basis of developments in other socialist countries and growing aspirations of the people for a better standard of living, Vietnamese model of industrialisation and modernisation of its socio-economic structures was evolved. Vietnamese leadership came to the conclusion that the road to transition from a backward agrarian socio-economic structure to a modern socialist system will be prolonged and there was no short cut to it.

In keeping with the rich heritage of the anti-colonial struggle, and the course evolved by Ho Chi Minh, the Vietnamese leadership evolved its own model with the main focus on transformation of human consciousness. That is one of the main reasons that despite internal and external pressures, Vietnam and its political leadership created political stability to move forward step by step on the basis of concrete experience to harness and develop its economic structures. This stands in complete contrast to the development of other socialist countries which collapsed under internal and external pressures. This perhaps is the biggest achievement of Vietnam during the last one decade of the present century.

To make an objective analysis of political and economic reforms of Vietnam, its theoretical basis should be recapitulated. In a backward agrarian society, the concept of "proletarian dictatorship" for building socialism has been given a new content. If one goes by the official documents, Vietnam is now building "a state of the people, by the people and for the people with the alliance with the working class, peasantry and intelligentsia".

This concept has far reaching political and ideological implications. Intelligentsia, has played an important role in the national revolution of Vietnam. But now its role has been upgraded.

The significance of this concept has to be understood in the context of the fact that intelligentsia from the working class and peasantry is still very weak in Vietnam. Quite apart from this aspect, in a period of technological and scientific revolution which the world is witnessing, no social transformation can take place without the active participation of intelligentsia. Thus, the social forces which are being galvanised for modernisation and industrialisation of Vietnam consist of these three social forces.

These two basic theoretical postulates, it appears are the foundations of the new orientation of Vietnam for its modernisation and industrialisation.

In the midst of euphoria in the former socialist countries and some of the developing countries, about dismantling public sector and state owned enterprises, Vietnam has evolved its own model of simultaneously building and consolidating various layers of economic structures in which public sector and state owned enterprises have been assigned an important role.

Vietnam has decided to develop and consolidate public and state owned enterprises in *key sectors* and *sub sectors* of economy, particularly in those sectors in which other sectors of economy are unable to invest or operate. The state sectors of economy are being restructured with new technology and modern administrative set up to make them efficient.

However, in case of those enterprises where state-run status is no longer necessary, their form of business and ownership is either being changed or they are being dissolved. In this process the problem of employment and living conditions of these employees are being given a top priority. Nevertheless, in totality of the situation in the policy of Vietnam both state-run and public sector enterprises have been assigned a "leading role" and function as an "instrument of macro-economic management".

This line of demarcation between Vietnam and former socialist countries must be kept in mind. This shows that in the new economic policy of Vietnam, the old policy of "unrestrained" development of state sector and the system of "state subsidies" are being replaced with new forms of economic structures, in which the state sector is to be modernised and made more efficient. This alone will enable the state sector to play a leading role.

This, however, is only one aspect of the economic reforms, which are mainly directed to make state sectors efficient, competitive, modernised, market oriented and democratic. These sectors of economy are proposed to be run with well trained cadres and will no longer be under the old bureaucratic control. However, it is too early to pass any judgement on this fresh approach to run the state sector.

Equally important is that, along with these changes in the state sector of the industrial economy, Vietnam has evolved a long term policy of "liberalising the entire industrial sector" with a view to develop what is called *socialist oriented multi-sector commodity* economy.

This multi-sector economy has various components. These can broadly be categorised as follows:

**(i) State Sector**

The state resources will be concentrated on developing the state economy in such vital branches and areas such as financial system, banking, insurance, important areas of production, trade and service establishments and a number of enterprises and undertakings relating to national defence and security. State enterprises in general shall be medium and large sized, equipped with advanced technology. These units will be run with efficiency to generate large budget revenues.

**(ii) Joint Sector**

Joint sector enterprises will have different forms. In some joint sector enterprises, the state will hold majority or dominant percentage of shares. With a view to set up new enterprises and expand the industrial base of the country, these shares will be sold both to the local population and foreign organisations and individuals. The joint sector will play an *intermediate* role in the industrialisation of the country.

### (iii) Co-operative Sector

Co-operative sector will be promoted and strengthened both in production and business. This sector will have various forms, from low-level co-operatives to high-level co-operatives, depending on the specific conditions and their area of operations.

### (iv) Individual and Small Ownership

Individual and small owner economy has an important position in the new economic policy of Vietnam. Assistance is being given to it to overcome difficulties in acquiring capital, modern technology and scientific knowledge. Above all, it is being given help in marketing. This sector of economy is being given help to set up co-operatives on voluntary basis. Steps have been taken to make this sector as ancillary units to the state sector.

### (v) Private Capital

Private capital has been assigned an important position in the industrial development of the country. To encourage private capitalists investments are taking place in the economy of the country on a long term basis. Their property rights and legitimate interests are protected. They are provided with favourable conditions. They are also being given help in modern management techniques.

All these components in the industrial sector, in trade and commerce and in finance and Banking have slowly though surely begun to generate a new atmosphere in the country. This has already begun to show positive results.

### Agrarian Sector

Land is held by the State and is leased out by the State to individual rural household on long-term basis. In the opinion of the political leadership of Vietnam "land must not be privatised" because it will lead to "major class polarisation". This would hamper planning and building of infrastructure and other material bases for the development of the country. However, one basic factor which has to be kept in mind is that due to certain historical conditions and terrain of Vietnam, the land ownership system in Vietnam is very complicated. Therefore, the land policy of Vietnam is that this system should not be disturbed because in the final analysis in the agrarian society of Vietnam, neither capital formation nor expansion of internal market would be possible without increasing the agricultural prodution within the framework of the fact that land belongs to the "entire nation".

Within this broad framework, a well-defined agrarian policy has been evolved, which has begun to yield positive results. The main elements of this policy can be summed up as follows:-

(i) Agriculture, forestry and fisheries are being developed in the direction of the commodity economy linked with processing industries to meet domestic demand and to promote exports. Vietnam has already become one of the major rice exporting country.

(ii) Agricultural production has embarked upon specialised cultivation with a view to obtain highest possible yield per acre. Intensive cultivation and crop multiplication are being promoted. Alongwith this, cultivation of cash crops have begun to show a steep upward trend.

(iii) Hydraulic system to solve the problem of drainage and irrigation in selective high concentration areas of food crops and cash crops is being introduced.

(iv) Fisheries are being developed to fully exploit different varieties of aquatic and marine resources.

The main orientation of these and other measures is to transform the face of rural Vietnam as an integral part of the new socio-economic policy.

The following table gives an idea how agriculture in Vietnam is being modernised and undergoing basic changes:

**Table 1**

**Projects investing in Agriculture, Forestry and Fisheries in 1998-2005**

| *Item* | *Number of Projects* | *Total Capital ($ Million)* |
|---|---|---|
| Cashew nuts and cocoa | 4 | 17.5 |
| Sericulture | 4 | 23.0 |
| Vegetable | 15 | 97.9 |
| Tea | 18 | 129.0 |
| Coffee | 13 | 136.5 |
| Cereals | 28 | 147.3 |
| Fisheries | 45 | 159.5 |
| Other Projects | 24 | 185.5 |

| | | |
|---|---|---|
| Sugarcane and sugar industry | 6 | 195.0 |
| Rubber | 16 | 246.7 |
| Animal husbandry and feed industry | 78 | 366.4 |
| Fruits and vegetables | 79 | 466.9 |
| Forestry | 69 | 2404.0 |

*Source:* Indo-Vietnamse Chamber of Commerce and Industry, News Letter, Vol. 9, No. 1, July-September 1998.

**Foreign Capital**

Due to certain historical reasons, prolonged struggle against colonialism, the biggest problem which Vietnam is facing is that of capital formation and capital accumulation. That being the situation, in the new economic policy of Vietnam, foreign investments are encouraged. However, this policy has been evolved keeping in the forefront that political and economic independence of the country are not weakened and these investments are made within the broad framework of the national objective of industrialisation and modernisation of the country. An important component of this policy is to raise the standard of living of the people interests of the workers in these industries.

Thirty-nine foreign capitalised businesses whose investors are from 14 countries world-wide have been granted licences to operate in Da Nang. They have a total investment capital of US$ 423 million, and legal capital of US$ 179 million. Of this the realised funds were US$ 127 million, accounting for 29.89 per cent of the total investment capital. Apart from this, Da Nang is now home to 22 representative offices for foreign organizations. In the first six months of 1997, the 39 businesses achieved a gross turnover of US$ 27 million, an expor turn over of US$ 20 million, equal to 95.2 per cent of that of the same period last year. Nevertheless, contribution by these enterprises to State taxes amounted to US$ 2,326,290 —1.35 fold higher than in the corresponding period of 1996. Sixteen out of 39 foreign capitalised businesses with a total capital of US$ 237 million (representing 56 per cent of total) engaged in industrial production, four businesses (US$ 30 million in investment capital, accounting for 7 per cent) are involved in construction and building materials, six units (US$ 107 million, 25 per cent) in hotel and restaurant trading, three projects (US$ 10 million, 2.3 per cent) in services, four aquatic farming and processing projects (US$ 6 million 1.4 per cent), three agricultural product and food processing projects (US$

28 million, 6.7 per cent), and three forestry product farming and processing projects (US$ 6 million, 1.3 per cent). Fourteen of the 39 projects are 100 per cent foreign capitalised businesses with a total investment capital of US$ 55 million and a legal capital of US$ 31 million. The other 24 projects are joint venture businesses with a total investment capital of US dollar 367 million, and the last is a business co-operation contract, having an investment capital of US$ 598,018. Vietnamese partners often contribute joint venture capital as land and water use rights and other material facilities. Foreign partners contribute capital as cash, equipment and machinery, and technology transfers. Notable among the 39 foreign investment projects in Da Nang are Vijachip, Sinaran, and Valley View. Last year Vijachip achieved profits of US$ 515,709 and provided 7,000 jobs, 3,470 of which contracted for six months or more, with an average income of US$ 44 per month. This gives an idea about the role of foreign capital in Vietnam.

French direct investment in Vietnam increased from US$ 870 million in 1996 to US$ 1.45 billion in 1997, pushing France from the tenth place to the sixth place in the list of the countries who make investments in Vietnam. According to the experts, this is the largest wave of French investments ever seen in Vietnam.

Vietnam has maintained a close trade investment relations with Hong Kong for many years. On July 1, 1997, Hong Kong returned to China. This created a sense of uncertainty about Vietnam's economic relations with Hong Kong. However, statistics show that economic relations between Vietnam and Hong Kong have not witnessed any change so far. Hong Kong is the fourth largest investor in Vietnam. In the first six months of 1997, Hong Kong had licensed 14 projects in Vietnam worth US dollar 148 million.

After Vietnam became a full fledged member of ASEAN, its economic relations with the countries of ASEAN witnessed a marked change. ASEAN investors have created a favourable impact on Vietnam.

According to one source, upto June 1997, the number of investment projects from ASEAN countries in Vietnam was 371 with a total capital of US dollar 8.3 billion.

Soviet Union-Vietnam relations stood on a different footing before the disintegration of the USSR. However, now Russian-

Vietnam economic relations are being restructured in the new historical conditions.

These selective facts show how Vietnam has to diversify its economic relations and how foreign capital has started playing an important role in its new economic policy.

**Exports**

In 1997, Vietnam exported agricultural products worth US dollars 2.4 billion equal to one-third of nation's total export value (US dollar 8.7 billion). This was an increase of over 10 per cent over 1996. However, this increase in 1997, was low in comparison with the average growth rate of 20 per cent of the country's export. In 1997, Vietnam exported 3.6 million tonnes of rice, a sharp increase over the last year. But there is one important factor which should be kept in mind. Financial crisis in South-East Asia had boosted rice exports. But Vietnam had to sell rice at a low price. The result was that its foreign currency earnings decreased. The total value of rice exports in 1997 was according to one estimate only US dollar 900 million against US dollar 850 million in 1996. Again coffee export increased by 26 per cent over 1996. However, the total value of the coffee export reached only US dollar 400 million.

As far as rubber export is concerned, China imports 70 to 75 per cent of Vietnam's rubber. Here again, Vietnam did not receive adequate price and is now looking for other markets.

This shows that as far as the policy of export of agricultural products to other countries is concerned, Vietnam is facing new problems. It has, therefore, to adjust its policies in a period of globalisation of economy. This decline in real earnings through exports of agricultural products has a direct bearing on the earnings of the rural population.

However, during 1997, the pace of setting up of foreign aided projects has accelerated. Nevertheless, as against this trend, statistics of Ministry of Planning and Investment show that by the end of 1997, the country has licensed 313 new projects and 137 projects are in the pipe line. This will increase foreign direct investment capital to US dollar 30 billion. It has been estimated that in 1997, the foreign direct investment (FDI) would be US dollars 6 billion. This will be around 2 billion US dollars less than 1996.

It may also be mentioned here that in the first 11 months of 1997, foreign invested enterprises made US dollar 1.85 billion in production value, an increase of 45 per cent as compared to 1996.

In the past, investment capital was mainly funnelled into oil and gas exploration (32.2 per cent) and hotel construction (20.6 per cent). But since 1995, the country has focused its investment on production, accounting for 80 per cent of the total investment capital, of which 60 per cent is intensive investment aimed at developing and upgrading the current production capacity. At present, areas ranking first in terms of attracting foreign investment are HCM City, Ha Noi, Hai Phong, Binh Duong, Ba Ria-Vung Tau and Quang Ninh. Though, investment capital has still mainly been funnelled into the three key economic zones, up to now, almost all provinces, including remote and mountainous provinces like Lai Chau, Kon Tum and Ha Glan have received foreign investment.

State-owned enterprises are the main partners entering foreign investment co-operation JVs, amounting to 96 per cent of the total number of projects and 99 per cent of the total investment capital. Presently, Vietnam is home to 700 foreign companies from 50 countries and territories worldwide, ranking first is

Singapore with US dollar 5.3 billion (172 projects),

Taiwan with US dollar 4.1 billion (306 projects),

Japan with US dollar 3.48 billion (216 projects) and

Hong Kong with US dollar 3.7 billion (196 projects).

The inevitable conclusion is that Vietnam is evolving the policy of industrialisation and modernisation on the basis of actual experience and is not influenced by old dogmas. Nonetheless, the basic parameters of transition from a backward agrarian country to building a modern Vietnam are still valid. This means that the Vietnamese model needs to be critically examined for it has its own lessons for all the developing countries.

## Foreign Investment in Vietnam

Five localities invested with US$ one billion upward of FDI

| *No.* | *Provinces* | *Projects* | *Reg. Capital* | *Ratio (%)* | *Average Project* |
|---|---|---|---|---|---|
| | | *($ Mil)* | | *($ Thousand)* | |
| 1. | DCMC | 697 | 8,857.5 | 29.6 | 12,708 |
| 2. | Hanoi | 345 | 6,885.2 | 23.0 | 19,957 |
| 3. | Dong Nai | 249 | 3,258.9 | 10.9 | 13,088 |
| 4. | Ba Ria-Vung Tau | 83 | 2,249.0 | 7.5 | 27,096 |
| 5. | Hai Phong | 88 | 1,456.4 | 4.9 | 16,550 |

63 countries and territories invest in Vietnam, including 10 investors with more than $ one billion in investment capital.

| *No.* | *Countries* | *Projects* | *Reg. Capital* | *Average Project* |
|---|---|---|---|---|
| | | *($ Mil)* | *($ Thousand)* | |
| 1. | Singapore | 185 | 4,845.7 | 26,193 |
| 2. | Taiwan | 354 | 4,168.5 | 11,775 |
| 3. | Hong Kong | 264 | 3,364.0 | 12,742 |
| 4. | Japan | 236 | 3,037.5 | 12,871 |
| 5. | South Korea | 223 | 2,960.7 | 13,277 |
| 6. | France | 119 | 1,705.1 | 14,329 |
| 7. | Virgin Is. of Britain | 66 | 1,667.4 | 25,264 |
| 8. | US | 74 | 1,095.4 | 14,803 |
| 9. | Australia | 72 | 1,080.8 | 15,011 |
| 10. | Thailand | 109 | 1,037.5 | 9,518 |

Apart from more than $ one billion investors, others with more than $500 million number five including Malaysia $943.9 Mil., Panama $673.2 Mil., Switzerland $618.6 Mil., Britain $569.1 Mil., Netherlands $565.4 Mil.

Eleven among 19 economic sectors have attracted FDI.

| No. | Sector | Projects | Reg. Capital ($ Mil.) | Ratio% | Average Project ($ Thousand) |
|---|---|---|---|---|---|
| 1. | Agri-Forestry | 233 | 1,195.6 | 3.8 | 5,131 |
| 2. | Fishery | 83 | 331.7 | 1.1 | 3,996 |
| 3. | Gas and oil industry | 39 | 1,611.6 | 5.1 | 41,323 |
| 4. | Heavy industry | 430 | 5,289.4 | 16.8 | 12,301 |
| 5. | Light industry | 608 | 4,645.3 | 14.8 | 7,640 |
| 6. | Construction | 221 | 3,677.1 | 11.7 | 16,638 |
| 7. | Hotel, tourism | 189 | 3,880.5 | 12.3 | 20,532 |
| 8. | Service | 191 | 7,410.9 | 23.6 | 38,810 |
| 9. | Transport and communication | 120 | 2,785.9 | 8.9 | 23,216 |
| 10. | Finance and banking | 26 | 182.8 | 0.6 | 7,031 |
| 11. | Culture, health care and education | 68 | 426.0 | 1.4 | 6,265 |

Grouped into three main categories, as follows:

| No. | Sector | Projects | Reg. Capital ($ Mil.) | Ratio(%) | Average Project ($ Thousand) |
|---|---|---|---|---|---|
| 1. | Agriculture, forestry and fishery | 316 | 1,527.3 | 4.9 | 4,833 |
| 2. | Industry and construction | 1,298 | 15,223.4 | 48.4 | 11,728 |
| 3. | Service | 594 | 14,686.1 | 46.7 | 24,724 |

As mentioned, sectors of industry and construction recorded the highest ratio of both number of projects and registered capital, the second rank was service and the lowest was agriculture-fishery.

## References

1. Communist Party of Vietnam 7th National Congress Document, Published by Vietnam Foreign Languages Publishing House, Hanoi-1991.
2. Communist Party of Vietnam 8th National Congress Document, Published by the GIOI Publishers, Hanoi-1996.
3. Various issues of Vietnam Economic News.

# 6

# IMPACT OF ECONOMIC REFORMS

V.D. CHOPRA

The economic reforms introduced by Vietnam in the 90s have begun to change the socio-economic structure of the country. This is confirmed by the fact that the average annual growth rate in the 1991-95, period was 8.2 per cent for the gross domestic production (GDP) (against a planned target of 5.5 per cent-6.5 per cent). 13.3 per cent for industry, 4.5 per cent for agriculture and 20 per cent for export volume. The economic structure experienced a measure of change. The ratio of industry and construction to GDP increased from 22.6 per cent in 1990 to 29.1 per cent in 1995; and that of services from 38.6 per cent to 41.9 per cent. Accumulation from within the economy started. The capital investment of the whole society accounted from 15.8 per cent of GDP in 1990 and for 27.4 per cent in 1995 (in which investment from domestic sources amounted to 16.7 per cent of GDP). By the end of 1995, the total registered capital of the FDI projects had reached over 19 billion US dollars, with almost one-third already put into operation. The inflation rate decreased from 67.1 per cent in 1991 to 12.7 per cent in 1995.

Scientific and technological activities have become more closely associated with the needs of socio-economic development and progressively adapted to the market mechanism.

Relations of production have been adjusted to better suit the development needs of the productive forces. The multi-sector commodity economy operating along a market mechanism with State management and a socialist orientation continues to build up.

The material conditions of life for the majority of the population have been improved. The number of medium-income and wealthy households has risen while the percentage of poor households has decreased. Each year, over one million more working people have found employment. Many dwelling houses and roads have been upgraded or built in both rural and urban areas.

The intellectual level and the extent of cultural enjoyment of the population have been heightened. Education, training and health care, cultural, artistic and sports activities. mass communication, family planning and many other social activities have seen development and progress.

Working people, liberated from the bondage of a good number of unreasonable mechanisms having their right to be the masters and their dynamism and creativity promoted, show greater initiative in seeking employment generating, additional income, and taking part in community activities.

The policy to pay the nation's debt of gratitude to those with meritorious service has elicited nation-wide support; the campaign for hunger eradication and poverty alleviation and philanthropic activities continue to expand, becoming a new and fine feature of the society.

The confidence of the population in the political system and the future of the country, and in the party and State, has been heightened.

However, one cannot ignore that Vietnam remains among the poorest countries in the world, with low levels of economic development, labour productivity, production and business efficiency, backward material and technical base, and a heavy degree of indebtedness. While its requirement for capital for development investment is very large and pressing, a number of State and Party institutions, economic organisations and a section of bureacracy and population are spending wastefully, consuming more than they can produce without saving for intensive development investment. The State is yet to adopt policies which can effectively mobilise capital resources among the population. In 1995, investment from domestic savings (including capital depreciation) in capital construction accounted for a meagre 16.7 per cent of GDP, in which investment from the State budget accounted for only 4.2 per cent of GDP which was very low compared with the need for economic development. "The utilisation of the resources was scattered and inefficient, indicating a lack of resolve to concentrate on the highly necessary socio-economic programmes and projects."

"Corruption, smuggling and the squandering of public property have yet to be checked. Serious lapses persist within the State and party apparatuses and people's organisations, and in State enterprises, especially in the fields of land and housing, capital construction, investment cooperation, taxation, import and export, and even in the operation of many law-enforcement bodies, etc".

The problem of generating employment remains acute. Polarisation of wealth has rapidly increased between the various regions, between urban and rural areas, and between different segments of the populations. The condition of life of part of the population, especially in a number of former revolutionary and resistance bases and in ethnic minorities' areas, remain very hard. The quality of education, training and health care is quite low in many places. Poor people cannot afford medical treatment and sending their children to school while financial sources from the State budget and other available resources that can be mobilised to respond to social welfare requirements remain both limited and poorly utilised. Traffic congestion, eco-environmental pollution and natural resources destruction all continue to grow. Noxious cultural articles are widespread. Social ills are on the rise, many complex problems still beset public order and safety. This frank assessment made by the Communist Party of Vietnam in its 8th Party Congress documents of 1996, shows how the weaknesses in the system are not concealed from the people.

What is more important is that instead of liquidating partially or wholly, public sector projects, Vietnam is engaged in the exercise of making these projects more efficient and profitable. It is this exercise which needs to be critically examined. Cooperative sector is also being revamped.

Quite apart from this number of policies aimed at providing incentives for private economy to promote its own potentials have not been properly handled, and at the same time, management of this economic sector leaves much to be desired. There have been many loopholes in the management of enterprises involved in cooperation and joint ventures with foreign countries.

The system of laws, mechanisms and policies are not yet well-co-ordinated, consistent and strictly implemented.

The operations in financial, banking, pricing, planning, construction scheming, and land management have shown many weaknesses. The pace of renewal in administrative procedures, etc., is slow. The State trade service has left vacant a number of important "grounds", while not yet effectively bringing to bear its leading role on the market. The management of import-export operations has revealed many loopholes, giving rise to negative phenomena some of which have adversely impacted production. Income distribution still suffers from many irrationalities. Budget over expenditures and trade deficit remain large. Inflation, though curbed, is still unsteady.

Removal of poverty, particularly in the rural areas is the main challenge which Vietnam faces today. Although, ten years of economic reforms has witnessed a general increase in people's income, poverty remains widespread in Vietnam. This is especially the case outside the major cities where, according to an ADB report, 90 per cent of the poor live. The UN resident coordinator Edward A. Wattez said an internationally comparable poverty line indicates that nearly 50 per cent of the population lives in poverty, while the Vietnam Government's lower poverty line suggests nearly 20 per cent live in extreme poverty. Only 45 per cent of the rural population has access to safe drinking water and 26 per cent to sanitation. Three million people, the majority in the Northern Uplands, Central Highlands and North Central Coast, suffer three hungry months a year and are sometimes forced to supplement their diets with roots and tree bark. This indeed is the grim situation.

However, most public investment has been directed to the largest cities, with Ha Noi and HCM City receiving three times more than other areas. The level of ODA allocated to poor rural areas, especially the poor Northern Uplands and Central Highlands, has been rising since 1995. However, the capital city continues to receive US dollars 18 of ODA per capital compared to the Northern Uplands 5 dollars, the Central Highland 4 dollars and the Northern Central Coast less than 2 dollars.

While conceding this fact, the Deputy Minister of Labour, War Invalids and Social Affairs, Nguyen Luong Trao said, the Vietnam Government is well aware of the problem and is trying its best to resolve the imbalance. In an effort to fight the urban-rural disparity, the Government recently launched a poverty alleviation programme with its chief focus on the 1,000 poorest communes in mountainous and remote areas. It is one of the seven programmes the National Assembly and the Government have approved in response to the 20/20 initiative. This initiative implies that 20 per cent of the State budget and 20 per cent of ODA should be devoted to the social expenditure.

The Vietnamese Government has committed to alleviate extreme poverty by the year 2001 and the general poverty in 2010. This shows that the first decade of the next century will be decisive in Vietnam's policy of economic reforms. That underlines the strategic importance of creation of jobs.

However, this commitment will be no easy task to implement. According to the UN's index of Human Development, Vietnam ranks only 121 of 175 countries in terms of overall human development, reflecting the need in further improving the people's general well-being.

Prime Minister Phan Van Khai, on 11th July, 1998, signed a decision approving the national employment promotion programme till the year 2000. According to experts from the Ministry of Labour, War Invalids and Social Affairs, creating five million jobs from now to the year 2000 requires many things.

Under the programmes, from 1997 to 2000, the national economy should be developed fast to create five million new jobs, train 4.5 million employees and raise the rate of trained labourers to 22-25 per cent by 2000 (the current rate is 12.2 per cent). The programme at the same time will lower unemployment in urban areas to five per cent (the current rate is 6-8 per cent) and increase labourer hiring from 72.1 in 1996 to 75 per cent in 2000.

Tran Huu Trung from the Ministry of Labour, War Invalids and Social Affairs thinks that to hit this target, it is necessary to do the following:

Assessing the effect of various policies on the decrease or increase of jobs; profiling and assessing employment criteria stated in State plans and socio-economic programmes; offering vocational training courses and jobs for one million people; granting loans to provide 925,000 jobs; and forming employment service centres in centrally governed cities and provinces and these centres' satellite establishments in towns, townships and concentrated industrial zones. Trung said that Vietnam suffers from a high unemployment rate and its employee training and distribution structures have revealed some weaknesses. Specifically, agricultural labourers account for 69.78 per cent, while those for the construction and industrial sectors account for only 10.55 per cent, and those for the service sector represent only 19.65 per cent of the total figure.

Some VND 4.8 trillion is earmarked for the programme. According to Trung, from now to the year 2000, it is necessary to promptly set up and submit to the relevant authorities, plans to grant loans from the national employment fund; choose partners and sign agreements with State credit organisations such as the Vietnam Bank for Agriculture and Rural Development, Industrial and Commercial Bank of Vietnam and State Treasury to grant loans which will generate jobs; assist the 550,000 people who registered at different employment service centres to find a good job; encourage businesses to grant loans to provide stable jobs to 370,000 unemployed people recommended by different employment service centres in accordance with developing small-scale enterprises and those processing agricultural and export products; help businesses using a large number of female workers get loans to assure stable jobs for 2,500 female workers and create 2,500 jobs for the disabled.

This shows the real content of "economic reforms with human face", however, this highlights the importance of foreign investments in Vietnam's economy.

A recent survey from the Ministry of Labour Invalids and Social Affairs (MOLISA) reported that nation-wide unemployment rose to 7 per cent of the labour force in 1997, with that average rising to 23 per cent in some rural areas. However, foreign investment is falling quickly; the amount of foreign direct investment pledged to Vietnam in 1998, is just 60 per cent of the amount received in 1997.

With the labour force growing by 1.1 million workers every year, getting people to work— no matter where— is crucial. This is leading to migration of workers to other countries—both skilled and semi-skilled.

Going to work in a foreign country is not a new concept for Vietnamese labourers. The Government began sending workers abroad in the early eighties under agreements with a host of Eastern-bloc countries. The declining economic power of the Soviet Union also prompted the Government to look for labour contracts in other non-aligned countries. Official figures from MOLISA indicate that between 1980 and 1990, over 250,000 people went to work in Iraq and Libya.

Under the terms of these agreements, Vietnamese workers were technically employed by the Vietnam Government, which then subcontracted their services to the host countries. The agreements were very profitable. Over the course of the decade, roughly VND 800 billion or 300 million dollars calculated at the 1990 rouble-to-dong rate, was earned for the state budget by the labour contracts. During an era when rice was rationed and there was not enough meat to go around, it was a good arrangement for everyone. "Vietnam was experiencing a serious crisis at that time", says Nguyen Trong Duc, a professor at the Hanoi Irrigation University who went to Iraq in the late eighties. "People had nothing to do and the government desperately needed to find jobs for us. They found them abroad."

Following the collapse of the Soviet Union, export emphasis has shifted to other markets, such as South Korea. The change in economic models also brought about a change in the export industry. For the first time, individual government bodies were allowed to market their workers and undertake contracts directly with private companies, usually through one of their subsidiary companies.

Under the present arrangement, these state-owned firms apply to MOLISA for quotas to export workers. The largest two labour exporting ventures are the Vietnam Construction Company under the Ministry of Construction, and the Labour Overseas Development Company (LOD) under the Ministry of Communications and Transport. Between 1990 and 1997, 54,000 labourers have been sent abroad under arrangements organised by these organisations.

Keeping tabs on actual figures for the past decade has also become much more difficult; many of the workers that went abroad in the eighties have yet to return. After the last of the inter-governmental agreements from the eighties ended, an estimated 200,000 Vietnamese guest workers remain unaccounted for, most of whom are working unofficially in their host countries.

They are also generating lots of unofficial business for their home country.

A recent survey conducted by MOLISA reports that between 1991 and 1997, Vietnamese working abroad officially contributed about 1 billion dollars every year to the Vietnamese economy. While exact numbers are not available for this grey industry, people involved in trade with relatives abroad say this number is plausible.

"I set up this workshop with the money my brother sent from Russia. We make garments that he orders, which we export to Russia", said Nguyen Tu Nam. Mr. Nam's shop has expanded and now employs 15 tailors in Hanoi's Hai Ban Trung district. According to a source from the Vietnam Chamber of Commerce and Industry (VCCI) hundreds of these small businesses have been set up with money repatriated by overseas workers. These establishments then create more jobs.

The growth in small-scale trade could be a blessing. As the effects of the regional crisis take hold around the region, the number of official labour contracts is beginning to taper off. The reason for the decline is simple: "In South Korea, there are so many unemployed natives right now," explains Kim Hyun-Myung, counsellor at the Embassy of the Republic of Korea in Hanoi, "No new guest labour contracts are being made".

Beginning in the early ninetees Sourth Korean companies began employing Vietnamese labourers. At the peak of the hiring in 1993, there were 50,000 Vietnamese guest workers in South Korea. But with almost 2 million unemployed workers in the country, it's hard to justify bringing more foreigners in. Kim says that South Korean companies aren't signing any new contracts and are ending present contracts through attrition. "Importing more foreign labourers will be difficult for the time being," He says.

Depressed economies aren't the only reason that Vietnamese workers aren't being invited back to their former countries of employment. "I am told that our office in Libya is planning to reduce the number of Vietnamese workers imported to Libya," says Jong Sun Lee, representative for the Dong Ah company in Vietnam. "There have been thefts of our supplies. This is a serious problem." Through a partnership with Vinaconex, Lee's company has sent more than 2,000 labourers to Libya.

This shows that job opportunities for Vietnamese workers outside their countries are shrinking. This will increase the pressure on Vietnam's economy. That is why in the new economic policy of

Vietnam, industrialisation, modernisation and commercialisation of agriculture have assumed new importance. Vietnam therefore has evolved a flexible and multi-dimensional policy of foreign investments in the country. The new policy of foreign investments should be seen in this context.

**LABOUR EXPORT FROM VIETNAM**

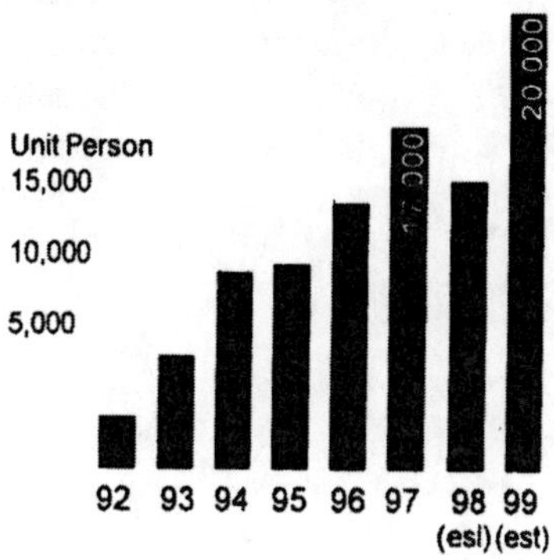


**LABOUR EXPORT DESTINATIONS**

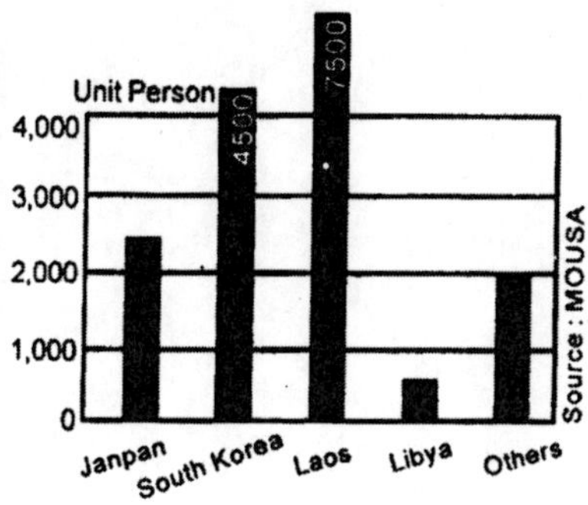


## References

1. *Vietnam Economic Times,* Issue 57, November 1998. p. 14-15.

# 7

# FOREIGN ECONOMIC RELATIONS

V. D. CHOPRA

Vietnam has evolved a policy of developing economic relations with other countries on a multi-dimensional basis. This policy has yielded tangible results. What is of relevance is that notwithstanding the serious financial crisis which the Asian countries faced in 1998, its economy continued to register an upward trend. But for this economic policy, Vietnam would have suffered heavily. The economy still posed a GDP growth of about 6 per cent and the country has maintained its socio-economic stability. In the context of the economic situation in neighbouring countries, these are substantial achievements.

However, every achievement has its negative aspect. Agricultural production grew by 3 per cent. But in this estimate the cost of irrigation to fight the drought and the damage caused by it to such cash crops as coffee and pepper have not been fully taken into account.

However, the 11.5 per cent increase in industrial production, despite Vietnam's limitations and stiff competition and more difficult distribution conditions, this indeed is significant achievement. But the improved output of crude oil and power has been offset by a decrease in the production of numerous other commodities hit by low rates of consumption, such as cement and steel, or competition from imports, such as ceramic sanitary wares. Local manufacture of urea fertiliser, in particular, suffered a serious setback due to high cost of production.

Production in the public sector has grown by 8.7 per cent, in the private sector by 6.3 per cent and in the foreign-invested sector by 22 per cent, proving that efficient production and goods with a sharp competitive edge can still secure a market share in a crisis-hit economy. Attempts at restructuring and cutting costs by the service sector, including tourism, aviation and post and telecommunications, could not prevent a major decline. The growth rate was, therefore, just 6 per cent. Given its high profile in the national economic structure (42 per cent of GDP), this disappointing result has considerably slowed down the national growth rate.

The most obvious effects of the economic crisis on Vietnam have been the reduction in exports and foreign direct investment. Exports have risen by about 0.3 per cent compared with 1997. Apart from the outstanding success of rice and crude oil, output of many manufactured and processed items have registered a steep decline. The primary reason for the fall in exports is contraction of traditional markets in Asia, the destination of up to 60 per cent of Vietnamese exports. Major trading partners such as Japan and South Korea have cut their imports of Vietnamese garments and textiles, leather goods and marine products.

Since supply exceeds demand in the world market, the price of many items, crude oil in particular, has sharply declined. Therefore, despite the increase in the quantity of crude oil exports, upto 34 per cent compared with last year, foreign currency revenue has actually fallen by 18 per cent— a loss in real terms of 588 million dollars. Other exports, such as garments and textiles and leather goods, have shown similar results.

The crisis has also meant that competition between countries in the region has become increasingly fierce in terms of prices, delivery conditions and so on. Vietnam has tried to find new markets for its exports in Europe and Australia, but these efforts have not made up for the slump in the Asian market.

Foreign investment has obviously decreased, the implementation of investment projects already licensed has slowed down, and a number of hotel and high-rise building projects have been put off. Total realised foreign investment capital is estimated at 1,735 million dollars in 1998, a fall of 40 per cent compared with 1997, but the real figure is lower if price rises are taken into account.

In December 1997, economic reforms were further intensified. The Government proceeded with an integrated programme to introduce numerous new policies, extended the list of businesses that oculd deal in direct exports, state-owned enterprises were reformed with greater autonomy to them.

This new thrust to economic reforms became necessary because the economy showed signs of a slow down in 1996, even more so in 1997. The current population growth of 1.64 per cent and GDP growth rate of 6 per cent pose a new challenge for Vietnam of how to balance its rate of consumption with its reserves. The reduction in exports has made the trade deficit a crucial issue. In particular, the imbalance in current account payments has placed pressure on the exchange rate of the *dong*. The fall in foreign investment has increasingly stemmed the flow of foreign currency, leading to the necessity for adhoc solutions such as limiting imports and making more effective use of foreign exchange for urgent requirements.

Exposure to competition has revealed weaknesses in the economic mechanism and management of the system. The 5th Plenum of the Communist Party of Vietnam in mid 1998, evaluated the cultural life of the country, focusing on ethics, corruption and the consumerist lifestyle. A number of government officials and company directors in particular were sharply criticised for this. The Plenum emphasised the dire need for thrift to combat the crisis.

Low productivity, high production costs and overheads which conceal a multitude of unnecessary expenses have made it difficult to corner even the domestic market.

Bureaucratic red tape and corruption are still prevelant. Large-scale economic scandals that have come to light in recent years are only the tip of the iceberg, and make a case for much deeper economic and administrative reform, it was underlined.

The stress that the Party's 6th Plenum in late 1998, placed on the agricultural sector indicates a major shift in the policy at the national policy making level. This sector will spearhead the government's efforts to deal with the crisis.

Growth rate targets for 1999, set GDP at 5 to 6 per cent, agricultural output at 3.5 to 4 per cent, industrial production at 10 to 11 per cent, the service sector at 4.5 to 5 per cent, exports at 10 per cent and imports at 2.7 per cent. These are all thoroughly considered objectives in view of the regional economic crisis and are based on the continued progress of firm and comprehensive renovation. Their ultimate aim is Vietnam's gradual integration into the international community.

The economic crisis can be overcome step by step, but it would be naive to rule out the possibility that things could get even worse.

Failure to seize the opportunity presented by the crisis will compound matters as countries in the region will be far more competitive than even before undergoing radical reforms. Without vigrous and in-depth changes at both macro and micro level, the economy of Vietnam will be in an even less favourable competitive position. Macro economic reform must focus on restructuring the banking sector, controlling foreign exchange and dealing with outstanding debt, in order to generate a smoother circulation of capital flow in the economy and provide the secure capital foundation which business requires. This is the main content of economic reforms in the last year of the present century.

The mobilisation of sources of funds must begin with land, which is still used in a less than efficient way and is often extensively misused. The programme to reform State owned enterprises will continue; the equilisation scheme is likely to improve the efficiency of this most important sector of the economy. Controlling monopolies and creating an environment for fair competition for business, especially the private sector, are urgent priorities.

But economic reform will be effective only if it is carried out in conjunction with administrative reform—streamlining the state apparatus and its staffing levels, radically improving working methods and cracking down more effectively on corruption.

These are testing times. But every Vietnamese knows that gold has to be refined by fire. History has shown that Vietnam have the will to prevail in the most adverse circumstances.

# 8

# SINO-VIETNAM RELATIONS: A NEW PHASE

V. D. CHOPRA

Sino-Vietnamese relations in the ninetees— political, economic and cultural have entered a new phase, which stand in complete contrast to the earlier phase. This process began when General Secretary of the Communist Party of Vietnam Do Muoi and Prime Minister Vo Van Kiet visited China in November, 1991, to lay the foundation for the "normalization of relations" between the two countries. Since then, about 18 high level meetings between the leaders of the two countries have taken place. The result is that a new phase of relationship between the two countries is clearly visible. Sino-Vietnamese relations have witnessed a steady development. This is evident from the last phase of talks between the leaders of the two countries in the last week of February, 1999. The significance of the latest round of talks between the two countries has to be seen in the context of the fact that this new trend of relationship between the two countries has begun to unfold itself when both China and Vietnam are making preparations to enter the third millennium with new opportunities and challenges. The leaders of both the countries have begun to evolve basis for new, stable and long-term basis for cooperation.

Economic cooperation ties between the two countries have been developing rapidly as two-way trade value has witnessed an annual average growth of 20 per cent from US dollars 266 million in 1992, to about US dollars 1.4 billion in 1998. China at present has 42 investment projects and 56 representative offices of its companies operating in Vietnam. Vietnam-China Economic-Commercial

Cooperation Committee set up in 1995, has contributed positively and is promoting bilateral trade and investment cooperation. This cooperation now is expanding and by the beginning of the next century, it has been stipulated that this two-way trade and economic co-operation should reach the target of US dollars 2 billion.

Significantly, China is increasing investment and participation in construction projects in Vietnam. Equally important is the fact that the leaders of the two countries are making serious efforts to solve their border problem. During the visit to China by the then Communist Party of Vietnam General Secretary, Do Muoi, in July 1997, top leaders of the two countries agreed to settle the land border issue in 1999 and to demarcate the Bac Bo Gulf between the two countries in the beginning of the next century. This decision was confirmed by the leaders of the two countries during their exchange of visits, the latest being the China visit by Vietnamese Prime Minister Phan Van Khai in October, 1998, and the visit to Vietnam by Chinese Vice-President Hu Jintao.

After six-day visit to China by General Secretary of Communist Party of Vietnam Le Kha Phieu from February 25 to March 2, 1999, a joint declaration was issued, which confirms that Sino-Vietnamese relations have already entered a new period. The main features of this joint declaration by Jiang Zemin, General Secretary of the Communist Party of China and President of the People's Republic of China and General Secretary of the Communist Party of Vietnam can be summed up as follows:

The leaders of the two countries discussed extensively, how to further consolidate and stregthen the friendly and co-operative ties between the two communist parties, the states and people of the two countries as well as regional and international issues of mutual concern. This shows that the relations between the two countries have been raised to a very high level and are no more confined to what is called in diplomatic jargon as "state to state relations".

Secondly, the leaders of the two countries confirmed that "these relations will exert a positive influence on peace, stability and developments in the region". This declaration, therefore, brings into focus the international and regional importance of these relations. It is relevant to quote some portions of this declaration to reinforce this argument.

The declaration has underlined that "the two sides expressed satisfaction at the constant consolidation and positive development of the friendly and cooperative relations between the two Parties and the two countries. This serves not only the fundamental interests of the two Parties and the two countries and peoples, but also peace, stability, co-operation and development in the region and the world as a whole. The two sides agreed that by continuing to observe the principles laid down in the joint communiques made public, since the normalization of Vietnam-China relations and the reaching of mutual agreement by leaders of the two Parties and the two countries, they will join efforts in building long-lasting neighbourly and friendly relations and comprehensive cooperation in the future. The two sides affirmed that on the basis of the principles of independence, sovereignty, full equality, mutual respect, and non-interference into each other's internal affairs, the Communist Party of Vietnam and the Communist Party of China will continue to constantly develop their friendly and cooperative relations and promote a comprehensive development of State relations.

The two sides agreed to look forward to the future by further exchanging friendly and cooperative visits and experiences in various forms between departments and branches of the two Parties and administrations as well as mass organizations and localities of the two countries, especially the exchange of friendly visits between the youth and children of the two countries to comprehensively develop the Vietnam-China friendship, and pass it to the future generations.

The two sides reaffirmed the agreements and common understanding reached during their high-level meetings since 1991, and share the view that an early solution to the territorial border issues between the two countries conforms to the fundamental interests and the common aspiration of the two peoples. At the same time, they express satisfaction at the positive developments of the bilateral negotiations in recent years. The two sides agreed to place the primary issues foremost, show sympathy and compromise with each other, conduct fair, rational and friendly consultations, and taking into account international laws and reality, try to satisfactorily settle the outstanding territorial border issues between the two countries through peaceful negotiations.

The two sides expressed their determination to accelerate the process of negotiations and raise their working efficiency for the signing of a land border treaty in 1999; to complete settlement of the issue on demarcation of the Bac Bo (Tonkin) gulf in 2000; and to join efforts in making their common borderline one of peace, friendship and stability.

"The two sides agreed to maintain the existing negotiation mechanism on the sea issues, and through persistent peaceful negotiations, try to find out a basic and long-term solution acceptable to both sides. Pending such solution, the two sides by proceeding from easy to difficult issues will actively conduct discussions to seek possibilities and solutions to implement bilateral cooperation on the sea in such areas as protecting the sea environment, hydro-meteorology, and natural calamity prevention and control. At the same time, the two sides should refrain from any actions that are likely to further complicate or widen the dispute, and from the use of force or the threat to use force. The two sides should promptly conduct discussions and satisfactorily solve any difference with a calm and constructive attitude without letting such differences affect the normal development of bilateral ties.

"The two sides expressed their satisfaction at the positive results in the expansion of trade, economic development, scientific and technological cooperation, as well as other domains between the two countries in recent years. The two sides hold that there is still great potential and bright prospect for further broadening economic, commercial, scientific and technological cooperation, and other domains between the two countries. On the principle of equality and mutual benefit and with emphasis on efficiency, quality and diversified forms for common development, the two sides are determined to join efforts in bringing into full play the key role of major companies, broadening bilateral trade ties to increase the volume and value of trade, encourage and support businesses of both sides to carry out major cooperation projects, create favourable conditions for their investment in each other's business, and boost healthy and orderly cross-border trade. The two sides will be active in finding out new ways and measures to broaden and deepen economic, commercial and scientific-technological cooperation and other domains, thus bringing cooperation to a new height of development".[1]

The two sides signed an agreement on economic and technical cooperation between the two governments.

The two sides reaffirmed the common understanding reached in the joint Vietnam-China communiques issued on November 10, 1991, November 22, 1994 and December 2, 1995; the Vietnamese side reiterates that Vietnam recognizes the government of the People's Republic of China as the sole legitimate government representing the whole of China; and that Taiwan is an integral part of China. Vietnam only maintains non-governmental economic and commercial exchanges with Taiwan without developing governmental relations with Taiwan. The Chinese side shows its understanding the appreciation of Vietnam's position. The Chinese side affirms that the Taiwan issue is merely an internal affair of China, and resolutely protests against any country which has established diplomatic relation with China while attempting to set up governmental relations in any form, or make any governmental contact with Taiwan.

"The two sides note with pleasure the great achievements obtained by the two countries in their renovation process, open-door policy, socialist construction and improvement of the people's living conditions. The Chinese highly value the achievements recorded by Vietnam in the renovation process and expansion of international cooperation for the goal of a rich people, a strong country, and an equitable and civilized society. The Vietnamese attach great value to China's achievements in the reform and open-door process, as well as in broadening its external relations and preserving and realizing national unity.

"The two sides expressed satisfaction over the wide range of common view-points they have reached on regional and international issues of mutual concern. The two sides share the view that maintaining and consolidating peace and stability in the region and the world, and enhancing bilateral, multi-lateral and regional economic cooperation are in conformity with the common aspiration and fundamental interests of the peoples in the region and the world. The two sides advocate working for a new fair, and just political and economic world order and will practically contribute to the maintenance and consolidation of peace, stability and development in the region and the world.

"The two sides hold that the financial-monetary crisis in Asia has affected to different extents the economy of many Asian nations; that the nations concerned should share the responsibility by enhancing their coordination and cooperation to overcome the crisis. The Chinese side highly appreciates Vietnam's active efforts toward the impact of the financial-monetary crisis in Asia and ensure a continual development of the national economy. The Vietnamese side highly values China's contributions to alleviating the impact of the financial-monetary crisis in Asia and stabilising the regional economy."[2]

These excerpts from the joint declaration of China and Vietnam bring out that the relations between these two biggest socialist countries of the world, which are engaged in modernising and industrialising their countries within the framework of what they call a "socialist oriented mixed economy" is of far reaching political and economic importance both for Asia and the world. In a way, this declaration represents an alternative to the western model of "free market economy": But there is something more to it.

This joint declaration of February 27, has clearly laid down parameters for resolving border disputes between the two countries through negotiations and peace on the principle of ground realities and mutual interests. In this sense this declaration lays basis for solving border disputes between the two countries on long term basis. It will not be therefore, incorrect to say that this declaration may become a pace setter for building Asian unity in a period when the transition from a unipolar world to a multipolar world has become more complex and in some regions even explosive.

## References

1. Vietnam News Agency, February 28, 1999. Vietnam-China joint declaration.
2. *Ibid.*

# 9

# OPEN-DOOR POLICY AND ECONOMIC RELATIONS WITH THE UNITED STATES

V. D. CHOPRA

Vietnam has evolved a multi-dimensional open-door policy of economic cooperation with other countries to industrialise and modernise its economy.

In 1997, Vietnam achieved a 9 per cent economic growth rate, the highest in South-East Asia. Despite adverse effects from the regional financial crisis and shrinking foreign investment, the country reached planned norms for industry, agriculture, import, export and inflation rate. Although, the value of the Vietnamese currency to the US dollar decreased by 20 per cent by the end of the year, massive withdrawals of deposits usually happening in previous years and in other regional countries at present were not seen last year. The consumer goods price index climbed at the end of 1997, equalling the previous year's figure, and thus speeding up goods circulation and benefiting production and business.

The donor conference held in Tokyo in December, 1997 pledged a donation of 2.4 billion dollars to Vietnam in the fiscal year 1998. The London Club conference which took place in Paris on December 12, 1997 also passed the decision to reduce Vietnam's debts by 53.9 per cent. Japan has proved to be the largest donor, with a pledged sum of over 700 million dollars.

Vietnam's stable economic growth, vigorous implementation of the Government's open-door policy and persistent market economic reforms have impressed donors and creditors.

Assistance funding for Vietnam in 1998, equals that of the previous year, regardless of the announcement by many countries to reduce donations due to their own difficulties. By September, 1997, total due date debts that Vietnam owed international banks and financial institutions accounted for 815.8 million dollars.

The project to use natural gas from offshore Ba Ria Vung Tau to develop 15 industrial plants; the project to construct oil refinery 1 at the Dung Quat bay of Quang Ngai Province; and the project to regreen stripped hills on a total five million ha area are believed to be the three largest projects that the National Assembly approved.

Following the National Assembly's new resolution, any project worth more than VND 10 trillion (about 800 million dollars) must be submitted to the National Assembly for approval.

The gas utilisation project involves nine thermo-electric plants; three gas related plants; a steel plant; a fertiliser plant and a methanol factory.

The oil refinery 1 project, with a yearly capacity of 6.5 million tonnes and a total investment of 1.5 million dollars is scheduled to become operational by 2001.

The reforestation project is due to be promoted nation-wide during 1998-2010.

In 1997, Vietnam ranked second globally in rice exports, exporting 3.6 million tonnes following Thailand and surpassing the US.

Despite damage and huge losses caused by floods and storms in the Cuu Long (Mekong) Delta, the country managed to yield 30 million tonnes of food, including 27.5 million tonnes of husk rice, the peak output so far. The northern delta now has surplus of rice for export.

Foreign Direct Investment (FDI) registered in 1997, amounted to 5 billion dollars against 8 billion dollars in 1996, a 37.5 per cent decrease. This decline is mainly attributed to decreasing attraction of foreign investment in the region as a whole. South-East Asia has endured the worst financial crisis over the past several decades, and Vietnam has been adversely affected by such a chaos. The drop in FDI is also caused by Vietnam's less attractive policy on foreign investment plus needless troublesome administrative procedures.

In November, 1997 tropical storm Linda slammed into the southern coast of Vietnam leaving widespread damage of about 500 million dollars. This savage storm not seen for the last 100 years caused nearly 500 deaths, destroyed more than 200,000 houses, sank over 3,000 fishing ships and seriously flooded more than 300,000 ha of rice fields.

Many domestic and international organisations, enterprises and businesses actively provided both spiritual and material support for Linda's victims. Hundreds of billions of VND coming from voluntary supporters across the country and millions of US dollars from international organisations and governments was handed over to storm victims.

The Vietnam-EU garment and textile accord signed by the end of 1997, allows Vietnam to export goods of this kind to EU estimated at 650 million dollars in 1998, a 35 per cent increase against 1997.

The Vietnam-Eu garment and textile accord ended with a total of 3.5 billion dollars in Vietnam's export goods which have gained an international reputation and have created many jobs for labourers.

The new accord will last until the end of 2001, allowing Vietnam to lessen categories and obtain more favourable provisions.

Exposing weaknesses, the banking system paid a heavy price A governor was relieved of his post, with three big cases involving banking activities. Three entities of Nam Dinh textile factory, Epco and Minh Phung are about to be heard.

Ex-governor of the State Bank of Vietnam Cao Si Kiem could not gain enough reputation among National Assembly members and thus had to retire, while general directors of the three companies are now waiting for trial charged with lending hundreds of millions of US dollars in an attempt to run fraudulent businesses and embezzle the money, pushing thousands of employees to the edge of unemployment and poverty.

This is the minimum amount of foreign currency needed to import two million bottles of alcohol which, by November 30, 1997, were declared and stamped.

Including non-trade and illegally imported bottles of alcohol, by the end of December, luxury goods of this kind amounted to more than 1 million dollars.

The campaign to stamp three types of goods: imported alcohol, bicycles and electric fans, launched in November 1997, is seen as one of the Government's efforts to vigorously control imports of deluxe items and boost locally made products. This is also regarded as a crucial first experiment for further stamping other kinds of imports. However, after two months of implementation, the price of these three items increased by 10-20 per cent.

The financial crisis in South-East Asia has adversely affected Vietnamese currency, to some extent. In an effort to strengthen Vietnam's competitiveness in exports, the State Bank has loosened the trading band between VND and US dollar from 5 to 10 per cent, which rocked the black market exchange rate. The value of Vietnamese currency to the US dollar decreased by 15 per cent 1996, from VND 11,600/1 to VND 13,500/1 dollars.

After six rounds of negotiation, a Bilateral Trade Agreement between the US and Vietnam seemed still out of reach in the last quarter of 1998. However, the negotiations are still going on and American business circles do not want to be left behind in capturing the market of Vietnam.

The round continued discussion on some key areas the two sides had raised in the last round held in Washington in May, 1998. At that time, Vietnam submitted a proposal that covers four areas including trading goods, intellectual property right protection, trading service and investment. These proposals according to the US official, basically accepted the outline of the US agreement.

Investment is the issue that created most controversy. Although, US investors entered the Vietnamese market later than Asians or Europeans, they are now included in the top 10 investors and very keen to urge Vietnam to improve its investment environment. According to one of Vietnam's negotiators and Deputy Head of the Ministry of Trade's Division for Europe-America Affairs, Nguyen Van Bih, the US side wanted to include an entire investment chapter to the agreement, while World Trade Organisation (WTO) does not require a separate agreement on the issue. Moreover, the Vietnamese side argued that the US requirements relating to investment environment improvement for US companies operating in Vietnam are even higher than regulated by WTO.

The most sensitive issue concerning the rights of US businesses to compete on an equal footing with Vietnamese companies remained deadlocked. Vietnam is firm not to equally treat foreign and domestic enterprises regarding land and fixed assets ownership, business establishment, business forms, etc; and this corresponds with the international practice.

Vietnam's officials maintain that in the trading service areas, the US requirements are also higher than those of WTO, for example, the requirement to totally liberalise some sectors in which the United States is very strong like telecommunications, finance, banking, insurance, etc. They also maintain that the Vietnamese side had given to the US side its commitment on services based on WTO principles.

The American representatives maintain that the progress made in the negotiation are impressive, the US official, however, conceded there are fundamental issues that need to be resolved as the two sides disagree on many points.

The US side questioned if Vietnam really understands how important it is for the country to have this agreement and take the next step in economic reform by integrating into the world market and facilitating investment of companies and enterprises in Vietnam. There are important issues which need to be resolved for integration of Vietnam with the US market. Obviously this is a major policy decision for Vietnam.

The agreement is needed for Vietnam to receive normal trade status. In the opening speech, US Ambassador Pete Peterson said it would be the most important economic agreement between the two countries for the next 15 years and it will determine the course of their economic relations for the future. Although, Vietnam's Trade Minister, Truong Dinh Tuyen, stated that negotiation process with the World Trade Organisation and the US on trade issues are separate and independent, still many believe that a Bilateral Trade Agreement with US would significantly boost Vietnam's chances of joining WTO.[1] However, the process of economic cooperation between the two countries has yet to gain momentum.

As against this French direct investment in Vietnam, in 1997, increased from US dollar 870 million to 1.45 billion pushing France from the tenth place up to the sixth on the list of countries and territories investing in Vietnam. This is the result of the official visit of French President Jacques Chirac, in November 1997, to Vietnam. According to investment experts, this is the largest wave of French investment, even seen in Vietnam, with numerous valuable contracts worth more than 696 million dollars signed with Vietnam during his visit. The first among these contracts is the 470 million dollars co-operative project between the Vietnam Post and Telecommunications Corporation and France Cables at Radio (FCR), a subsidiary of France Telecom. The project will install and develop a local telecommunications network, including 540,000 telephone lines for the eastern region of HCM city, over a 15 year period. The construction of this network is scheduled to last for five years. France Telecom will assist Vietnam in terms of technical examination, management work, staff training, and technology transfer.

Also in HCM City, Suez-Lyonnaise des Eaux Corp. has signed a 110 million dollars contract to construct a 300,000 cu.m/day water plant, which will supply tap water to more than one million inhabitants and rectify the permanent water shortage in the City.

FCB an offshoot of Fiver Lilles Corp. has also gained an investment licence worth 130 million dollars to provide equipment for the Hoang Mai (Hghe An), 1.4 million tonne per year cement plant. In addition, Caisse Francaise de Development (French Development Fund) has approved a credit agreement to fund about 19 million dollars for a sugar factory in Quang Ngai Province and around 36.9 million dollars for the project to grow Arabia Coffee by the 'Vinacafe' Company. A financial letter of credit worth about 53.7 million dollars has also been concluded. The French 150 million dollars project for an asphalt production plant in the South is now waiting for approval. French firms: Alcatel, Matra Macom, and Aerospatiale are now also waiting for approval of a 200-250 million dollars satellite telecommunications project. According to a French press source, during his visit, President Jacques Chirac encouraged French energy oriented companies such as GEC-Alsthom to get involved in the construction of the Phu My Thermo-electric Plant 2 and the Pha Lai Themo-electric Plant 2.

The visit to Vietnam of President Chirac is cited as a good start for further deals by French businessmen and investors in Vietnam.

**New Thrust**

At the second session of the 10th National Assembly, great attention was paid to the report by Prime Minister Phanvan Khai on

Vietnam's socio-economic development in 1997. This report underlined the importance of the new economic policy.

Khai's review on 1997's socio-economic situation pointed out that: The economy continued to maintain the development pace of previous years. However, difficulties have emerged in view of keeping the growth rate stable. Only five out of the total of eight norms laid down by the National Assembly were expected to be realised, regarding GDP growth rate; increase in agricultureal output; food; inflation; and population growth.

The planned industrial growth rate is 14-15 per cent; services 12-12.5 per cent; and export turnover 0.27 per cent. Yet, the real figures may fall to 13.2; 9.5; and 20 per cent, respectively.

This explains why Khai said "We must look straight into the truth to find the right solutions to accelerate the renovation cause". He stressed the economy is now exposing some main weaknesses, low economic efficiency and decreasing competitiveness; modest accumulated revenue due to worthless extravagant expenses; improper investment in the economic development; and irrational allotment relations, leading to an increasing gap between the rich and the poor, as well as the big gap among different regions throughout the country.

He attributed these shortcomings to an unsound economic structure and a slowly renovated economic management apparatus. The Prime Minister assessed: "The processing industry is growing slowly. Processed export products make up a minor portion". The State-run sector, the so-called key economic area, has not received appropriate investment in technology and capital regardless of its own entanglements in management structure, resulting in less efficient operations.

In regard to major solutions and economic tasks for 1998, Khai particularly focused on renovations in institutions and policies.

The Prime Minister stated that untangling obstacles and difficulties in regulations and procedures which had hampered business registration and investment development were key steps in motivating all resources and attracting investment.

Khai announced that the Government will soon introduce a new decree providing guidelines for the implementation of the Domestic Investment Encouragement Law. Laws and decrees on private businesses, as well as the Company Law will be adjusted and added to support investment and business in such fields that are not prohibited or restricted.

To gear up domestic production, vital measures are needed to strengthen the competitiveness of Vietnam made products together with a rational production protection policy, it was emphasised.

In the years to come, large investment, including that from foreigners and the State, will concentrate on infrastructure construction. Small and medium-scale investment will be preferred. For large-scale projects, conditions and feasibility, as well as efficiency of projects should be contemplated carefully. Special attention will be paid to projects able to create many jobs and generated high export revenue. The Prime Minister also stressed that construction and efficiency of industrial and export processing zones will be enhanced. A pilot project to set up special economic and free trade zones at suitable locations is scheduled to be formulated.

In particular, for the purpose of intensifying exports, an essential part of the economic structure, the State, as Khai indicated, "will create the most favourable facilities for exports of all kinds of goods (excluding those subject to State ban and control) in all economic sectors. On the basis of realised export turnover, credit policies will be amended in favour of exports."

For the State-run Sector, the Prime Minister affirmed: "Renovation of State-run businesses will be continuing" through specifying different types of State-owned businesses, including 100 per cent State-invested establishments (mainly those operating for the purpose of public interest); businesses with main shares of which the State only needs to hold small shares and will diversify the remainder in many appropriate forms.

This will serve as a solid base of the enlargement of private businesses, alongwith which the aim of privatisation is believed to be boosted. In addition, the Government will add new regulations on selling holdings to different organisations and individuals aimed to diversify property. Pilot sales of share to foreigners will be included. For small and medium sized businesses suffering from continuous losses with out-dated technology and playing a less important role in the country's economy, the State may suggest diverse variations, according to specific cases. Accordingly, these businesses might be incorporated to others, or be subject to privatisation and public tenders, or even be required to go bankrupt in accordance with legal stipulations.[2]

This shows how economic reforms in Vietnam have begun to unfold a new dimension.

## References

1. *Vietnam Economic News*. September 28 - October 4, 1998, p. 5.
2. *Vietnam Economic News*, 5-11 December, 1997, p. 5.

# 10

## VIETNAM AND ASEAN

### V. D. CHOPRA

Vietnam's economic relations with ASEAN Association of South-East Asian Nations have evoked conflicting assessments for obvious reasons. Vietnam is a backward agrarian country surrounded by developed asea. This poses new challenges.

In fact, the integration into ASEAN and the implementation of CEPT (ASEAN'S integrated tax program) is a great challenge for Vietnam's economy, since the level of economic development and technology in Vietnam is well behind that of other ASEAN countries. However, this does not mean that Vietnam's economy will be unable to cope with this problem. Vietnam has proved this simple truth many times throughout its history.

Integration into ASEAN gives Vietnam an opportunity to develop more quickly its economy, particularly to attract more foreign investment which is vital to the industrialization and modernization process. Since Vietnam became a full ASEAN member, the investment of ASEAN companies in it has been continuously increasing.

Coming later than many other countries, ASEAN investors have created a favourable impact on Vietnam. According to one estimate up to June 1997, the number of investment projects from ASEAN countries was 371 with a total capital of 8.3 billion US dollars.

Five of six ASEAN countries are included in the list of the top 20 foreign investors in Vietnam. At present, Singapore is the number one with 167 projects valued at 5.2 billion US dollars. Malaysia is in the seventh place with 62 projects and capital of 1.6 billion US dollars. The figures for Thailand are 105 projects and nearly 1 billion

US dollars, for Indonesia— 17 projects, US dollars 250 million and for Philippines— 20 projects, 225 million US dollars.

It is significant to mention that the success rate of ASEAN investment projects is high in comparison with other countries. Up to 1997, only 43 ASEAN projects have been revoked, accounting for 11 per cent of the total number and just 1.4 per cent of the total ASEAN investment capital. As against this the number of all revoked projects is 352, accounting for 17 per cent of all projects and 10 per cent of the total capital.

Singapore, Malaysia and Indonesia are considered as the most effective investors. Singapore has 8 revoked projects with revoked capital accounting for just 0.4 per cent. For Malaysia the figures are 3 and 0.25 per cent; for Indonesia : 2 and 1.2 per cent. Malaysian investors have focused on the development of industry, with 69 per cent of capital and 44 per cent of projects. More than 90 per cent of Malaysian investment capital has been put into operation. That's why Malaysia is considered as one of the most successful investor in Vietnam.

Thus, beginning with a few small-scale projects aimed to search Vietnam's market in the early 90s, ASEAN'S FDI in Vietnam has expanded quickly over recent years. However, ASEAN projects do not affect Vietnam's economy greatly, since most of them are small or medium in size. With a few exceptions, the majority of ASEAN projects have total investment capital of 1 to 8 million US dollars. But, the increasing number of projects and capital show the true interest of ASEAN investors in Vietnam's economy and markets.

Being a full ASEAN member, Vietnam becomes more attractive for ASEAN investors. In the recent years, total ASEAN investment capital has been double that of the period from 1989-1995. Singapore has the highest growth rate of investment. Indonesia has had approved the largest project, with total capital at 2.1 billion US dollars.

Although, ASEAN investment volume is significant, it is mostly in the field which do not require high technology. Most of its projects are in real estate, hotel, tourism, and assembly and processing industries. More than 50 per cent of FDI from Singapore, the country with highest technology level in ASEAN, is in the field of hotels and tourism. It is clear that hi-tech industries are not targets for ASEAN investors.

Some specialists are critical of ASEAN'S investment strategy in Vietnam. They say: "If we consider hi-tech as a major factor accelerating the economic growth rate of developing countries, then we must also see that the economic effectiveness of ASEAN investment, is low". They propose that Vietnam have more incentive policies to attract more hi-tech investment, vital to the industrialization and modernization process. This would enliven the competition between ASEAN and other investors in the Vietnamese market.

At present, Singapore is the biggest investor in Vietnam, though in 1995, it was still in the fourth place. ASEAN investors do not dominate the Vietnamese market, and the competition between ASEAN companies and others becomes fiercer. Japanese, Taiwanese and Hong Kong investors came to Vietnam very early and have cemented their position in the market. By mid 1997, Taiwan had invested more than 5 billion US dollars. Australia has also proved to be a strong investor in the field of oil and mineral exploration, metallurgy and other high-tech areas. American companies are also becoming stronger competitors. Just one year after the lifting of the US embargo, US investors jumped from 24th place to 13th, and now are at 6th place.

ASEAN companies are not as strong in capital and technology as others in the developed countries. In fact, ASEAN countries, including even Singapore, have at times had to invite foreign investment to cover capital shortages, and to improve technology levels. Therefore, there is little likelihood that ASEAN investors will come to dominate in Vietnam, according to one expert. Presently, ASEAN investment in Vietnam accounts only for 18 per cent of all projects and 25 per cent of the total investment capital internationally.

Theoretically, Vietnam will expand its market to about 400-500 million consumers when it implements the ASEAN integrated tax program CEPT, creating impetus for foreign investment. But in reality, Vietnam does not gain much from this programme, becuase it must now compete against other ASEAN countries for investment flow. Vietnam has little chance in this struggle, since its economic development level is well below that of other ASEAN countries, and its investment environment is still not favourable for foreign investors. In his recent visit to Vietnam, the EU ambassador revealed that Vietnam is not attractive enough for EU investors. They can find better investment environment in other ASEAN countries.

Therefore, one of the most important tasks before Vietnam is to improve the investment environment. According to Nguyen Trong Xuan from the Economic Institute, Vietnam's FDI Law is quite attractive for foreign investors compared with other ASEAN countries. However, many foreign investors complain about uncertainty in the Vietnamese Government's policies, and call for greater stability and predictability.

Nevertheless, ASEAN investors believe that they have a future in Vietnam. A survey during a seminar organized by the Thai Embassy showed that 90 per cent of Thai investors are confident that their investment in Vietnam will bring profit.

In totality, however, Vietnam's economic relations with ASEAN have opened a new chapter in regional economic cooperation.

Vietnam has maintained a close trade-investment relationship with Hong Kong for may years. On July 1, 1997, Hong Kong returned to China. This development did not have any negative impact on economic relations of Vietnam with Hong Kong. Unexpectedly, in the last two weeks of June, just before Hong Kong returned to China, five Hong Kong investment projects, totalling 100 million US$, were granted licences, double the value of projects licensed to Hong Kong interests in the first five months. Nevertheless, according to investment experts, this should not be taken to mean that Hong Kong's investment pace in Vietnam will increase. Meantime, there are no signs that Hong Kong's investment will flow to China instead of Vietnam.

According to the Investment Department of the Ministry of Trade of Vietnam, by early July 1997, Hong Kong had 267 licensed projects worth a total of 2.8 billion US$.

Hong Kong is the fourth largest investor in Vietnam. In the first six months of 1997, Hong Kong had 14 projects totalling 148 million dollars licensed. Hong Kong investors are concerned mostly in hotels, entertainment sites, light industry (garments, textiles, and footwear), and agricultural product processing. Hong Kong's largest investment project so far is the 75 million dollars JV to construct and run businesses in the Hai Phong EPZ. Hong Kong was also the first and the second largest investor in the other two EPZs of Tan Thuan and Linh Trung with 9 projects producing garments, textiles, shoes, and packaging, totalling 57 million dollars.

In response to the question, whether, Hong Kong's investment activities are likely to change after July 1, 1997, the Deputy Head of the investment Department of MPI, Tran Quan Ngoc, said that Hong Kong authorities have the complete right to steer investment into any country they desire, according to the policy "one country, two systems" which China is now imposing on Hong Kong, a special administrative region. Thus, Hongkong investors may continue to invest heavily in Vietnam because they will continue to need the Vietnamese market.

This statement seems to accord with the speech of Raymond Xip, the director of the Hong Kong Trade Development Council in the Asian region: "Hong Kong will not only decidedly maintain its investment policy for Vietnam, but will also want to boost the bilateral trade relationships after July 1." He also emphasized: "Hong Kong will strengthen and maintain its strong investment position as presently. Vietnam will become the door to countries in the Mekong River region".

Will the handover impact Hong Kong businesses currently operating in Vietnam? The director of cathay Pacific Vietnam, Sidney Kwok says: "The transfer of Hong Kong will not affect Cathay Pacific's operations, including our existing JVs with Vietnam Airlines". Hong Kong Bank's transactions director Tim Slater also remarked: "The return of Hong Kong to China will not influence Hong Kong Bank's activities in Vietnam. We also hope to help Vietnamese companies accelerate trade activities between Vietnam, Hong Kong, and China, as economic relations continue to be developed".

At one time, Hong Kong was nearly the only gateway for Vietnam to other countries in terms of trade. Now, Vietnam has many such gateways. However, Hong Kong continues to be a major trading partner of Vietnam. In 1995, Hong Kong ranked sixth in trade with Vietnam, with a total of $814 million in bilateral trade. In the first half of 1997 alone, bilateral trade amounted to $474 million. Vietnam's Deputy Minister of Trade, responsible for external economic issues, Mai Van Dau, noted: "Hong Kong will remain an important trading partner for Vietnam". Dan also noted that presently 8-9 Vietnamese companies are operating in Hong Kong engaged in a wide range of business, from trade, transport to finance and tourism. Furthermore, Vietnam, has set up a Consulate recently in Hong Kong.

Vietnam Hong Kong trade relations are likely to continue to flourish, as they have in the past. These relations will get a new boost after improvement of Sino-Vietnamese relations.

## References

1. Dang Hong Nga — Asea and Investment in Vietnam, p 20, 21, Vietnam Economic News, No. 33, Vol VII, August 15-21, 1997.
2. Hai Nam — Vietnam — Hong Kong Relations after the Handover. *Ibid* p. 22.

# 11

## VIETNAM AND RUSSIA

**V.D. CHOPRA**

Relations between Vietnam and the Soviet Union were traditionally based on friendly cooperation, in which goods and commodities were exchanged between the two sides largely through barter. The seventies and eightees were a golden era for the two countries' trade activities with total trade values worth more than 1 billion dongs/ roubles a year. Vietnam's imports from the Soviet Union were three-fold to its exports to that country. The Soviet Union was a market for 80 per cent of Vietnam's foreign trade.

After the Soviet Union's break-up, Russia became a member of the Commonwealth of Independent States (CIS) and the relations between the two countries moved to a new chapter involving international trade practices such as using international prices and convertible foreign currencies.

"I consider the level of current cooperations not equal to the significant potential of our bilateral relations", Russian Prime Minister said when he visited Vietnam in November, 1997. In analysing the cause of this, Russian Ambassador to Vietnam, Victor V.Ivanov remarked, "There are political and economic reasons in Russia that do not allow the country to maintain old relations", for example, a strong shipping fleet in Black Sea, which formerly based on Odessa, now belongs to another country. Many Russian private enterprises lack capital, affecting Russia's trade activities with Vietnam.

Vietnamese Ambassador to Russia Ngo Tat To said that first of all, the ways Vietnamese businesses are operating are unsuitable with Russia's existing situations. Second, Vietnam's marketing methods are not effecive and the range of products is not diversified.

Third, since Russia has expanded its foreign trade activities with new markets in Western Europe and North America, the country has reduced its trade volume with Vietnam.

As of October 27, 1997, Russia has directly invested in some 30 projects in Vietnam with a total investment capital of US $ 109.6 million, ranking 19th in the list of foreign countries, investing in Vietnam. To date, the joint venture of Vietso Petro is regarded as Russia's most successful project in this country. This joint venture had turned out a total oil production of 50 million tonnes in October 1997.

During discussions, the Governments of Russia and Vietnam planned to continue to develop this joint venture as well as to set up a new joint venture capable of transporting oil by sea. In addition, the two sides are pushing for some other projects, including an agreement between Kamaz Holding Group with Vietnam's Machinery Import Export Corporation (machine import) to build up a joint venture for assembling and distributing Kamaz automobiles in Vietnam.

Most business people in both countries feel Vietnamese goods need the Russian market and vice versa. Speaking of the existing Russian market, the Deputy Minister of Trade, Ho Huan Nghiem said, "Through practical studies, Russia has been a big market, with very significant potential for Vietnamese exports. In addition to traditional export items, such as, agricultural products, fruits, food stuff products, and handicrafts, Vietnam has recently added more items to its export list, such as, garments, footwear, home electronics, fans, and construction materials."

Meanwhile, many major projects in Vietnam that received support from the former Soviet Union have long been operating, such as, hydroelectric power stations of Hoa Binh, Tri An, Thac Ba, Thermo-electricity Factory of Pha Lai, and Bim Son Cement Factory, and these projects are in dire need of importing Russian-made components and parts to keep them operating. Vietnam's consumers are also very familiar to such Russian products as steel, fertiliser and specialised machinery.

In addition to business, the two governments are interested in improving diplomatic relations. In a speech made to the Russian Parliament, the Russian President Boris Yeltsin said, "Russia will continue to re-establish active relations with traditional trading partners like Vietnam". And this has been also confirmed by the Russian Prime Minister.

"During 1980s, Vietnam was the fourth largest trading partner of Russia in Asia (After Japan, China and India). We see no reason to not improve this position," the Russian Prime Minister said.

During his visit to Vietnam, the Russian Prime Minister held talks with the Prime Minister Phan Van Khai to discuss ways to strengthen the two countries' trade activities and enhance co-operation in other fields such as energy, oil exploration and production.

The two governments signed agreements to increase co-operative relations in such fields as economy, commerce, science and technology, tourism and veterinary science.

It is certain that through efforts implemented by both sides, the relationship between Vietnam and Russia will attain new developments in the future in terms of quality and quantity, meeting a real wish of business communities in the two countries. Thus, Russian-Vietnamese economic relations are being reconstructed on new basis.

**Vietnam's Relations with Czech**

The two countries have a long established and co-operative relationship which have been growing in strength from generation to generation. The Czech Embassy was established in Vietnam in 1954, and a large number of Vietnamese have since worked and studied in the Czech Republic.

Regrettably, Czech companies were unable to respond to the needs of Vietnam's economy in the early 1990s, when competition was not as fierce as at present. In the light of the two countries' traditional relationship, many Czech enterprises thought they would receive preferential treatment in Vietnam. In fact, Vietnam has proved to have a less favourable environment than other countries. Over the years, the investment environment for Czech businesses has not grown as quickly as the investors expected. This is partly due to the differences in the modes of business, production, construction and markets between the two countries and the mutual problem of capital shortages.

In the recent years, the number of Czech businesses that have shown an interest in Vietnam has been on the increase.

The Czech Republic currently has two joint ventures (JV in Vietnam, the Bohemia Crystal Ha Noi JV, producing crystal ware, and the Skoda Isovina energy JV).

In the short term, the Czech Republic intends to focus investment on the transport and communications industry. The Czech Republic will supply locomotives and spare parts to the railway branch. It will also assist in manufacturing irrigation machinery and assembling refrigerators for the processing industry. Additionally, preparations for two projects to supply and jointly manufacture water supply and discharge equipment are now underway. The Czech Republic has recently been involved in two projects for water supply and discharge in the coffee growing areas of Dak Lak and Tay Nguyen (Central Highlands). Furthermore, during a recent meeting of the Joint Committee, the issue of joint production of mechanical machines for agricultural cultivation was discussed.

Since 1986, the Vietnamese Government has persisitently pursued the renovation policy in the direction of market economy. In view of the fundamental changes that the commercial sector has undergone, the Czech Republic is hoping to further stabilise trade and economic co-operation with Vietnam. In terms of sales of Czech goods in Vietnam, once a sound goods supply structure is established, Vietnam's current low solvency is rectified, and payment transactions are formalised, Czech will be able to supply Vietnam with complete technological equipment for breweries and cement plants as well as power projects. It will also include separate mechanical equipment, such as, weaving, printing, cutting and shoe making machines and vehicles.

To further boost economic cooperation Czech will be seeking to harness the skills of those people who have been trained and worked in the Czech Republic. Czech will earmark considerable non-refundable development assistance for Vietnam. Specifically the Czech government will give Kc 45 million to build a centre for handicapped children in Bac Thai Province and Kc 20 million in non-refundable aid to develop Vietnam's railway. Excluding Russia, the Czech Republic is the only country which previously belonged to the union of socialist countries which is assisting Vietnam. China's economic relation with Vietnam stand on a different footing.

## References

1. Nam Huyen — Russia wants a worthy position in Vietnam, p. 23, 24, Vietnam Economic News, No. 49, Vol VII, December 5-11, 1997.

2. An interview by Mark Skolil, Czeh Ambassador in Vietnam, *Vietnam Economic News*, No. 45, Vol, VIII, November 2-8, 1998.

# 12

# ECONOMIC TRANSFORMATION AND NEW ECONOMIC POLICY

PROFESSOR B.D. ARORA

The emergence of a united SRV in July 1976, was a significant event in South-East Asia. It marked a victory of Vietnamese nationalism, independence and unification against the French, the Japanese, and the Americans. It was in a way the culmination of serious efforts launched since May 1941, when Ho Chi Minh had established Viet Minh (Vietnam Independence League). Positively, it became a source of inspiration to the peoples of Asia and other regions fighting for freedom and independence from Western colonialism. It had some negative elements as well. In April 1975, the U.S. defeat at the hands of battle-toughened Vietnamese soldiers created a hurt psyche and a severe anti-Vietnamese feeling. On its part, China viewed the unification of Vietnam, and that too with the active military support by the Soviet Union, as a threat to its own perceived security and its aspiration for a regional power status. In the conflict between the Pol Pot-led democratic Kampuchea (established since April 1975) and Vietnam in December 1978 and January 1979, China saw a valuable opportunity to browbeat Vietnam. Its "teaching a lesson" to Vietnam through its invasion, in February 1979, gave clear hints to the emergence of a new alignment of forces antithetical to the *SRV*. With the ASEAN giving signals of joining hands against Vietnam, there emerged a sort of strategic convergence of views among the United States, China and the ASEAN countries (with Thailand in the front rank). The main objective of this consensus was to "bleed Vietnam white".

These negative elements left no choice for Vietnam except to increase its dependence on the Soviet Union. For a decade or so, since its armed action against Democratic Kampuchea, for its survival as also for its geo-strategic objectives of promoting "special relations" with People's Republic of Kampuchea (established after the Pol Pot-led Democratic Kampuchea was overthrown) and Laos (LPDR), Vietnam denied itself the opportunity of launching development schemes necesary for the interest of the people. This was the time when people, weary of the war since 1946, onwards [8-year war between France and Vietnam (DRV) beginning this year], wanted peace and development. All these years, however, defence preparedness, national unification and geo-strategic objectives in Indochina received urgent attention of the policy makers in Hanoi, whereas peace and development remained at a low priority. It was only when the Vietnamese agreed to withdraw all their forces stationed in PRK that peace could be established and development programmes launched for the welfare of the people.

Although, the Vietnamese withdrew their forces in September 1989, the process of reforms had been initiated in the mid 1980s. One of the major reasons was a sharp decline in economy. While in the thick of the trade and economic squeeze imposed by Washington, Beijing and the ASEAN capitals as also the Cambodian quagmire, the Vietnamese leaders realized the gravity of the situation in which people's needs were demanding more and more attention and hence could no longer be shelved. An important factor which compelled them to recast their priorities away from defence and geo-strategic activities to economic development purposes was the Soviet disinclination to pump in more and more aid and loans, both for military hardware and economic development on earlier and easier terms. Because of a mess in its own economy, the Soviet Union could no longer be expected to foot the Vietnamese bill in the virtually unwinnable war against the Chinese backed Khmer Rouge.

In order to understand the new economic policy and transformation of Vietnam it would be meaningful to go into the nature and extent of decline that had set in. The Vietnamese leaders had to contend with the problem of food shortages, unemployment and under-employment of the people. In 1975, the import of grains amounted to 645,000 tons. By 1980, it reached 924,000 tons. At the end of this year, according to a report by the FAO team, the biggest problem was food shortages. Between October 1980 and September 1981, there was a deficit of about 4.4 million tons of rice. Although, there was an improvement in food production, the problem was compounded by typhoons and tropical storm. It was this situation that made the life of the people miserable.

Failure to remove shortages of food grains was, in a serious way linked with the economic recession in the country. The situation became grave because 80 per cent of the people worked in and were based on agriculture. The socialization process in southern part and collectivization in the northern part compounded the difficulties of the people. The opening up of new farm lands, called New Economic Zones, as a major effort to bolster food grain production, failed to deliver the goods. Furthermore, the Government's closing down of all businesses in the South including those of Chinese or Vietnamese of Chinese origin, fomented China's ill-will towards Vietnam. As regards industrial development the Vietnamese had neither the capital nor technical knowhow. They also lacked experience in economic management. Moreover, continuing war had never allowed them to use their energies and will power to remove poverty of the people and improve upon the backwardness of the economy.

The decline in economy in 1986 onwards could also be seen from the conditions in which the masses found themselves. The basic wage of a worker was around US $ 1 a month at the black market exchange rate of 'dong' (the Vietnamese currency), about $ 25 at the inflated official rate. The inflation rate which was 700 per cent in 1986, reached about 1000 per cent in 1987. By April 1988, a captain in the army was receiving 10,000 dong. At the then free market exchange rate, this was equal to a mere three US dollars. Even a bicycle, most people's only form of transport could, as per reports, cost as much as $ 100.

The Vietnamese spirit of resistance to colonialism and imperialism was getting eroded. The State and the system based on State, subsidized production and distribution were failing to meet even the day-to-day needs of the people. They wanted a change, a sort of transformation of State policies which were people-oriented.

The people's miseries increased as a result of the rigid doctrinaire approach to Marxist-Leninist path of economic development through rhetoric for austerity rather than tangible incentives. Simultaneously, the entrenched Party (CPV) bureaucracy had created bottlenecks in the path of development.

The prevailing situation demanded an urgent overhauling of economic and social policies troubling Vietnam. The Communist Party of Vietnam, in this connection, had to relax ideological rigidities, change scale of priorities, diversify relationships with various countries, especially China, the United States and the ASEAN group, promote a situation at home which could attract foreign capital, and so on. All these measures required the Government to initiate a process of reconciliation in the region. This could be achieved only by withdrawing its forces from Cambodia. Disentangling itself from the situation in that country would enable Vietnam to devote its attention single-mindedly to the daunting economic and social problems. The path, however, was difficult and even tortuous. But, the options were seriously limited. A degree of regional and international acceptability could be gained only by pursuing confidence building measures. Simultaneously, for the sake of economic development, state subsidies would have to be drastically reduced, if not fully withdrawn, in order to increase labour efficiency and productivity. Besides, a new set of rules and regulations assuring reasonable returns on foreign investment, would have to be drawn up and implemented.

Keeping in view the gravity of the situation, and in the hope of arresting the sharp down turn in economy, the Government decided to launch policies and programmes different from the earlier ones. It was expected to transform both the economy and polity.

To overcome serious problems of economic stagnation, increasing inflation, budgetary, balance of payments, imbalances resulting from the rigid centrally planned and controlled economy, the 6th Congress of the CPV, in December 1986, recognised the need to introduce market-oriented reforms. The structural reform measures called 'doi moi' in Vietnamese included (a) floating of the currency, (b) introduction of banking system, (c) fiscal reforms, (d) decollectivization of land, (e) decontrol of prices, and (f) development of laws and administrative systems to govern the establishment of business and commercial transactions in a market economy. The objective of the reforms was to free the economy from State control and Government intervention.

While implementing economic reforms, the Vietnamese faced numerous difficulties. The country, however, succeeded to an extent, in attracting foreign direct investment (FDI) for development purposes. Encouragingly, it continued to grow year after year. Side by side, it received considerable amount of aid from both bilateral and multilateral sources. Japan's contribution was the highest. In the decade that followed there was all-round development. The GDP rose from 6 per cent in 1991, to 9 per cent in 1995. During this period, the industry and services registered increases in growth from 2.2 per cent to 5 per cent and from 8.2 per cent to 10.2 per cent respectively. There was what is called 'Big-Bang' of liberalisation in 1989. Vietnam's economy was no longer ailing. Investments and exports were up. So was the vigour of private enterprise and rising incomes. This was evident from north to south.

In early 1996, number of telephones grew to 800,000 from 100,000 in 1990. The country had 1,000 taxis instead of none two years ago. An importer of rice in 1995, it became, world's third leading rice exporter. In 1996 itself, the economy was expected to grow more than 9 per cent. Inflation which had soared to 600 per cent and higher was down to around 12 per cent. Nearly $18 billion in foreign investments had been recorded. On the other hand, Vietnam had established diplomatic relations with the United States, set up a framework for relations with European Union and joined the ASEAN. Thirteen years of bitterness with China had already melted. In 1991 itself, Vietnam had succeeded in normalising relations.

The development had, in its trail, brought serious social problems. There were persistent poverty, drug abuse, prostitution, corruption, smuggling and growing incidence of crime. At the same time, gaps between the rich and the poor had widened. So had the gap between the fast-developing cities and the lagging country-side. The Government was unable to increase funds for education and health-care of the poor, which were deteriorating.

Simultaneously, in view of these growing social problems, debate within the CPV that had been raging since the adoption of 'doi moi' (reform programme) in 1986, got reinforced. For several members in the politbureau, 'perestroika' was acceptable but under restraint and 'glasmost' was not at all so. For the radicals, who the western media dubbed as 'conservatives', wanted the CPV control over the market place, were ensured. Also, according to them, plural democracy (in politics) would still further distort the aims and objectives of development.

Hence, Vietnam must remain a single Party dominant state. This alone, for them, would ensure stability and development in the country.

Keeping in mind the reforms which have been initiated and implemented and the results that have accrued for the polity and society in Vietnam, one has to comment on the term 'transformation'. It means, I understand it correctly, a change in form, nature and structure. Looking at the transformation that has been taking place has certainly put certain question marks. This is particularly so in the case of a developing society in the process of modernization. Moreover, development cannot be compartmentalised where economic development is 'Yes' and political development is 'No'. This inhibits the growth of overall development of an individual, society and country. But, one could understand the difficulties in the process of development and modernization. The only thing necessary to keep in mind is that while transformation is under way, the basic interests of the poor and the have-nots must not get ignored.

# 13

# ECONOMIC RELATIONS WITH OTHER COUNTRIES IN THE POST-COLD WAR ERA

UDAI BHANU SINGH

Vietnamese economy is going through a period of trial. Its economic development has been through a number of phases. The legacy of colonial rule and a prolonged war with the United States created a situation in 1975, where the country's economic infrastructure was completely devastated. According to Hanoi, there were 10 million refugees, 362,000 war invalids and 3 million unemployed in the south alone.[1] Added to this was the problem of the incorporation of the south with the north and there was no Marshall plan for South East Asia either, to absorb the aftershocks.

There were two strands of thinking that emerged on how to tackle the economic problems of the day. One was the dominant orthodox socialist view that sought to extend the system instituted in the North (in the 1950s) to the South. The reformers in the light of the changes sweeping the socialist world and the changes occurring in Vietnam itself increasingly questioned this view.[2] Previously, war time morale and a little aid from the Chinese allies had helped the Vietnamese tide over their many economic difficulties. But, when friend turned into enemy (China invading Vietnam in 1979) the crisis that Vietnam faced had been doubled.

Economic crisis led to popular discontent, which prompted the Government to give in to change, which it had earlier resisted. It was the Communist Party's Sixth Party Congress in December 1986, that the plan for deregulation of Vietnamese economy or doi moi (renovation) was enunciated. This has meant a shift from centrally planned economy to a market oriented one in which

Vietnamese businesses can cooperate with foreigners. It got a boost after Vietnam withdrew its troops from Cambodia. It launched its *doi moi* (renovation/economic liberalization) policy in December 1986 and the transformation of this nation had begun.[3] Inevitably, certain individuals have had a leading role in shaping history. General Secretary of the Vietnamese Communist Party, Nguyen Van Linh, nicknamed, the Gorbachev of South-East Asia injected new ideas, overturning the concept of a centrally planned system.[4] The Socialist Republic of Vietnam is tasked with the objective of achieving rapid economic transformation as it adjusts itself to the political environment in the post-Cold War world. It is doing this at a time when some of the miracle economies of East Asia are facing the brunt of the financial crisis. This historic moment could be a blessing in disguise for Vietnam if it is handled judiciously.

The necessity and desirability for change had begun to be felt during the last several years in Vietnam, but certain developments have added momentum to the course cf events. On February 3, 1994, President Clinton of USA finally lifted the 19 year old trade embargo against Vietnam and announced the opening of a liaison office in Hanoi.[5] This followed the US decision in July 1993, to cease all opposition to the flow of multilateral funds to Vietnam, totalling $ 600 million. With this an era ended.

It is a measure of Vietnamese statesmanship that they are attempting to successfully carve out a place for themselves in the post-Cold War world despite all odds. The Vietnamese are a fiercely nationalistic people, who became victims of the historical process. The *Economist*, quite significantly, called them South-East Asia's Prussians. It is noteworthy that the people of Vietnam who in recent history have fought and won some significant wars against the established military might of the French, the Americans and the Chinese are now fighting a new kind of war. This time the war is against economic stagnation and underdevelopment caused by years of colonial exploitation and falling prey to Cold War politics. They have undertaken, in a rapidly changing global environment, the daunting task of structuring a hybrid 'socialist market economy' while preserving the dominance of the Communist Party.

According to the Vietnamese Prime Minister Phan Van Khai, the three weak points that require immediate attention are:

* The economy's low competitiveness.
* Red tapism.
* Social evils, particularly drug trafficking and abuse.

The Prime Minister outlined six major tasks for 1999 focusing on:

* Developing agriculture and rural areas.
* Removing obstacles to industrial production, thereby maintaining the economic growth rate.
* Mobilizing and effectively utilizing all sources of investment.
* Enhancing external economic rèlations while ridding the finance and banking sectors of all negative features.
* Solving urgent social issues and reforming the national administrative system.

If Vietnam today is beset with so many economic problems, it is in no small measure due to the legacy bequeathed to it by some of the Western powers. Firstly, with the collapse of the Soviet Union, an important ally on whom it depended so much has disappeared suddenly. The friendship with the Soviet Union had been at the cost of China and the United States. A point of contention Vietnam had with the United States, China and ASEAN had been its intervention in Cambodia. With the Cambodian troops withdrawn, the process of building bridges of friendship had begun. It resulted in Vietnam's admission to Pacific Economic Cooperation Council (PECC) and later ASEAN and APEC.

The sixth plenum of the Central Committee of Vietnam Communist Party formulated the economic strategy for 1999, when it met from 13th to 17th October 1998, in Hanoi. Despite the many financial and other difficulties, it noted, the country had remained socially and politically stable and managed to achieve a GDP growth rate of six per cent which was regarded as a "big success" which vindicated the correctness of the Eighth Party Congress.[6]

**Table 1**
**GDP: Growth Rate**
**(per cent)**

| 1980-89 Average | 1990 | 1991 | 1992 | 1993 | 1994 | 1995 | 1996 | 1997 | 1998e | 1999e |
|---|---|---|---|---|---|---|---|---|---|---|
| 5.0 | 4.9 | 6.0 | 8.6 | 8.1 | 8.8 | 9.5 | 9.3 | 9.2 | 5.0 | 6.5 |

*Source : Asian Development Outlook,* 1998,
*World Economic Outlook,* May 1998 (IMF),
*Regional Outlook:* South-East Asia, 1998-99.

However, the plenum was realistic enough to acknowledge the problem. It candidly admitted that economic growth had slowed down and that production and trade were down. Unemployment, both urban and rural has been increasing, though the employment rate in 1997 was 3.5 per cent of the labour force.[7] In rural areas there is underemployment and in urban centres unemployment, as high as 7per cent. Poverty still stands at 17.4 per cent. In an introspective tone it admitted that the inner strength—the potential resources (including the overseas Vietnamese)—of the economy had not yet been tapped. The race for efficiency resulted in many workers in State enterprises being laid off while the withdrawal from Cambodia resulted in demobilisation of half a million soldiers. However, Vietnam exudes a certain confidence in the path of renovation that it has adopted, which has resulted in its integration with the regional and world economies.

**Table 2**
**Vietnam: Inflation Rate**
**(per cent)**

| 1990 | 1991 | 1992 | 1993 | 1994 | 1995 | 1996 | 1997 | 1998e | 1999e |
|---|---|---|---|---|---|---|---|---|---|
| 36.0 | 81.8 | 37.7 | 8.3 | 9.5 | 16.9 | 5.7 | 3.2 | 4.0 | 4.0 |

*Source: Regional Outlook: Southeast Asia,* 1998-99 (ISEAS).

Besides the unemployment, there is inadequate domestic capital accumulation and a growing budget deficit. The burden of economic responsibility has gradully shifted to the non-State sector which now accounts for the bulk of the GDP and of the total employment. But, the helping hands that these enterprises require in the nascent stage of development are not so visible. Access to credit is not easy as banks are still relatively underdeveloped and state enterprises in any case are given priority. Some enterprises in urban areas have however benefited from the foreign capital that has trickled in.

The infrastructure that is so necessary for making any economic headway is slow to emerge. Paved roads and bridges which are regularly repaired and maintained, ports with adequate facilities, and a regular source of electric supply— are some of the essentials. Perhaps, what the Vietnamese are lacking in physical infrastructure, they make up for in the high degree of motivation among their technocrats. There is a great willingness to learn, even at the highest levels of office, whenever modern economic or technological know-how is on offer. This may be indirectly related to the fact that Vietnam has among the highest literacy rates in the world. But, now declining State subsidies and insufficient investment, which have already affected social welfare and medical facilities adversely have hit the education system as well. One of Vietnam's strengths—its high literacy rate could be endangered in the future because of the high dropout rate and a growing aversion to the teaching profession. A commendable attempt has however been made by the Government to link schools with industry that could yield desirable results in the area of vocational training.[8]

The tenth SRV National Assembly approved the goal of 5 to 6 per cent GDP growth, a 3.5 to 4 per cent growth in agricultural production, and a 7 per cent increase in exports.[9]

According to a senior Vietnamese economist and advisor to the Government, Le Dang Doanh, "Nineteen ninety-eight is the most challenging year for Vietnam since the reform process started". He said, "The regional crisis will have a real impact on us"[10]. Similarly, the IMF's representative in Vietnam, Erik Offerdahl warned that without a comprehensive package of measures the good macro-economic performance of high growth and low inflation[11] could easily be lost.

**Agriculture:** The Communist Party leadership in the latter part of 1998, sought to decollectivise agriculture in order to encourage large-scale commercial farming. But, the 450-member national assembly turned down the proposal to amend the 1993 law that would have increased farm sizes and extended rural leases. This marked a defeat for Communist Party reformers.

Hanoi lays great emphasis on food security. Hanoi hosted the conference of ASEAN Ministers on Agriculture and Forestry held on September 17-18, 1998, in Hanoi.[12] later, in November, it hosted a conference on food security (3-6 Nov). This emphasis becomes necessary as 13 million of its 77 million populace live in poverty (i.e., those unable to get a diet of 2,100 kilo calories per day). The deputies in the National Assembly in its fourth session also affirmed the significant role of agriculture and rural development and wanted the government to increase investment in agriculture in 1999 (especially more in irrigation projects and farm produce processing and marketing). Agricultureal output has been growing at the rate of three per cent. Vietnam's annual production of an estimated 31.3 m tonnes of paddy food this year must touch 40 m tonnes by 2000 if it is to meet its domestic and export requirements. It is significant that Vietnam became a rice exporter in 1989. According to the US Department of Agriculture, Vietnam would produce 18 m tonnes of rice in 1998-99 crop[13] and it will become the second largest exporter of rice next year with 3.5 m tonnes.[14]

**Industry:** Industrial production increased by 11 per cent.[15] There are plans to add new industrial zones.[16] Vietnam is making notable headway in the exploration of oil and gas, not least because it has a dispute in the South China Sea with China. Vietnam has a joint venture with the Russians in the *Vietsovpetro* for exploiting crude and gas from offshore oil fields.[17] Vietnam is also collaborating with Norway in this field.[18] In the fishery sector the Asian Development Bank has granted $70 m to build 10 fishing ports across the country.[19]

**Trade and Investment:** Vietnam had an export turnover of US $ 740 m in September 1998, which was a 4.1 per cent increase when compared to the same period the previous year.[20] The trend has been subdued for some time: exports grew only 5.8 per cent (instead of the projected government target of 25 per cent) from $ 616 m in January 1997 to $ 650 m in January 1998[21].

**Table 3**
**Vietnam: Balance of Trade**
**(Unit: million US$)**

| | 1990 | 1991 | 1992 | 1993 | 1994 | 1995 | 1996 |
|---|---|---|---|---|---|---|---|
| Balance of Trade | -41 | -63 | -60 | -547 | -1190 | -2345 | -3150 |
| Export | 1731 | 2042 | 2475 | 2985 | 4054 | 5198 | 7330 |
| Import | 1772 | 2105 | 2535 | 3532 | 5244 | 7543 | 10480 |

*Source: Regional Outlook: Southeast Asia,* 1998-99 (ISEAS)
*Asian Development Outlook,* 1998.

Vietnam's exports had touched $2.5 billion in 1992, recording a 19 per cent growth with rice, petroleum, marine products, coffee and rubber constituting the major export items. The depression in Vietnam's traditional export markets as a consequence of the dissolution of the Soviet Union and the Council for Mutual Economic Assistance (CMEA) did not, however, adversely affect its balance of trade. In fact, as its market diversified to include such countries as Japan, Singapore, Hong Kong, as its major trade partners, Vietnam was able to achieve a favourable balance of trade for the first time since independence.

**Table 4**
**Top Ten Foreign Exporters to Vietnam**
**(Unit: million US$)**

| *Countries & Territories* | *Export Turnover* | *Ranking* |
|---|---|---|
| Sourth Korea | 923 | 1 |
| Japan | 601 | 2 |
| Taiwan | 545 | 3 |
| Thailand | 500 | 4 |
| Hong Kong | 376 | 5 |
| Malaysia | 169 | 6 |
| Singapore | 139 | 7 |
| France | 95 | 8 |
| United States | 88 | 9 |
| Russian Federation | 48 | 10 |

*Source: Vietnam Information Bulletin,* January 1999 (New Delhi: Embassy of the Socialist Republic of Vietnam).

Vietnam is attracting considerable foreign investment. In June 1990, the National Assembly passed the Law on Foreign Investment which further liberalised foreign investment procedures. Foreign investment has fallen.[22] The structure and geographical pattern of investment have also diversified over the years.[23]

**Table 5**
**Top Ten Foreign Investors in Vietnam**
**(Unit: million US $)**

| *Countries & Territories* | *Number of Projects* | *Capital* | *Per cent* |
|---|---|---|---|
| Singapore | 181 | 6,477 | 20 |
| Taiwan | 309 | 4,268 | 13.3 |
| HongKong | 184 | 3,734 | 11.6 |
| Japan | 213 | 3,500 | 11.4 |
| South Korea | 191 | 3,154 | 9.8 |
| France | 96 | 1,465 | 4.6 |
| United States | 70 | 1,401 | 5.1 |
| Malaysia | 59 | 1,372 | 5.0 |
| Thailand | 78 | 1,109 | 4.0 |
| B.V. Islands | 54 | 1,063 | 3.9 |

*Source: Vietnam Information Bulletin*, January 1999 (New Delhi: Embassy of the Socialist Republic of Vietnam).

## Economic Ties with Other Countries

### *USA*

The US is the tenth biggest investor in Vietnam with investment totalling US $ 1.1 billion[24]. There are more than 500 US companies operating in Vietnam since the two countries established diplomatic ties in July 1995. US has more than 70 projects valued at $1.1 billion ranking 12th among foreign investors[25]. The American businessmen are now urging Washington to sign a trade agreement with Vietnam to facilitate large-scale investment and trade with that country.[26]

The waiver of Jackson Vanik amendment[27] has created a favourable opportunity to further improve economic and trade relations between the two nations.[28] The two-way trade value between Vietnam and US stood at US $1 billion in 1997.[29]

### *Russia*

Vietnam's defence cooperation with Russia, meanwhile, has been revived. Vietnamese President Tran Duc Luong went on a four day visit to Russia in September 1998, to boost defence and economic ties.

The Soviet Union had been a major aid donor and trading partner with assistance amounting to 9 per cent of GDP between 1988 and 1990. It had been a conscious, deliberate decision to opt for Russian aid instead of Chinese aid. Once Soviet Union disintegrated, Vietnamese decision-makers were faced with major dilemma. Soviet Union's successor states went to the market with their military hardware to the consternation of Vietnam. Russia sold Su-27 interceptors to the Chinese, which the latter promptly deployed on the island of Hainan.[30]

### *China*

The Vietnamese leadership claims that the relations with China are better than before. The two sides had agreed to settle peacefully all issues relating to the border, including the Bac Bo (Tonkin Gulf) by the year 2000.[31] Prime Minister Phan Van Khai visited China in October 1998, where he exchanged ideas with the Chinese Premier Zhu Rongji regarding their experience with reform and liberalization and the socialist method of coping with the Asian financial crisis.[32]

Sino-Vietnamese relations began improving in 1991, for various reasons. First, the fall of communism in Eastern Europe pushed these two communist countries together. Second, PRC had resolved to discontinue its military aid to the Khmer Rouge by September 1991, following Vietnamese withdrawal of troops from Cambodia in September 1989. Third, it was economics as much as politics which was behind the coming together. China itself suggested that the two countries shelve the dispute over the Spratlys and start "joint development". In November 1991, Sino-Vietnamese political relations were restored with the visit of Vietnamese Prime Minister Vo Van Kiet to Beijing and the gesture was reciprocated in November 1994, with Chinese President Jiang Zemin's visit to Vietnam.

It is understandable that Vietnam's recent accession to ASEAN alone would not prove to be the best insurance against a resurgent China. Rather, its economic integration with China (which provides the world's largest single market) which will be the major stabilising factor.[33] Sino-Vietnamese cooperation is also important from the point of view of proximity to the Golden Triangle and need for greater surveillance against spread of narcotics and small arms in both countries. Closely connected is the spread of HIV-AIDS which the two countries are concerned about.

### *Japan*

Vietnam's relations with Japan also improved in 1991. Japan resumed aid in November 1992, after a gap of 14 years with a grant of 45 billion yen (US $ 364 million) in commodity loans. In March 1993, Vo Van Kiet became the first Vietnamese Prime Minister to pay an official visit to Japan and the Japanese Prime Minister Tomiichi Murayama reciprocated in August 1994. Japan readily extended aid and also welcomed Vietnam's entry into ASEAN.

### *India*

When such path breaking developments were occurring in the region, it should have been easier for India to build up on its traditional good relations with Vietnam and give a boost to the economic ties. Several Indian companies like TC, Birlas, Mafatlal and Modi groups, Ashok Leyland, and Max India have already begun operations in Vietnam. India's Oil and Natural Gas Commission (ONGC) has undertaken gas and oil exploration in Vietnam successfully and Indian railways exported coaches for use on the line between Hanoi and Ho Chi Minh cities. India is also helping and assisting in the infrastructural development of Vietnam by setting up many rural telephone exchanges and by making some headway in the automobile sector. Other areas in which India has made inroads are engineering goods, tyres, drugs and pharmaceuticals. Some of these companies have realised the potential of Vietnam as a market in its own right and as a gateway to the larger ASEAN market.[34]

With India's elevation to the dialogue partner status in ASEAN and Vietnam's inclusion as the seventh member of the ASEAN, Indo-Vietnamese relations climbed to newer levels of cooperation. More recently, India exported machinery worth $ 33 million in 1997-98, according to Engineering Export Promotion Council (EEPC) President P.K. Shah.[35]

**Table 6**
**Vietnam: Trade with India**
**(million US $)**

| | 1991 | 1992 | 1993 | 1994 | 1995 |
|---|---|---|---|---|---|
| Imports | 12.87 | 18.63 | 29.05 | 58.5 | 124.88 |
| Exports | 38.03 | 66.03 | 45.80 | 53.97 | 15.68 |

*Source:* Embassy of India, Hanoi. Cited in *Vietnam Economic Times*, March 1998.

### *Regional Cooperation*

Vietnam's economy will gain as much credibility as its polity when the Sixth ASEAN summit meets in Hanoi on December 15 and 16, with all the prominent ASEAN leaders expected to attend.

In 1997, East Asia absorbed approximately 60 per cent of Vietnamese exports. But now because of the East Asian economic crisis, Vietnamese exports will be negatively impacted because of reduced demand in East Asia and less competitively priced products.

The Lao President Khamtay Siphandone led a high level delegation to Vietnam from 4th to 7th January 1999.[36] Among other things, they agreed to :

* Give priority and preferential treatment and to facilitate the exchange of goods and assist each other in the regional and global integration of their respective economies.
* Stressed that regional and non-regional countries should enhance their cooperation and mutual assistance to overcome the economic crisis.

During the visit also the Laos-Vietnam and Vietnam-Laos Cooperation Commission was held on 5th January, in Hanoi when Vietnam agreed to grant aid worth 67 billion dong to Laos.[37] Earlier, during the visit to Vietnam by the Lao Prime Minister Sisavath Keobounphan in July 1998, an agreement was signed by which Vietnam will start buying electric power from Laos in 2003. A memorandum for the construction of Vung Ang Port and a road leading from it to Laos was also signed.[38]

Hanoi sought to enhance cooperation and develop confidence with neighbouring Myanmar when its Deputy Prime Minister and Foreign Minister Nguyen Manh Cam recently went to Myanmar to attend the Second Vietnam-Myanmar Joint Commission meeting. They focussed on trade, agriculture and forestry.[39]

The Mekong River Commission Council (MRCC) seeks to optimise the management of water resources for better use and environmental protection through cooperation among the Mekong basin countries.[40]

Singapore which had been one of the staunchest critics of Vietnam during the Cold War, sent its former Prime Minister Lee Kuan Yew to Vietnam to offer advice on managing the economy. Then Prime Minister Goh Chok Tong lifted the ban on the foreign investment in Vietnam. Singapore is the biggest foreign capital investor in Vietnam with 22 projects valued at US $ 792, followed by UK, Taiwan, Hong Kong and Japan.[41] The two granted each other Most Favoured Nation (MFN) status and signed a pact to develop bilateral trade.

## Conclusion

Vietnam is at the crossroads like the rest of South-East Asia. The issues facing the region remain much the same. The basic question is how much opening up of the economy is prudent. The budget deficit (at 2 to 3 per cent in 1997) needs to be curtailed, but if State spending is cut, then the infrastructure projects— roads, ports, and highways automatically get delayed. If the cuts are made in the social sector the long term impact in terms of a healthy and skilled manpower may be debilitating for the nation. An insufficiently developed infrastructure does not bode well for the health of the economy. Hanoi still has the problem of attracting foreign investment. If FDI is not forthcoming, the Five-Year Plan (1996-2000) growth targets may not be reached. The debate in Vietnam over reform will have far reaching effect not only for that country but the region as well. Yet, Vietnam has the advantage of more reaction time because the economic crisis has not struck it in quite the same way as the rest of East Asia has been. The challenge that Vietnam faces may be the opportunity it has been seeking in its years of unfair history.

## References

1. *Vietnam Ten Years After* (Hanoi: Foreign Languages Publishing House, 1985), p. 6
2. *Ibid.*
3. For details see, Dorothy R. Avery, "Vietnam in 1992: Win Some; Lose Some," *Asian Survey,* Vol. 33, no. 1, January 1993, pp. 71-72 and Douglas Pike, "Vietnam in 1993: Uncertainty Closes in", *Asian Survey*, Vol. 34, no. 1, January 1994, pp. 65-66.

4. Zain Amri, "Post Cambodia Vietnam: Some Economic Security Considerations," *Asian Defence Journal,* no. 5, 1994, pp. 45-49.
5. See George Esper, "Clinton lifts 19-year trade embargo on Vietnam," *Pioneer* (New Delhi), Feb. 5, 1994; Michael Elliott, "Exorcising the Ghosts", *Newsweek,* Feb 14, 1994, pp. 14-15,; Thomas W. Lippman, "Senate Votes to Free Vietnam Trade", *Guardian Weekly,* Feb. 6, 199, p. 17.
6. BBC/SWB/FE/3362, B/6, October 20,1998. Also see, BBC/SWB/FE/3361, B/4, October 19, 1998. The World Bank estimates the GDF growth at 3 per cent.
7. Many businesses were forced to cut down production because of reduced demand. One $18 m joint venture car company was forced to reduce production from 10,000 cars to only 2,800 cars per year. Vietnam Motor Corporation had to downsize its plant in Hoa Binh from 910 workers to only 318 due to declining sales.
8. Andrew Ranara, "In Old Saigon, a Raw Resiliency," *International Herald Tribune,* August 13, 1993.
9. BBC/SWB/FE/3374, B/9, November 3, 1998.
10. "The gathering storm", *Vietnam Economic Times,* March 1998, p.12.
11. Faith Keenan, "Vietnam: No Rubber Stamp", *Far Eastern Economic Review,* December 10, 1998.
12. *Vietnam Information Bulletin, November,* 1998.
13. BBC/SWB/FEW/0562, WB/4, November 4,1998.
14. Vietnam exported 3.5 m tonnes of rice in 1997. BBC/SWB/FE/3376, B/8, November 5, 1998.
15. BBC/SWB/FE/3361, B/4, October 19, 1998.
16. The country has a target of 70 Industrial Zones by the year 2000. Refer, BBC/SWB/FEW/0559, WB/3.
17. BBC/FEW/0562, WB/3, November 4, 1998.
18. *Ibid.*
19. BBC/FEW/0561, WEB/2, October 28, 1998.
20. BBC/FEW/0559, WB/4, October 14, 1998.
21. *Vietnam Economic Times* (Hanoi), March 1998, p. 6.
22. Vietnam received an additional 178 foreign investment projects valued at US $1.7 in the first nine months of 1998, which is 42 per cent of the figure obtained in the same period last year. See BBC/SWB/FEW/0560, WB/3, October 21, 1998.
23. BBC/SWB/FEW/0365, WB/1, January 4, 1995.
24. SWB/FE/3356, B/5, October 13, 1998.
25. BBC/SWB/FEW/0564, WB/3, November 18, 1998.
26. It was in that context that the President of the US Chamber of Commerce Thomas J. Donahue visited Vietnam in October, Refer, BBC/SWB/FE/3356, B/5, October 13, 1998.

27. The amendment denies countries which restrict emigration, government sponsored credit, or investment guarantee.

28. The Vietnamese Foreign Ministry spokesperson told the press on July 31, that this decision was an active development in restoring normal economic ties between the two countries.

29. SWB/FE/3356, B/5, October 13, 1998.

30. *Asia Pacific Defence Reporter,* 1994, Annual Reference Edition.

31. BBC/SWB/FE/3427, B/6, January 8, 1999.

32. BBC/SWB/FE/3363, G/1, October 21, 1998.

33. For details, see, Udai Bhanu Singh, "Recent Trends in Sino-Vietnamese Relations", *Strategic Analysis,* May 1996, Vol. 29, No. 2.

34. Refer, Udai Bhanu Singh, "Vietnam's Economy and Foreign Relations in post-Cold War Era", *Strategic Analysis,* October 1994.

35. BBC/SWB/FEW/0562, WB/3, November 4, 1998.

36. BBC/SWB/FE/3425 B/6, January 6, 1999. For Joint Statement, see BBC/SWB/FE/3428, B/6-B/7, January 9, 1999.

37. BBC/SWB/FE/3432, B/5, January 14, 1999.

38. *Vietnam: Information Bulletin,* October 1998 (New Delhi: Embassy of the SRV).

39. *Ibid.*

40. Towards this end, the MRCC met on 27th to 28th Oct 1998, in Hanoi where officials from Cambodia, Laos, Thailand, the UN Development Programme, Australia's Murray-Darling Commission Council and the Mekong River Secretariat attended. See, BBC/SWB/FEW/0562, WB/2.

41. BBC/SWB/FEW/0560, WB/3, October 21, 1998.

# 14

# CHANGES IN POLITICAL SYSTEM

GANGANATH JHA

The contemporary history of South-East Asia has testified that the Vietnamese are dynamic in their approach and realistic in their policies. They are pursuing the policy of *Doi Moi* in their system and consequently political institutions are rapidly reformed to keep pace with the changing world. Hence, the role of the Party, National Assembly, Army, Bureaucracy and the Press have undergone transformations in tune with the democratic trends in the region. Though, the nature and function of the major political institutions are changing but the scrutiny of the changes suggest that the Vietnamese believe in continuity and change. One-party rule of the Communist Party remains but the evolving system has endeavoured to promote democratic way of life without diluting the principle of "dictatorship of the Communist Party".

Nobody can deny that Vietnam remains a communist country, but at the same time they cannot deny that they are cultivating democratic way of life by introducing the features of liberal society, i.e., decentralization, privatization, free trade, etc., to prove that Vietnam is an ideal partner of the Association of South-East Asian Nations (ASEAN).

Socialist Republic of Vietnam occupies 130,000 square miles of the territory and has the population of 78.7 million. The annual birth rate is around 1.9 to 2 per cent and the family planning drives are not very successful. Though, there is a committee on Family Planning to minimise growth of population and policies have been adopted for late marriage and two-children families, etc., but they have yet to produce desired results.[1] The ethnic Vietnamese comprise the majority community, but simultaneously, there are ethnic Chams, Khmers, Tais, Hoas, Hmongs, Montagnards and heterogeneous tribal groups.[2]

Vietnam has a history of warfare against the Chinese for one thousand years from 111 B.C. till 939 AD. It emerged as a powerful Kingdom in the 13th Century AD after annexing Champa and subduing the Khmers. It lost its sovereignty only after the end of the opium war (1842), when France, as a colonial power, emerged on the South-East Asian horizon. France colonised Vietnam in 1858, and expanded their rule over Cambodia, and Laos, but the Vietnamese did not accept colonial rule gracefully, and continued to struggle against it. Hence, it has a long and chequered history of struggle and warfare against colonialist forces.

The communists under the banner of the Indochina Communist Party (1930-42) and the Vietminh (1942-54) led the freedom movement and defeated the colonial powers.[3] The United States in pursuance of the policy of containment of communism, replaced the French to oppose freedom and independence of Vietnam in 1954. Ignoring the nationalist nature of the communist movement, the Americans helped the process of temporary partition of Vietnam. It organised and aided anti-communist forces and sent its security forces to defeat communist guerrillas. The US involvement in Vietnam thus started growing and between 1964-75, 7 million tonnes of bombs, three times the tonnage used in World War II, had been dropped on Vietnam.[4] Besides, napalm and phosphrous boms were also used. The tragedy of this phenomenon for the US was its defeat. It had to withdraw its forces lock, stock and barrel in April 1975. Besides, it had to accommodate thousands of Vietnamese refugees in the US. Vietnam war indeed proved very costly for the US, in which the US lost the lives of 56,559 servicemen and an expenditure of US $ 150 billion.[5] Though, millions of Vietnamese also died, but they were victorious finally in defeating the colonial forces and in uniting the two parts of Vietnam under a common political system. The communist ideology worked as a cementing force to unite the people of North and South Vietnam against external enemies.

The Communist Party of Vietnam (CPV) has special status because it led the nationalist movement against France and anti-colonial struggle against the U.S. successfully. Whether it was Indo-china Communist Party (ICP) or National Liberation Front (NLF), their mobilisation and strategies were decided by the communist cadres. The role played by the communists were so much nationalistic that communism began to be equated with nationalism, and communist endeavours were projected as nationalist goals.

The victory over the US in 1975 boosted the morale of the Vietnamese. As it was under the stewardship of the CPV, the then leaders attached prime importance to it in the political system. Hence, they adopted one-party rule and the Constitution adopted in 1980, entrusted it with supreme powers of rule making and rule application. That did not work properly and therefore, there were some modifications when 1992, Constitution was passed. Now the attempt was made to separate the legislative, executive and judicial powers of the Government and thereby moderate the powers of the CPV. Though the consensus continues to be in favour of one-party rule of the CPV, but the Constitution enacted in 1992, has definitely curtailed the role of the party to a great extent. Article four states that "CPV, the vanguard of Vietnamese working class, the faithful representative of the interests of working class, the working people and the whole nation, following Marxism-Leninism and Ho Chi Minh's thought, is the force leading the state and society."[6]

At the same time, the reforms are accelerated under the slogan of "we the people are fundamental". All party organisations including Communist Party, operate within the framework of the Constitution and the law. The people, therefore, exercise power through the National Assembly and the People's Councils.[7] The new Constitution, though, recognises the leadership of CPV, and guarantees that it is the one and only legitimate political party, but the overall situation is changing.

Mentioning the continued leadership of the Communist Party, however, is unique, because other socialist countries in the process of reorganisation and reform in the post-Cold War era, particularly in Eastern Europe left out the provisions dealing with the role of the Party, Vietnam has shown its courage by attaching importance to the CPV constitutionally even in the changed context and it continues to project it as a vehicle for development and modernisation.

The critics of the Vietnamese political system have been very active. They believe that Vietnam is unchanged as far as Doi Moi in political matters are concerned. They are unable to understand the rationale of one-party domination. They have been saying that the CPV conservatively clings to the right of leadership role and unless this situation is changed, Vietnam cannot evolve a democratic way of life. Notwithstanding, an objective assessment of Vietnamese politics that the leading position and role of the CPV has been agreed by the Vietnamese revolutionaries in the past five decades. The CPV leadership has been acceptable to the masses and without its leadership, it is difficult to promote nation building and at the same time promote reforms with efficiency and legitimacy. The CPV is relevant even in the changed context and plays its part in promoting liberalism and market economy.

Vietnam has accelerated the process of development and endeavoured to be a "market place". It wants foreign collaboration and investments and this factor was realized first by the CPV, which in its Sixth Party Congress, in December 1986, took momentous decisions that were beyond the scope of conservative communist thinking. The CPV, under the leadership of Nguyen Van Linh, adopted the policy of Doi Moi. This accelerated the reform process to open Vietnam to the outside world while projecting credentials of Vietnam as a peaceful country.

**Doi Moi**

Doi Moi is a unique way of bringing changes in the socio-economic life of socialist country and revolutionary in its own way. It is a means to social change and economic development, to the introduction of certain aspects of liberal democracy.[8] The various steps under Doi Moi have paved the path of development and the undergoing changes are appreciated at the global level.

Doi Moi has a wide meaning and it is being defined in various ways. Japan's Tetsusaburo Kimura analysed that Doi Moi has a wide range of contents, but it can be understood in three parts. The first is market opening measures including the abolition of the Central Government's monopoly of trade, encouragement of foreign investment and a shift to floating exchange rate system. The second part of Doi Moi is through which autonomy has been given to farmers, merchants, and enterprises in terms of manufacturing and sales. The third is the abolition of price control and use of interest as macro-economic variable.[9]

On the other hand Akie Ishda has said that Doi Moi is a legal reform in conformity with policy changes from a centrally planned economy to market-oriented economy. It is aimed at recognising multi-sector structure in the economy, operation of market mechanism and expansion of external economic relations.[10]

Ishida and Kimura both have stated that the emphasis of Doi Moi is reforms in the economic system, but its long-term impact on politics is a subject of speculation. Thus, Kimura says that Doi Moi is not to renovate everything in the short-term, but it is a process to study and experience trial and error. It is a repetition of an advance and retreat. It is different from perestroika and glasnost in meaning and texture, and a unique contribution of Vietnam under a communist order.

Doi Moi has proved advantageous in accelerating economic growth rate which has been around eight percent since 1992. The measures under Doi Moi have enabled the government to control inflation rates and Vietnam is exporting 1.5 to 2 million tonnes of rice to the outside world. It has emerged as a third biggest rice exporting country. Besides, it is exporting crude oil, coal, tin and marine processed products. Agricultural exports also include groundnuts, wine, rubber, coffee, and tea. Again textiles and handicrafts production are rapidly rising. Thus, it has contributed to the factors for regional stability and prosperity.

While attending economic restructuring, Vietnam also locked towards some political institutions which have interconnections with management and economy. Hence, the role of the party, National Assembly, army and the press are changing. These transformations are complimenting the effectiveness of the economic institutions and helping the process of liberatisation and market economy. Here an attempt is made to analyse briefly the changes in the role of the Party, National Assembly, Army and the Press to prove that the political system too is in the transitional phase, and it is changing to cope with the challenges of economic development and globalisation.

**Communist Party**

Though, the new Constitution of Vietnam says that the CPV is the force leading the state and society, its powers have been reviewed as a result of the corresponding increase in the powers of National Assembly. Now it is not necessary to be a member of the Communist Party to be a member of the National Assembly. Nguyen Xuan Oanh, a member of Vietnam's National Assembly spoke to International Herald Tribune that the election for National Assembly in 1987, brought major change: 60 per cent of those elected were new to the legislature. They came from a variety of backgrounds. About 10 per cent of those did not belong to the Communist Party. Independent candidates are encouraged to fight and as they have opted for multi-candidate election, the electorates have choice of alternatives.[11]

The 1992, Constitution has attempted to define the limits of the role of the Party by stating that the people are the masters, the state is the manager and the party is the leader. While affirming the leadership in the CPV, the Constitution has pointed out its obligations to the state and society. For the party to lead does not mean, "try to impose its will", or "to do everything in place of the state bodies and social organisations". All party organisations should carry out activities in the framework of the Constitution and law.

The CPV has thus set for itself the reformative measures for the daunting tasks ahead. Its has sought to raise the standard of its leadership and for building and developing an economy along the line of market mechanism. The party's guidance is designed to promote people's right of mastership, to raise the managerial skill and effectiveness of the state and role of the Front along with that of the people's organisations and social bodies, to mobilise the whole political system in society, thereby creating the strength of social democracy.

Though, the style of functioning of the CPV is changing, yet the demands for introduction of multi-party system have cropped up. This is because of the pluralist culture and historical legacies of Vietnam. Tonking, Annam and Cochin-China had three separate systems and there were cultural differences between the people inhabiting in the north and south. Saigon was the centre of business and trade during the Colonial period. The Americans propped up business culture of Saigon further and it was considered an ideal trading centre during 1954-1975. When the two parts of Vietnam were united in 1975-76, Saigon (Ho Chi Minh City) had medium sized factories for production of consumer goods. It had a large service industry and an efficient commercial banking system. On the other hand, northern areas had communist infrastructure, where collectivisation of agriculture and a weak industrial base existed. With the unification, socialist drives started everywhere for integration of the economies as well. The CPV leadership ignored the ground realities in the process. Centralisation came in place of privatisation and collectivisation of agriculture was promoted in the south as existing in the north. It disturbed the entrepreneurial initiative of the people. Hoas, the business class of Chinese origin felt victimised so much so that they began to desert their homes to seek asylum elsewhere.

Vietnam soon became one of the poorest countries of the world. With rapid deterioration in the economy, people felt restless. They started questioning the leadership of the country and this tendency was witnessed at various forums of the government in due course. By 1986, the situation deteriorated to an extent that a number of leaders including Prime Minister Pham Van Dong resigned, to pave the path for reformists to take over. Hence Doi Moi process began.

Though, review of the existing rules and overhauling of the system have been promoted, Vietnam is not yet prepared to nurture a culture to tolerate dissent. Ross Range of *New York Times* reported in May 1995, that harsh sentences are meted out for the slightest show of dissent, such as, "15 years sentence" given to a man, named Phan Van Quang for waving the flag of the former South Vietnam during the Ho Chi Minh City international marathon in 1992. Ross Range, at the same time has reported that "although government-controlled, the press is relatively uppity, reporting all manners of corruption, scandal and general incompetence local television is heavily westernised. On my first night in the town, I was stunned to see 'Apocalypse Now' showing on the main channel followed by Operah, Popeye, the Master's tournament and the NCAA final etc."[12]

Thus, the western culture through media is welcomed and this would gradually influence the people. A number of westernised Vietnamese who have been doing business overseas are returning back. They have new thinking and new awakening and they symbolise new culture. They are interested in restoring Vietnam as an ideal trading centre and hence they would like to promote democracy and free trade. As multi-party system is an important element of democracy, it would naturally be encouraged advertently or inadvertently.

There are indeed some Vietnamese leaders who advocate the case for multi-party system and demanding more democratisation in the political process. Prominent amongst them are Tran Xuan

Bach (former Politburo member), Bui Trinh (former Vice-Editor, Nhan Dan), Phan Dinh Dieu (mathematician), Duong Thu Huon (Novelist) and the Club of Resistance Fighters (an organisation of Veterans in the southern part of Vietnam). Again some pressure groups in the name of the Scientific Socialist Party (1990), the Form of Freedom (1993), the United Buddhist Church, and the Organisation of Catholic Church have time and again criticized the leadership and the system.[13] The influence of these groups are, however, confined to certain areas only and nationwide support is required to transform one-party rule to multiparty system.

**National Assembly**

Prime Minister Nguyen Van Linh and Vo Chi Cong strengthened the powers of the National Assembly. They believed that it was wrong to turn it as a rubber stamp and therefore while restructuring the system paid particular attention to make National Assembly vibrant and a strong institution of the government. Vo Chi Cong stated that "it is necessary to allow the National Assembly to represent the people and to give it responsibility for solving important problems in the life of the people".[14]

The powers and functions of the National Assembly have been effective in the Doi Moi era. Though, the old Constitution had also projected National Assembly as the highest organ of state power and the sole organ to legislate laws, it was virtually a rubber stamp till the adoption of new Constitution in 1992.

The new Constitution says that the National Assembly is the people's highest representative agency, and the highest organ of state power, exercising its supreme right of supervision over all operations of the state. It elects the President and Vice-President, the Prime Minister and senior judicial officers, and ratifies the Prime Minister's proposals for appointing members of the government. It decides the country's socio-economic development plans, national financial and monetary policies and foreign policy. The term of each legislature is five years. The National Assembly Standing Committee supervises the enforcement of laws and the activities of the government. Amendments to the Constitution may only be made by a majority vote of at least two-thirds of the Assembly's members.[15]

Again the Prime Minister has to be a member of the National Assembly, but this is not necessary for other ministers. The Prime Minister is responsible to the National Assembly and his term of office is the same as that of National Assembly. Again the term of office of the presiding judge of the Supreme People's court corresponds to the term of the National Assembly and he or she is responsible to the National Assembly. The important point to be noted is that the National Assembly has started asserting its powers and this trend is encouraged.

The National Assembly before 1992, was ineffective because it was convened semi-annually merely for five days and its representatives merely raised their hands in favour of proposals made by the Council of Ministers. This practice was changed in 1993 and now each session continues for at least 29 days. As a result of the extended session, the time for discussion is longer and substantial. The representatives express their opinions and reservations freely and authorities have to answer their questions. If any bill is not discussed in the house, the representatives are empowered to reject it. The members of the National Assembly are also empowered to voice the concern of their respective constituencies and make important resolutions for consideration of the government.

The changes in the nature of National Assembly is not only due to the powers that the new constitution has given but also because of the electoral reforms through which non-party and independent members depend on their performance in the National Assembly. So, they have to be vocal and fearless to voice the opinion of the people. They are not afraid to express their concern for the omissions and commissions committed by the government officials. They are playing important role in the nation building and modernisation processes.

**Armed Forces**

Vietnam is trying to impress that it is not chauvinistic as projected in the past. It has peaceful intentions. It fought wars in the past because it was compelled to fight. Now that there is crusade for economic development at the regional level and Doi Moi is the desirable goal, Vietnam abolished conscription under which men between 18 and 35 years and women between 18 and 25 years had to go compulsorily for military training. Vietnam also reduced the number of its armed forces by 50 per cent in 1987 and it further reduced it in conformity with peace time needs. In 1988, the strength of the Vietnamese armed forces comprised eight per cent of the total population, but the government endeavoured to reduce it to one per cent of the total population. The military spokesman, Lt. General Nguyen Quyet is stated as saying that the military have undertaken a basic change in both direction and strategy. It is being streamlined into a defensive force consistent with peace time needs. The ultimate aim is to have an army numerically small but high in quality.

Vietnam has thus succeeded in creating a new image and the world view regarding Vietnam has become positive. The Vietnamese no longer see the world in terms of two mutually antagonistic camps, but endeavouring to link Vietnam's economy with global economy. Foreign Minister, Nguyen Co Thach (1986-91), talked about interdependence in international matters and in May 1988, he was instrumental in passing a resolution which had deep-rooted impact on strategic thinking of Vietnam. The CPV politburo passed resolution 13 which officially accepted interdependence factor in international relations. While explaining resolution 13, Zachary Abuza says that it provided a new holistic paradigm for national security: One that included 'a strong economy, a peaceful international situation, "sufficient defence" and an increase in bilateral relations with countries in all three worlds.[16]

Thus, Vietnam adopted comprehensive security approach which included three components:

(a) to foster good bilateral relations with all countries, including former enemies, i.e., the U.S. and China,

(b) to have no alliances, nor a reliance on a super power, and

(c) to maintain a peaceful external environment so that all resources can be spent on developing the economy.

**The Press**

The outlook of the Vietnamese press has changed in the past one decade. Though, censorship has altogether not been relaxed, the journalists are encouraged to report investigative articles and about wrong-doing of the officials. They keep a watch on bureaucrats and ministers this development has irked some CPV stallwards. The government has given directives to the press to reflect not merely "the voice of the party" but also the "voice of the people". It has permitted the press to expose dark areas of socio-economic life and investigative pieces are given incentives.

Premier Nguyen Van Linh had set a new tone of the press by stating that they should not bend their pens in order to please officials. He said that "if a person is unable to write as they wish, they should do research and enhance their knowledge, till the suitable time comes for free and fair reporting".[17] He clearly said that the press should not write opportunistic pieces. His successors also promoted investigative articles and this has helped in the better performance of the government and better image of media.

**Conclusion**

The socio-economic and political developments in Vietnam are indicating that the changes are substantial and it would ultimately promote pluralism. Though, the people's faith in one-party rule remains, but the adoption of market economy do provide a choice between alternatives. Hence, alternatives to one-pary rule also cannot be ruled out.

However, if we analyse the existing realities of the South-East Asian Polity, we can easily predict that there is no immediate threat to the CPV leadership. Two neighbouring countires, i.e., China and Laos have one-party rule of the Communist Party. On the other hand, Indonesia with Golkar, Singapore with People's Action Party (PAP), and Malaysia with United Malay National Organisation (UMNO) have one-party rule, without the adoption of one-party system. All the above-mentioned parties have often been viewed authoritarian, yet they continue to remain in power. The notable reasons for their success is that they have performed well, and have led their countries on the path of modernisation and development. They are popular in their respective countries and the mere adjective of being "authoritarian" cannot destabilise them. Similarly, CPV may be projected authoritarian, but if it performs satisfactorily and so long as it contributes to increasing influence and affluence of Vietnam, it cannot be replaced. The political system is changing but the Vietnamese believe in continuity and change and hence, the process is gradual and substantial.

It is noteworthy that the changes in the political system have long-term implications on Vietnam's foreign policy and relations. It has been unique on the part of Vietnam to diversify its relationship from the erstwhile Soviet Union to the countries in Asia-Pacific. After the break up of the Soviet Union, with which it had cultivated intimate relations for decades, it adjusted astutely as a trustworthy partner of the countries in Asia-Pacific. Hence, the polemics of the cold war era was forgotten and realistic assessment of the international situation began. As trade with former communist allies declined, Vietnam was quick to forge new commercial links with Asian tigers. At the same time, initiatives were taken to promote trade links with the countries in the European Union and the United States. Murray Hiebert reported in *Far Eastern Economic Review* in May 1992, that Vietnam escaped the clutches of economic disaster by turning to its Asian neighbours to replace the collapsing Soviet Union, its major trading partner so far.[18]

Singapore, Japan and Hong Kong, which together accounted for half of Vietnam's trade in 1991, were the biggest beneficiaries of the Soviet collapse. Official Vietnamese statistics in mid, 1992 showed that two-way trade with Singapore shot up from $111 million to $868 million, with Japan from $309 million to $709 million and with Hong Kong from $182 to $502 million.[19] Thus, Singapore emerged Vietnam's biggest trading partner in 1992, accounting for 26.7 per cent of imports and 33.7 per cent of exports. Vietnam and Singapore thus granted "most favoured nation" status to each other and signed a series of agreements to boost trade and investment relations. Other ASEAN countries also came forward to forge commercial links with Vietnam and subsequently became important trade partners and investors in Vietnam.[20]

Moscow, for decades, had controlled more than half of Vietnam's foreign trade and had provided Hanoi with more than $ 1 billion in aid and concessionary trade arrangements. It was difficult to envisage anything without the Soviet aid and assistance in Vietnam for decades, but it was smooth and admirable effort to diversify it. Vietnam succeeded in finding new markets, new allies and new donors in the post-1991 era.

The widespread changes in Vietnamese politics had implications on the attitudes of the US also. The Americans, which proved the stubborn enemy of Vietnam from 1945 to 1991, began to review its policies and adopted a favourable posture. President Clinton decided to remove the US veto on Multilateral lending to Vietnam in 1993 and paved the way for IMF, World Bank and ADB lending and operations. In 1994, the US lifted trade embargo and evinced interests in resuming diplomatic ties. In August 1995, Secretary of State, Warren Christopher initiated the resumption of diplomatic ties at the level of charge d' affairs and full diplomatic relations were established in May 1997.

Vietnam has earned the friendship of the ASEAN also due to changes in its system. This grouping, which had adopted anti-communist postures right since its inception, and had ostensibly worked for isolating Vietnam for decades, changed their attitudes rapidly. The ASEAN as a group was advertently supporting "bleed Vietnam white" policy ever since December 1978 and was critical of Vietnamese intervention in Cambodia. The Communist system was being ridiculed and they were projected as barbaric monsters. But changes in the Vietnamese political system, followed by the dissolution of the Soviet Union, changed the attitudes of the ASEAN countries. Hence, the ASEAN first offered observer status to Vietnam in 1992 and thereafter full membership in 1995. Though, Vietnam remains a communist country, but this reality does not inhibit its becoming relations with the ASEAN partners.

The ASEAN leaders have very positive opinion regarding Vietnam and they admire the latter for worthwhile partnership. They are genuinely interested in Vietnam's locational advantages, mineral resources and its chaep and relatively well-educated labour force. Above all, Vietnam is considered important for ASEAN solidarity and regional consensus.

It is noteworthy that ideology, which perennially proved an irritant in Vietnam's interaction with the ASEAN and East Asian neighbours, is not considered a threat in the present context. The Communist Party of Vietnam is working as a facilitator to promote business and trade with the outside world. It is not at all interested in exporting revolution and does not talk of Indo-Chinese federation. Hence, it is unwilling to interfere in the affairs of Laos and Cambodia. It voluntarily withdrew its forces from Cambodia (1988) and is a silent spectator in view of the anti-Vietnamese rhetoric of the Khmer Rouge.

Vietnam now believes in peaceful resolution of the conflicts and is acting as a trustworthy and responsible neighbour. Above all, it has displayed good understanding of regional realities and simultaneously introduced structural changes to accommodate regional interests in tune with regional consensus. To conclude in the words of Vietnamese ambassador, Pham Sytam, "the objective of reforms in Vietnam is indeed the policy of openness and integration into the world, selecting and adapting the world's essence with due regards to the trends and spirits of the present time. It is also a process in which whatever attained by modern science and technology is useful for this people and country would be taken in. The previous policy of "closed door" resulted in stagnation. International cooperation has become a common trend of the time now and an important condition for development too. The Doi Moi process is to befriend all nations for peace, independence, and development."[21]

## References


1. Nguyen Xuan Oanh, "Hanoi is moving towards more pragmatic socialism", *The Times of India,* New Delhi, 3rd January, 1989.
2. For an understanding of Vietnamese society and politics, see Melanie Beresford, *Vietnam: Politics, Economics and Society,* London, 1988 and J. Buttinger, Vietnam, *A Political History,* London, 1969.
3. For an analysis of this aspect see William J. Duiker, *Rise of Nationalism in Vietnam, 1900-1941,* New York, 1976 and Nayan Chanda, *Brother Enemy: The War after the War,* London, 1986.
4. Nirmala Laxman, "Vietnam: Poised for a Boom" *The Hindu,* Madras, 25th April, 1993.
5. *Ibid.*
6. The 1992 Constitution continues to affirm leading role of the Communist Party of Vietnam, *Vietnam Information Bulletin,* New Delhi, Vol. 30, no. 6, 1992, pp. 1-3.
7. Tsutomu Murano, "Can the Communist Party Maintain its Dominant Position?", *Dynamic Vietnam,* Tokyo, June 1995, p. 27.
8. Ganganath Jha, "Politics of Perestroika in Vietnam 1986-1990", *International Studies,* New Delhi, Vol. 28, 1991, pp. 373-88 and; Gareth Porter, "Politics of Renovation in Vietnam", *Problems of Communism,* Washington, D.C., Vol. 39, May-June 1990, pp. 72-89.
9. Tetsusaburo Kimura, "Access to International Division of Labour", *Dynamic Vietnam, IDE Spot Survey,* Tokyo, June 1995, p. 2.
10. Akie Ishida, "Legal Aspect of Renovation Policy", *Dynamic Vietnam,* pp. 21-24.
11. Oanh, *Times of India,* 3rd January, 1989.
12. Ross Range, "20 Year's on : Vietnamese are Looking Forward", *The Times of India,* 10th May, 1995.
13. Alan Dawson, "Battlelines are Drawn: Conservatives opposed to Doi Moi", *Bangkok Port,* 13th & 15th April, 1989.
14. *Straits Times,* 3rd February, 1990.
15. *Constitution of Vietnam,* 1992.

16. Zachary Abuza, "International Relations Theory and Vietnam", *Contemporary Southeast Asia*, Singapore, Vol. 17, no. 4, March 1996, pp. 406-19.
17. *Vietnam Courier*, no. 1, 1988, p. 12.
18. Murray Hiebert, "Vietnam looks to Asia after Soviet Collapse", *Far Eastern Economic Review*, 14th May, 1992, p. 56.
19. *Ibid.*
20. *Ibid.*
21. Pham Sytam, "Vietnam: continuity and commitment to the Renewal", paper presented in a seminar on Vietnam, India International Centre, New Delhi, 13 December, 1998.

# 15

# FOREIGN POLICY OF PEACE, DEVELOPMENT AND INDEPENDENCE

NGUYEN SI XUNG

In July 1995, Vietnam, in its strive for regional integration, became a full member of ASEAN whose member countries and others in East Asia now take up 70% of Vietnam's foreign trade and an equivalent 70% of foreign investment.

Vietnam today has diplomatic relations with 167 countries; trade relations with over 100 countries; more than 50 different economies have been effectively investing scores of billions of dollars in Vietnam. Not only has the blockade inhumanly and wrongly imposed on Vietnam been broken up but also the international position of Vietnam has been acknowledged and enhanced.

The traditional good neighbourly relations with China were restored in 1991; relations with the United States were formally normalized in 1995; and the time-tested traditional relations with friends near and far were consolidated and expanded.

Vietnam is one of the co-founders of the Asian-European cooperation mechanism known as ASEM. While actively promoting this mechanism, Vietnam extends its support and infact encourages friendly countries including India to join as well.

In November 1997, a first international summit ever hosted by Vietnam—the 7th Francophone Summit (of the Association of French-speaking countries) was successfully organized in Hanoi.

Vietnam has become a full member of APEC, an inter-regional co-operation forum with 21 member countries. This organization that has a 2.2 billion population and GDP of over 13 billion US dollar or 54% of world GDP, takes up 55% of global income, and 46% of world trade, is obviously playing a very crucial role in the world economy. As globalization of the world economy has become inevitable, Vietnam has been actively negotiating her accessation into the World Trade Organization (WTO).

Not only is Vietnam an active member of the Non-Aligned movement and the United Nations organization but also gaining creditibility from the world community: Vietnam was elected one of the Vice-Chairman of the 52nd Session of the UN General Assembly; member of ECOSOC— the second most important organ of the United Nations after the Security Council.

The above-mentioned records in Vietnam's international relations have proved that Vietnam's foreign policy undertaken over the past decade is correct and well grounded on the basis of historical, scientific and practical analysis.

Vietnam was heavily ravaged after hundreds of years under severe domination and heavy exploitation by foreign colonialism and imperialism and repeated wars against Virtnam by biggest adversaries of the times with largest human killing and devastating machineries. More than ever, Vietnam needed to have favourable conditions to recover and reconstruct the country. No one can embark upon national reconstruction in the atmosphere of continuous confrontation and instability.

Moreover, the physical demands in terms of technology and capital for recovery and reconstruction after the war was too big for Vietnam to rely only on herself. While self reliance is of vital importance, experience gained in the cause of national salvation has taught us that obtaining help, assistance and co-operation from others is also of great significance.

From a scientific analysis, Vietnam started its renovation when peace, stability and development became an inevitable trend of time. They have been for ages the aspirations of mankind, imperatively demanded and earnestly desired by nations in the present context of swift and complicated changes in the world.

We are living in a world in which interdependence among nations has become a striking phenomenon. Technological revolution is fast developing, affecting every aspect of our life. And globalization of the world trade and economy has become a fundamental characteristic of world affairs. In such a world, openness is a must for any foreign policy and diplomacy.

Vietnam's policy of being a friend to with all nations striving for peace, independence and development is a foreign policy that continued and inherited from the traditional foreign policy throughout the history of thousands of years of nation building, safeguarding national salvation for independence and freedom. Imbued with the belief of preserving our national characteristics, the Vietnamese people always cherish the good neighbourliness, are eager to enter cooperation for the sake of mutual benefit, and lofty purposes of mankind. Truthfulness and loyalty.

When we are refering to this here today, our minds go back to the days almost 30 years ago, from this country— the Great India, we in Vietnam heard the slogan from the bottom of the hearts of millions of Indian friends: Mera Nam! Tumhara Nam! Vietnam!

The policy of being a friend with all nations striving for peace, independence and development with all its practical, scientific and historical values will remain as guidance in Vietnam's diplomacy in her continued march into the next century. It helps to tackle challenges from the outside. Challenges by the globalization coupled with the ones caused by the financial and monetary crisis in East Asia now spreading to other parts of the world, highlight the urgent need to be put on the top agenda of the world community to increase cooperation among the developed and developing countries, such cooperation helps the affected countries and economies to get out of difficulties, and also leads the world economy to stable and durable development for the benefit of all nations.

At the time when many differences and conflicts remained unsolved or are being solved through peaceful means, Vietnam's positions has always enjoyed support from friends near and far. Vietnam is for peaceful solution of all differences and conflicts on the basis of sovereignty, equality and mutual respect and the benefit of the people of each side and for the common interest of world.

In conclusion, the policy of being a friend of all nations striving to peace, independence and development has been an unswerving foreign policy of Vietnam. The policy has been tested through time and made enormous contribution to the success of every stage of the nations' revolution and been confirmed as a continued foreign policy.

# 16

# FOREIGN POLICY IN THE POST-COLD WAR PERIOD

SHANKARI SUNDARARAMAN

The period following the cold war witnessed far reaching changes in the spheres of foreign policy postulations and the development of relations among global actors. What had been the norms during the cold war, with the division of groups in a bipolar world, was slowly replaced by other patterns both regionally and internationally to give newer prospects and dimensions to international relations.

When one looks at Vietnam's history from 1945 onwards it is evident that it is a history of conflict. Both, the first and second Indo-china wars took a toll of the country's development, interestingly during both these phases, the inherent problems in the region in terms of relations with Cambodia and Laos had remained submerged, in the context of fighting a war with a common enemy that is both the French imperialist rule and later the American presence in the region. After 1975, with the defeat of the common enemy, the differences emerged and this led to a new phase of bitter conflict between Vietnam and Cambodia under the ultra-radical Khmer Rouge. Another outcome of the Vietnam Cambodia problem was the Sino-Vietnamese War of February 1979. When placed in the context of such a history, it is easy to understand why Vietnam's foreign policy during these years were confined to close relations with the Soviet Union and to a strategic alliance with its two closest neighbours—Laos and Cambodia. From 1978 onwards, one of the major drains to the Vietnamese economy was the continued presence of its troops in Cambodia and this continued till about 1990. Thus, the contributing factors to changing the economic policy within the country came from poor economic management, the heavy burden of maintaining troops in Cambodia as well as the changes in the international environment—these produced the pressures for Vietnam to bring about a change in its policy.[1] The factors that governed this change in Vietnam's policy were both internal and external. Internally, the country moved to a phase of political and economic 'renovation' which has been called as the 'doi moi'. This phase of change at the internal level had a bearing upon the foreign policy as well— especially the economic policy that began to influence the foreign relations.[2]

## Historical Background: Factors that Ushered in a Change

In order to get a complete understanding of the issues that changed the internal complexion of Vietnam, it is significant to briefly view the historical dimensions that set about the transition. With the end of the Second-Indochina War in 1975 and the subsequent reunification of Vietnam in 1976, there was a belief in the invincibility of the Vietnamese strength. This belief in the political strength of Vietnam also encompassed the economic realm where the members of the politburo felt that having defeated the French and the Americans, Vietnam could then revive the plans for 'rapid force industrialisation' that had been a part of its economic agenda. This had been a part of the decision to reunify the country—that is a political and economic reunification of the North and South.[3] In fact, this decision to reunify the North and South, both politically and economically was met with a great deal of reservations from some members of the party. After the reunification of Vietnam, the severity of the economic problems continued and the Vietnamese Communist Party had believed that the efforts of post-war reconstruction and economic revival could once again be met with the assistance from the Soviet bloc, China and the West. The Vietnamese expectations were not met along these lines due to several reasons—first, the Cambodian situation flared up as a result of which there was tension with China. The Sino-Vietnamese War of 1979 ended with whatever assistance was coming from China. Second, the aftermath of the war led to the complete breakdown relations with the United States and the West. The embargoes placed upon Vietnam by the US crippled the system so greatly that Vietnam was left solely dependent upon the Soviet Union for aid.[4] Thus, from around the end of the seventies to the mid-eighties, Vietnam remained solely dependent upon the USSR for support.

The mid-eighties, in that sense, becomes a watershed in the development of Vietnam's economic policy, and from this period onwards the country embarked upon a period of economic renovation which was triggered off by two factors—the other socialist countries had started to follow a market-oriented policy. The Chinese liberalisation programme had been initiated since the 1978 and the Soviet Union under Gorbachev had begun the change with the perestroika and the glasnost. This was a major inducement for change within Vietnam. The other factor was that, within the South-East Asian region itself, Vietnam had remained economically backward while the countries of the Association of South-East Asian Nations (ASEAN), had furthered their economic policies. Both these contributed to the revision in Vietnam's policy and the change in the system automatically led to the expansion of the foreign relations because of increased economic contact.[5] It was the belief that nations that had greater economic linkages with others, had more capability to further economic development which became the single dominant factor for the change in attitude. These new levels of economic development became the single dominant factor for the change in attitude. These new levels of economic linkages would assist in 'gradually breaking down the barriers' of cold war political military alliances by creating mutual economic interdependence, which in turn created security interdependence.[6] Therefore, the change in Vietnam's foreign policy and its expansion of ties with other countries must be seen within this context of internal change.

### Vietnam's Foreign Policy in the Post-Cold War Period

Vietnam, since the end of the Second World War, has followed a foreign policy which has been considerably influenced by its revolutionary struggle, especially since it had to retain a position in an environment that was quite hostile. The struggle against the French imperialists and the Americans is well emphasised in this regard. The emergence of Communist China in 1949, strengthened the case of the fledgling Democratic Republic of Vietnam and the only two countries with which it had any firm ties were the USSR and China. The international environment dictated these initial foreign policy moves— the formation of ASEAN in 1967, made it very evident that it (ASEAN) was a regional grouping of non-Communist states and this difference in ideological perception was the first stumbling block in developing better relations. Another factor was that there was an outflow of refugees from the Indochina region and the tensions with ASEAN states increased. Moreover, the continued US embargo upon Vietnam, which was only lifted by President Clinton in 1994, also furthered the isolation of Vietnam. As the problem between the Vietnamese Communist Party and the Democratic Kampuchea regime increased, Vietnam's ties with China was also slowly replaced by an over-dependence upon the Soviet Union.

From the late eighties there was an overall policy shift and the approach seems to have been a dual one in that the Vietnamese Communist Party promoted economic liberalisation while at the same time tried to maintain the dominance of the VCP which would ensure political continuity. This approach is amply indicated in a statement made by the General Secretary of the VCP, Nguyen Van Linh. In his report to the 7th Congess in June 1991, he stated that Vietnam's overriding external relations task would be the maintenance of peace, security and cooperation which would create favourable international conditions for the building of socialism. In this report as well as in the address of the General Secretary Do Muoi to the Party's Third Plenum in June 1992, the significance of foreign relations was well emphasised. The June 1991, report maintained the centrality of the relations with the USSR and hinted that the furtherance of the Soviet-Vietnam relations would always be an issue of priority for Vietnam. The collapse of the Soviet Union had altered this position. Within the region of Indochina there has always been a stress on the 'special relations of solidarity and friendship' that it shared with Laos and Cambodia. The consolidation of "relations of friendship, solidarity and cooperation for mutual benefit and on an equal footing with Cuba and other socialist countries" was an important feature that indicated that Vietnam was keen to expand its ties in a multi-dimensional way—that is the normalisation and furtherance of ties with China and the expansion of co-operation with South-East Asia, the Asia-Pacific, the West and Japan. Two areas that were keenly endorsed were the normalisation of ties with the United States and the stress that was placed on the long standing relations that Vietnam shared with India.[7] The relations with the USSR (later Russia), the United States, and China are the angles that will be explored in the following sections.

**Regional Dimensions**

This section is devoted to analyses of Vietnam's relations with the region of South-East Asia and is approached in two parts. Part one deals with the Indochina states—that is, Laos and Cambodia while part two deals with its relations with the ASEAN states. As far as the relations with Laos and Cambodia was concerned it is important to understand the unique nature of the ties that bound this entire region of Indochina together. The Laos-Vietnam equation was different than the one that Vietnam had with Cambodia, since Laos looked to Vietnam as the senior and more dominant player in the strategic concerns of the Indochinese region. Cambodia differed in this sense since its history under the Angkor dynasty was resonant with granduer and glory. The weakening of the Angkor kingdom coincided with the encroachment upon the territory by the Vietnamese and therefore, the age old battle between Vietnam and Cambodia had always remained. Therefore, the Cambodian relations with Vietnam is far more complicated than that with Laos.[8]

**Laos and Cambodia**

The region of Indochina is one with which Vietnam shared a special relationship. During the colonial period the whole of Indochina had been administered as a single entity and even later, they were not viewed as separate states of Laos, Cambodia and Vietnam but more as a single strategic unit. As early as 1930, there was an indication of this when the newly formed Vietnamese Communist Party changed its name to the Indochinese Communist Party. Though, the name suggested the entire region of Indochina, the party remained largely Vietnamese in character.[9] The change of name was carried out under the instructions of the Comintern in the belief that the earlier name would have 'promoted narrow national chauvinism while down playing the importance of proletarian internationalism.'[10] The name as suggested by the Comintern was adopted on the basis of the premise that although, the three countries were different with respect to race, language, traditions and so on, they were concentrated in their efforts against a common united force which, therefore, made it impossible for the existence of separate, independent revolutionary movements.[11] In fact by 1950's, the idea of a combined revolutionary character for the entire region of Indochina also extended to the basis of the notion that viewed Indochina as a single strategic unit. The Vietnamese General Giap wrote that,

> Indochina is a single strategic unit, a single battlefield. For this reason and especially becuase of the strategic terrain, we cannot consider Vietnam to be independent as long as

> Cambodia and Laos are under imperialist domination, just as we cannot consider Cambodia and Laos to be independent as long as Vietnam is under imperialist domination.[12]

In the post 1975 period, the Pathet Lao came to power in Laos and the Democratic Kampuchea regime in Kampuchea. At this juncture the concept of a special relationship among the three states of Indochina, and the added emphasis to the Indochina federation idea did not meet with much enthusiasm from the Democratic Kampuchea regime. With Laos, it was a different story, in that the Pathet Lao had identified Vietnam as its main ally and so in 1977, the two states concluded a treaty of friendship. This treaty was signed on July 18, 1977 and in Article 1 it captures the nature of the twenty-five year agreement on friendship that these two are accepted as the basis for the ties between them. It stated that:

> The two sides undertake to do their best to defend and develop the Laos-Vietnam special relationship, to constantly strengthen solidarity and mutual trust, long-term cooperation and mutual assistance in all fields in a spirit of proletarian internationalism and on the principles of complete equality, respect for each other's independence, sovereignty and territorial integrity as well as each other's legitimate interests, and of non-interference in each other's internal affairs.'[13]

The treaty focussed upon 'extensive cooperation between the two governments and communist parties'. The relations between the two emphasised three categories of contact—party-to-party, military-to-military and government-to-government. Vietnam also agreed to provide considerable aid and advisory network to the government and approximately 50,000 Vietnamese troops were to be stationed in Laos. There was no friction between Laos and Vietnam at this point only because the foreign policies followed by the two countries during this period was not divergent from one another.

This was the difference between the Cambodian and the Laotian cases as a result of which the clash between the Khmer Rouge and the Vietnamese Government was very bitter.[14] In the case of Cambodia it was a very different approach altogether— the relations became entangled in long standing suspicion and mutual mistrust which led to intense conflict that finally caused the Vietnamese intervention in December 1978. The intervention caused grave concerns for the security implications and the entire region was divided along the fault lines of cold war *realpolitik*. The belief that the intervention was a precursor to the setting up of the Indochina Federation, an idea that had earlier been mooted by the Vietnamese was taken seriously by the rest of South-East Asia and this is what sustained the survival of the anti-Phnom Penh regime at that point.[15] By June 1982, when the three fighting factions along the Thai-Cambodia border joined to form the Coalition Government of Democratic Kampuchea (CGDK), the support that was provided to these groups kept the stalemate alive for a long time to come. The Vietnamese throughout the period of the eighties continued its close ties with the two states—in a Joint Communique that was released during the Indo-china Summit in 1983, the states reaffirmed their intention to protect against any kind of manifestation of superiority and stated that the relations were based on the legitimate interests and independence of all three which in turn was based on equality and free consent.[16]

The significant change in Vietnam's foreign policy occurred when there was a breakthrough in the Cambodian peace process—the eighties showed a period of intransigence on the part of all actors concerned as a result of which the peace efforts never really took shape. But the changes that led to the peace process were both at the global and the internal levels and this automatically led to a change in the nature of Vietnam's relationship with its two immediate neighbours. By the early nineties Vietnam's military presence in the region had reduced greatly and along with this so had its advisory role. Each state in the Indo-china region had embarked on a policy of market oriented reform and this had a profound impact on global relations too. For example, Laos had opened its economy and expanded wider ties with other states— especially Thailand, which soon replaced its sole dependence upon Vietnam. Laos also expanded its ties with China and this further reduced the Vietnamese influence. In the case of Laos, a major boost occurred when it became a member of the ASEAN in 1997, along with Myanmar. Vietnam, which had already become a member in 1996, welcomed the idea and the relations in the period that followed have developed along these lines, where both are a part of a larger regional grouping.

In the Cambodian context, the Vietnamese foreign policy became far more flexible than it had been during the years of the stalemate. The change in the perceptions of the Phnom Penh government was also a case in this regard. By 1989, The National Assembly of Cambodia had adopted a declaration that it sought to have a permanent policy of neutrality and that it would not be a party to any treaty or agreement ran counter to this policy— this automatically made invalid the previous agreement with Vietnam.[17] The response of the Vietnamese was positive and it stated that it would uphold the Cambodian Government's policy of neutrality. Several added factors influenced Vietnam's decision to sign the Paris Peace Treaty. First, the Chinese had indicated that they would not expect a dominant role for the Khmer Rouge in the post-treaty scenario; the United States said that it would be willing to accept Vietnam as part of the negotiations for the settlement of the Cambodian conflict and also the fact that Vietnam had become less dependent on Soviet aid and assistance. By the time the treaty was signed the Soviet Union had collapsed and the change that came about left very little choice for Vietnam but to accept more flexibility. The UNTAC period saw some tension between the two— especially close to the election time when the Khmer Rouge dropped out of the election process and carried out a genocide of the ethnic Vietnamese along Cambodia's eastern borders. This led to some strains in the ties but the Vietnamese endurance prevailed on the matter. Due to the lack of effective monitoring the situation proved to be far more complicated. The Khmer Rouge continued to make claims about the illegal presence of the Vietnamese and were also critical of the fact that several troops of the Vietnamese had stayed back in Cambodia. The border tensions between the two are also not completely resolved and this has been adequately studied by the International Border Research Unit (IBRU).[18] As the peace process took more concrete shape and the elections were conducted under the auspices of the United Nations, the internal problems within Cambodia became far too complicated. This did not allow for any major shifts in foreign policy and the relations with Vietnam remained more or less the same. There were however a few developments— Vietnam, Cambodia and Laos agreed to 'sustainable development' of the Mekong under the United Nations Development Programme (UNDP). Other areas of cooperation among the three are in issues relating to CBM's, preventive diplomacy and conflict resolution mechanisms.[19]

### Vietnam and the ASEAN

Within South-East Asia, Vietnam's foreign policy with the ASEAN states has also undergone some very significant changes since the end of the cold war. If one looks at the policy towards the ASEAN in three different phases the change becomes even more marked and crucial. The formation of ASEAN in 1967, occurred when the region of Indochina was in the throes of the war against the Americans and in this period, the ASEAN was seen to be merely an extension or replacement of the South-East Asia Treaty Organisation (SEATO). As such the Democratic Republic of Vietnam had very little contact with the ASEAN and there was a sense of hostility towards the ASEAN as a regional grouping. In the post-1975 period, the ASEAN seemed to take a more conciliatory approach towards Vietnam— it was very difficult to bridge the difference, since the ASEAN was seen as a bloc of non-Communist states in a region that had been threatened by the Communist ideology. Each individual member had battled insurgency at the national level and the response to Vietnam was seemingly open but the undercurrents in the ties remained.[20] In the initial period this was not too obvious but as the tensions between Vietnam and Cambodia increased and the Vietnamese intervention occurred, the ties between the ASEAN states and Vietnam completely deteriorated. With Vietnam's intervention in Cambodia, Thailand became a frontline state and the position of ASEAN rallied around the security concerns of Thailand.

On an independent level each state of ASEAN viewed Vietnam differently. It is important to bear in mind that the view of Vietnam varied in accordance with their view of China. Those that considered China to be the main threat to the region were more sympathetic to the security concerns of Vietnam, especially in regard to the issue of the Democratic Kampuchea regime's collusion with the Chinese and its impact upon Vietnam-Cambodia relations. In this context Malaysia and Indonesia were seen to be 'soft' on Vietnam. On the other hand the policy of Thailand and Philippines were different in that these two states were closely associated with the American war against Vietnam and were supportive of the United States policy there. What remains significant, however, is that Thailand was able to project its security interests as the *raison d'etre* in the aftermath of the Vietnamese intervention and any other consideration of the ASEAN states were put aside in preference for the Thai view and this is what dictated ASEAN policy in the years when Vietnam had its troops in Cambodia. The ASEAN role in the conflict rallied around the issue of mobilising support within the United Nations on the Cambodian issue and keeping it in the forefront of debates that raged therein. Moreover, the ASEAN also supported the formation of the CGDK in 1982 and gave recognition to the CGDK even within the United Nations.[21] In spite of the collective stand against the Vietnam presence in Cambodia, the ASEAN states followed a policy of pluralism and pursued independent approaches to Vietnam. Indonesia was probably closest to Vietnam in this regard and had even maintained low-key relations with Vietnam since 1964. Even in the period during the Cambodian stalemate, Indonesia remained as one of the major players from the ASEAN that had contact with Vietnam and its role in bringing about a solution through the efforts of its diplomacy can never be underemphasised.[22]

From the nineties the climate of dialogue changed rapidly with the overall changes that were occurring. Within the South-East Asian regional context, the most significant was the normalisation of ties between China and Indonesia as well as with Singapore. As far as Thailand was concerned, the period under the leadership of Prime Minister Chatichai Choonhavan was a crucial phase in Vietnam's relations with Thailand. Prime Minister Chatichai's famous speech in which he stated that the battlefield should be converted to a market place led to a changed attitude towards Vietnam. The aim was to pursue US and Thailand's common endeavours in trade with an investment in third countries, especially Indo-China and Myanmar (Burma). There was an increase in business relations and bilateral ties after this. Vietnam's policy towards ASEAN also changed and it began to follow a policy of closer ties with the ASEAN. A Vietnamese commentary of 1990, gave emphasis to the high economic growth rates in the ASEAN states and added that it would be worthwhile to supplement the ties with broader economic relations with the ASEAN states. Vietnam also indicated its intention to follow the ASEAN model of development.[23] The year 1992 was a landmark in the development of relations between Vietnam and ASEAN. There were several high level visits from the ASEAN states to Hanoi and Va Van Kiet also visited Malaysia, Brunei, Philippines and Singapore. At this time, the ASEAN states showed a keen willingness to develop the ties further, and a number of agreements were signed to this effect. The high point of this period was that Vietnam signed the

1976 Bali Treaty of Amity and Concord and this gave Vietnam an observer status in the ASEAN.[24] This was later changed and Vietnam became a dialogue partner in 1994 and finally a full member of the ASEAN in 1996. Membership to the ASEAN had both economic as well as strategic implications. The economy received a boost in the initial years and the effect of the financial crisis on Vietnam has not been as profound as in the other states. In the case of the security scenario, Vietnam was a part of the ASEAN Regional Forum that provided a plank for Vietnam in multi-lateral security arrangements. In conclusion, it can be said that the suspicions and hostilities that dominated Vietnam's relations with the ASEAN states have been replaced by a sense of shared interests.

**Extra-Regional Dimensions**

In the context of Vietnam's foreign policy, the most crucial area is the regional level. This is followed by its relations with other extra-regional powers among whom the most important are Russia, the United States and China.

**Vietnam's Relations with Russia**

Vietnam's relation with the former Soviet Union and later with Russia has been a significant one in which several parameters have changed. It is important to note that the Soviet Union was the mainstay of the Vietnamese foreign policy and the relations between the two countries have moved between several phases. When one views the history of the Soviet relationship with Vietnam, it is evident that the Communist Party of the Soviet Union did not rank Vietnam as a high priority in the 1940's and the 1950's. The Soviets did provide aid to Vietnam and from 1958 onwards, they surpassed even the Chinese as the major aid donors.[25] During the Second Indochina War, Vietnam was largely dependent on Soviet economic and military aid, but it maintained a kind of equidistant policy with both the USSR and China and its relationship with both varied at different phases. As the Sino-Soviet split became more evident, the Vietnamese clearly shifted towards the Soviet Union. After 1975, this relationship intensified and in November 1978, the two countries signed the Treaty of Friendship, which initiated a new phase and closer-ties developed between the two.

The Soviet-Vietnamese ties seem to have been a symbiotic one— in return for substantial amounts of aid the Soviets gained in strategic importance. Soviet assistance to the Vietnamese economy, especially for the Second, Third and Fourth Five-Year Plans amounted to approximately $ 21.5 billion.[26] In the aftermath of the Vietnamese intervention in Cambodia till the mideighties, the Soviets provided the military aid to the tune of dollars one billion per year for the maintenance of Vietnamese troops in Cambodia. For the Soviets the ties with Vietnam led to securing bases in Cam Ranh Bay which by the late eighties had been expanded to a considerable capacity. Cam Ranh Bay was well equipped with communications installations, missile loading equipment, fuel storage capacity as well as base facilities for reconnaissance, anti-submarine and strike aircrafts. The establishment of signals intelligence network at Cam Ranh Bay and its link to Danang and Hanoi proved to be very effective monitoring capacities for the Soviets.

The change within the internal political system in the Soviet Union was ushered in by Mikhail Gorbachev and in the post-1985 period, some fissions became evident in the Soviet-Vietnamese relations. These seem to have emanated from the Soviet move towards repproachment with China and the Soviet willingness to ease the tensions in regional conflicts. The change at this juncture was not so much in the Vietnamese thinking but emerged within the changing dynamics of the Soviet political thinking. Two factors became significant— first, the Soviets were ready to renounce the concept of confrontation as a principle of foreign policy and second, there seemed to be a willingness to give up the ideologising of inter-state relations. The first evidence of Soviet policy shift occurred when the Vietnamese and Chinese clashed in the Spratly's in the late eighties and the Soviet Union adopted a balanced stance on the issue.[27] By the beginning of the nineties, the Soviets announced their readiness to give up its use of Cam Ranh Bay for an American withdrawal from its bases in the Philippines and also specified that it would withdraw all military presence from Vietnam. Developments in the following period occurred with rapidity—economic aid to Vietnam was cut sharply and the agreement on military aid ended after which no new agreement was signed.[28]

The collapse of the Soviet Union was viewed with dismay by Vietnam as a loss to the communist and workers movement in the world. Vietnam recognised the Common wealth of Independent States and tried to salvage the economic mileage that it had in the region. With Russia, there has been an improvement in the eonomic ties— the two sides signed a joint communique on labour cooperation; a protocol on commodities exchange and expedite agreements on aviation, fisheries, etc. The question of defence cooperation remained uncertain since the geo-strategic equations have undergone very significant changes. It is very crucial for Russia and the other CIS states to strengthen their economies before Vietnam will show a keenness to base any potential ties with the region. Finally, the orientation of Vietnam's foreign policy in the post-cold war period shows a distinct shift towards the Asian region and its ties with the states of the former Soviet Union must bear the promise of lucrative dividends for it to attract Vietnam's interest.

**Relations with the United States**

In the years following the American debacle in Vietnam, the relations between the two countries remained extremely strained and tense. American foreign policy towards Indochina during the initial years was based on the premise of 'keeping their eyes and ears open and their mouth shut'. Thus, the United States quietly watched the changes that occurred in Indochina after the war. The atrocities of the Khmer Rouge regime and the border conflict between Cambodia and Vietnam, as well as Vietnam's intervention in Cambodia did not elicit much of response from the United States. After the intervention however, the United States strongly condemned the action and also gave vent to its earlier contention that the domino theory would affect the security of the entire region. The intervention made Thailand a frontline state and this caused the United States to react, since Thailand was a close ally. Just prior to the Vietnamese intervention in Cambodia, Vietnam had attempted to normalise its relations with the United States in 1978 and this had failed due to lack of US initiative.[29] The US embargo against Vietnam continued for 19 years and caused severe damage to Vietnam's economic recovery programme. In the first stage of the war, the embargo was imposed only upon the DRV, that is North Vietnam. But in the aftermath of the US defeat, it was extended to the entire country. One of the outcomes of the US embargo was that Vietnam was even denied aid packages through the international financial institutions such as the International Monetary Fund, the World Bank and the Asian Development Bank. Moreover, countries that were closely allied with the United States also followed the embago and Japan featured prominently in this. Another factor that pre-occupied the American thinking at this time was the issue over the Missing in Action (MIA) persons. After the Vietnam war, there were several persons who could not be accounted for and this further created very emotional reactions and complicated the process of normalisation of ties between the two countries.[30]

The changes that affected the global environment did not have any immediate impact on the US policy. In fact the climate of change had been in the offing for considerable time before the US foreign policy showed any signs of change towards Vietnam. The Cambodian situation had by then reduced in intensity and the first sign of US willingness to cooperate came in July 1990, when the United States which had till then supported. The CGDK of which the Khmer Rouge was a member, suddenly derecognised the Khmer Rouge and showed a keenness to include Vietnam as a party to the negotiations of the Cambodian settlement.[31]

The scope for the United States business interests in Vietnam also began to change in a very significant way. Many countries that had been closely allied to the US policy on Vietnam started investing in the Vietnamese economy since the opportunities were worth exploring. The Unites States did not see the logic of remaining out of this and by 1994, the United States embargo upon Vietnam was lifted and trade relations between the two countries have been resumed. However, normalisation of political relations still has not been up to the expected levels. After the embargo was lifted political ties also resumed from 1995 onwards. In August 1995, Secretary of State, Warren Christopher initiated the resumption of diplomatic ties between the two countries and for some time it functioned at the level of charge d'affaires. Full diplomatic ties were established in May 1997. Inspite of this, the relations between the two still leaves a great scope for development and both sides have sought to expand this relationship.[32]

**Vietnam's Relations with China**

A study of Vietnam's relations with China goes back a long way and the relations between these two states have always been a tense one. For over one thousand years, Vietnam had remained under Chinese domination and China, for its part, had always regarded Vietnam and Indochina as its 'soft underbelly' and policies that have been initiated in this regard have had an impact upon the two. As stated the root of the problem, a legacy of mutual suspicion and periodic conflict, goes back 2,000 years to the first emergence of direct ties between organised governments in the two countries'.[33]

During the period of the first and second Indochina wars, the relations between the two governments were good. In fact, China was one of the main aid donors to Vietnam. Vietnam's policy of maintaining equi-distance between China and the Soviet Union allowed it to maintain good ties with both the Communist giants. After 1975, the relations between Cambodia and Vietnam rapidly deteriorated and the backing which the Democratic Kampuchea Government received from the Chinese, led to tensions between Vietnam and China too. The Vietnamese too leaned towards the Soviet Union and all these factors contributed in adding further strain to the ties between the two. The ties were at its worst immediately after the Vietnamese intervention in Cambodia and as a measure of retaliation, the Chinese launched a massive offensive against Vietnam in February 1979, which was aimed at 'teaching Vietnam a lesson'. This was a brief period of conflict between the two countries. During the year of the Cambodian stalemate China was the principal backer of the Khmer Rouge and the very sustenance of the coalition forces against the Phnom Penh government and the Vietnamese troops, was due to the support that China, the United States and ASEAN provided. China's policy at this time centered around the need to provide support to the fighting factions in an attempt to 'bleed Vietnam white'.

As mentioned earlier it was the change in the global scenario that led to a shift in the foreign policy approach. The break in the Cambodian conflict led to certain changes. In September 1990, Li Peng visited the South-East Asian countries. During this visit China indicated its willingness to dump the Khmer Rouge. The Chinese policy of not seeking a dominant role for the Khmer Rouge in the peace settlement was one of the factors that set the momentum for the Cambodian peace process. The process of the Sino-Vietnamese *detente* also received an impetus from the expanding border trade. However, there were also several issues that remained as a potential source of conflict between the two. First, the border issue is one such problem that was triggered off in 1992. The Vietnamese claimed that China had occupied roughly 8,000 hectares of Vietnamese land and the tension was further increased since there was firing across the borders. This was resolved after bilateral talks, but other issues remained pending.[34] The dispute over the South China Sea Islands—the Spratly's and the Paracels remain and this has not yet been amicably resolved due to the number of contenders.

In spite of these differences the process of normalisation of ties between the two countries continued and Li Peng's visit to Vietnam in 1992 was a watershed in Sino-Vietnamese ties. At this visit, the leaders in the two countries pledged to resolve their border conflicts. In summer 1997, the two sides carried out talks on the disputed area in the Gulf of Tonkin. This dispute had been going on for a considerable period of time but in March 1997, a Chinese oilrig was moved into the contested area, thus eliciting a strong response from the Vietnamese. The talks that took place allowed the two sides to express freely their views and this helped to get a better understanding of each other's position on the matter.[35] There is some degree of ambivalence in the ties but the two countries have resolved to interact at a greater level where they can gain in mutual interests. This includes party-to-party cooperation and the exchange of many delegations between the two. There is no doubt, however, that the ties between Vietnam and China have significantly improved, and this process should remain for some time to come. It must be borne in mind that in both cases, the dictates of economic benefits have been very crucial to the normalisation of relations and as long as this fact remains in the forefront there is likely to be greater improvement of relations between the two.

In conclusion, it is important to identify the key areas that Vietnam today considers as its priority with regard to its security concerns. Interestingly enough, these are all related to the development of the internal dynamics of the country. In fact, there seems to have been a major change in perception the thrust that now occupies the Vietnamese political mindset, is one of economic backwardness and the rapid changes that economic development will result in.[36] Finally, it is believed that Vietnam has felt safest in one of three scenarios—firstly, when China itself was weak or divided; secondly, when China was preoccupied with its neighbours in the north -- Russia; and thirdly when Vietnam was at peace with its smaller neighbours and on good terms with the rest of the world. The present state of Vietnamese foreign policy is resounding with this final scenario.

## References

1. Frank Frost, "Vietnam's Foreign Relations: Dynamics of Change", *Pacific Strategic Papers* (ISEAS), Singapore, 1930, p. 2.

2. *Ibid.*

3. For details see, David G Marr, "Where is Vietnam Coming From?", in Dean K. Forbes *et al* (ed.), *Doi Moi: Vietnam's Renovation Policy and Performance* (ANU, Canberra, 1991), p. 15.
4. Frank Frost, n. 1, p. 5.
5. For details see, Gareth Porter, "The Transformation of Vietnam's World-View: From Two Camps to Interdependence", *Contemporary South-East Asia,* Vol. 12, no. 1 (ISEAA, Singapore, June 1990), pp. 1-19.
6. *Ibid.*, pp. 11-12.
7. BBC. SWB. FE/1109C1/11, 27th June, 1991.
8. Joseph J. Zasloff, "Vietnam and Laos: Master and Apprentice", in Joseph J. Zasloff (ed.), *Post-War Indochina: Old Enemies and New Allies* (Washington, 1988), p. 38.
9. Nayan Chanda, *Brother Enemy: The War After the War* (New York, 1986), p. 119.
10. Huynh Kin Khanh, *Vietnamese Communism 1925-1945* (Cornell, New York, 1982), pp. 126-28.
11. *Ibid.*, See also, Brown Mac Alister, "The Indo-chinese Federation Idea: Learning From History," in Joseph J. Zasloff (ed.), n. 8, pp. 85-86.
12. Nayan Chanda, n. 9, p. 120, See Also Gareth Porter, "Vietnamese Policy and Indochina Crisis" in David W.P. Elliot (ed.), The Third Indochina Conflict (Boulder, Westview Press, 1981), p. 88.
13. Treaty of Friendship and Cooperation between the Laos People's Republic and the Socialist Republic of Vietnam, July 18, 1977 (Ministry of Foreign Affairs, Vientiane, 1978), p. 2.
14. Joseph J Zasloff, "Vietnam and Laos: Master and Apprentice" in Joseph J Zasloff (ed.), n. 8 pp. 37-62.
15. The concept of the Indochina Federation was one that emerged from the idea of the Indochina Communist Party and was also a product of the vision that the region was to be considered one strategic unit which therefore indicated the possibility of a wider amalgam among these three states. Both the struggles with the French and the Americans was done in a collective fashion, but after 1975, Vietnam did not show any signs of ever initiating this concept. The very view that Vietnam wanted to establish such a structure would have met with severe opposition from the other two states. This theory became more of a rhetoric with the chauvinistic regime of the Democratic Kampuchea government and was also discussed at length in the official Black Paper: *Facts and Evidence of the Acts of Aggression and Annexation of Vietnam against Kampuchea,* Ministry of Foreign Affairs, Democratic Kampuchea (Phnom Penh, September 1978). See also Mac Alister Brown, n. 8, pp. 77-101.
16. Hollis C. Hebbel, "The Special Relationship in Indochina", in Joseph J. Zasloff, n. 8, pp. 103-114.
17. Immediately after the Vietnamese intervention a pro-Vietnamese government was set up in Phnom Penh. In 1979, the Vietnamese government had concluded a Treaty of Friendship with the Kampuchean

government. Once the state of Cambodia adopted the neutrality policy, it made the former agreement void.

18. Boundary and Security Bulletin, International Border Research Unit, Vol. 5, no. 2, Summer 1997 (University of Durham, UK), pp. 80-91.
19. The Economist, 8th July, 1995, p. 17.
20. One of the reasons for this was also the exodus of refugees from the region and the implications that it had on the entire region. This greatly weakened the relations between Vietnam and the ASEAN states. See Frank Frost, "Vietnam, ASEAN and the Indochina Refugee Crisis", *Southeast Asian Affairs* 1980 (ISEAS, Singapore, 1980), pp.347-67.
21. John Macbeth, "One for All and All for one", *Far Eastern Economic Review*, July 1982.
22. Indonesia took the lead role in trying to offer the ASEAN diplomacy as a plank where the conflict could be resolved. The cocktail diplomacy that it tried to initiate between the SOC and the CGDK was a major breakthrough in getting the factions together. Another significant move was the Jakarta Informal Meetings of 1989 and 1990, in which Indonesia used its good offices to achieve a breakthrough.
23. *The Nation* (Bangkok), 18th June, 1991.
24. Dorothy Avery, "Vietnam in 1992: Win Some; Lose Some", *Asian Survey*, Vol. 33, no. 1, January 1992, p. 73.
25. Carlyle A Thayer, "Vietnam and the Soviet Union: Perceptions and Policies", in Pushpa Thambipillai and David Matuszweski (ed.), *The Soviet Union and the Asia-Pacific region* (New York, 1989) pp. 134-53.
26. From 1976 to 1990, aid was given for the five year plans; $5-6 billion for the third plan and $12-13 billion for the fourth plan which amounted to almost 35 per cent of the total assistance to the third world. See, Robert C. Horn, "Soviet Policy in South-East Aisa in the Gorbachev Era: Change or Continuity", in Thambipillai and Matuszweski (ed.), n. 23, pp. 60-75.
27. *Far Eastern Economic Review*, 8 June, 1988.
28. Frank Frost, n. 1, p. 27.
29. *Ibid.*, p. 41.
30. *Ibid.*, p. 43.
31. *The Hindu* (Madras), 25th July, 1990.
32. Homepage of the United States State Department, internet Edition.
33. William J. Duiker, "Locking Beyond Cambodia: China and Vietnam", Indo-China Issues, no. 88, June 1989, p. 1.
34. *Frank Frost*, n. 1, p. 38.
35. *Boundary and Security Bulletin*, n. 14, pp. 48-49.
36. Nguyen Vu Tung, "An Initial Analysis of Vietnam's Concept of Security", in Mohamed Jawahar Hassan and Thangam Ramnath (ed.), *Conceptualising Asia-Pacific Security* (ISIS, Malaysia, 1996), pp. 55-60.

# 17

## PRESENT POLICY ON NATIONAL DEFENCE AND SECURITY

**DO TAT THI**

For more than ten years now, thanks to its renewal policy, Vietnam has emerged from a socio-economic crisis, its political situation has been stabilised and national defence maintained secured.

As the result of its foreign policy of openness, diversification, and multilateralisation of external relations, together with the leaps forward in the development process, Vietnam's status on the world arena and in the region has been enhanced. Vietnam has triumphed over the policy of blockade and isolation imposed by foreign factors against it for decades.So far, Vietnam has established full diplomatic relations with 167 countries including all the major powers and great centers in the world including five permanent members of the UN Security Council. Vietnam is also taking part in many international and regional organisations, in particular, it became a full member of ASEAN in 1995 and joined APEC in November 1998. Because of all the above factors Vietnam enjoys an international environment more favourable to the interests of its national construction and defence than in the preceding years.

Nevertheless, firmly maintaining sovereignty, national security and territorial integrity is still our first and most important task in defending our socialist Homeland of Vietnam. Those are sacred and inviolable rights achieved by numerous generations of the Vietnamese people who have shed their blood for them.

Being a country that has experienced fierce and protracted struggle for freedom and national reunification, Vietnam now strongly needs to create an environment favourable to its cause of national construction, economic development and raising the people's living standards. Moreover, Vietnam is still backward in agriculture with a low starting point, and a low level of development. Thus it is facing the danger of economically lagging further behind many countries of the world, and even of the region. That theat is becoming more and more acute in the very fiercely competitive environment of the global race in economic, scientific and technological fields. In addition, social problems such as red tape, bureaucrats, corruption and other social vices are of great challenges to the whole people's unity, political security, as well as social safety snide order.

The plots to take advantage of such pretexts as "human rights" or "democracy" in order to interfere into Vietnam's internal affairs, the intrusion into this country by means of culture and ideology and through various attempts and manouevres of the wicked forces, the actions of lending a hand to violent disturbances, activities of subversions are destabilisation for the purpose of replacing the current, political and social system of Vietnam, are all of great menaces to its security and national defence.

Disputes on the question of borders, land and maritime territories, particularly the disputes over the East Sea, have greatly affected the security and vital interests of Vietnam.

The illegal immigration and emigration, unlawful fishing in Vietnam's sea waters, crossborder, trafficking, illegal trade and movement of weapons and drugs also constitute menaces to the country's security and national defence.

As a sovereign state, Vietnam has a clear policy of national defence. Peace and self-defence are the features of Vietnamese national defence. National defence building is a process of inheriting and promoting the traditions of striving for peace, independence and freedom from the Vietnam ancient history.

The national defence of Vietnam is designed to defend the national interests, independence, autonomy, comprehensive sovereignty, and territorial integrity of the Socialist Republic of Vietnam.

The national defence viewpoint of Vietnam is to safeguard peace, to maintain and develop relations of friendship, cooperation, and joint development with other countries, to broaden national defence diplomacy, increase mutual understanding, build confidence in relations with neighbour countries, as well as with those in this region and the world over, regardless of their socio-political systems.

The national defence of Vietnam effects a policy of safeguarding national security, of combating all types of aggressions and encroachments upon the national territory, and of countering violent turbulences and subversions.

The national defence strength of Vietnam is built upon its national resources and manpower, in combination with availing itself of friendly and cooperative relations with other countries, jointly struggling for peace and security in the region and world wide.

The national defence of Vietnam defends the security interests of the country and, at the same time, respects the security interests of others, sincerely wishing to be a friend of countries struggling for peace, independence and development. The security of Vietnam contributes actively to the regional security which in turn positively impacts on maintaining the national security.

The national defence of Vietnam devised on the basis of the economic, political, military, diplomatic and humane interests of the country, while taking for reference and learning valuable international experience. Thus, the national defence of Vietnam will be consolidated in conformity with the development pace of the country and the world alike.

The national defence of Vietnam brings into play the strength of our whole people and political system, gradually builds and enhances its defence potential, firmly builds an all-people's national defence, and a posture of all-people's national defence linked to that of people's security, as well as raises the quality of the armed forces. Building national defence potential and real power should be closely linked to the overall economic, scientific and technological development of the country and with the national industry. The economy should be combined with national defence.

To be strong enough for self-defence and for the defence of its land, Vietnam has the legitimate right to build military strength and build an army provided with ever better weapons, equipment and techniques in accordance with the people's war fighting patterns of Vietnam. Proceeding from Vietnam's situation, in general, the work of providing the army and the armed forces with weapons and technical equipment should be done step by step in conformity with Vietnam's real capacities. With regard to weapons, the general guideline is good maintenance, durable use, economy, perfection and quality improvement, with self-reliance and resilience as the mainstay, in combination with considered procurement and selective cooperation.

National defence strength is used mainly for firmly protecting the independence, sovereignty and territorial integrity of the country, defending its people and political stability, curbing and foiling all the schemes and all activities of socio-political destabilization, encroachment on independence, sovereignty, territorial integrity detrimental to the national construction and development, effectively preventing and punishing criminals of all types, and properly safeguarding social order and safety.

At present, Vietnam is facing problems of territorial sovereignty, the boundaries of its exclusive economic zone and continental shelf which should be settled with the neighbouring countries. The maritime space and islands of Vietnam in the East Sea, including the Paracels and the Spratleys, are an integral part of the Vietnam. They lie within the Vietnamese national territorial boundaries founded for millennia. The exclusive economic zone and continental shelf claims of Vietnam are recognized by international conventions.

For the common interests and for the benefit of the concerned parties, Vietnam is ready to negotiate peacefully for the settlement of the historical issues as well as the newly arising ones. The national defence of Viètnam is one of peace in relations with all countries world-wide, including those involved in disputes with Vietnam concerning territorial borders, islands, and continental shelf.

In the new era, Vietnam advocates gradual integration into the regional and world community, and enhancing friendship and cooperation with other countries for joint development. The national defence of Vietnam contributes to the policy of openness, diversification, and multilateralisation of external relations, without aligning with one country against another, without confrontation and offensive against any country, but ready for self-defence against all types of aggression, of violent disturbances and subversions, without an arms race but still preserving the right to build forces for national defence. Vietnam puts its national security in the framework of regional security, and actively contributes to the overall world security. Vietnam neither joins any military alliances nor engages in any military operations contrary to the spirit of safeguarding peace, nor in any operations of deterrence.

The Vietnamese all-people's national defence originated from the history of the people and of the country. In the present time, it continues the fine historical traditions, and at the same time brings them to a stage of perfection and gradual modernization.

Consolidating the all-people's national defence of Vietnam should be closely associated with consolidating the people's security. A posture of all-people's national defence means that all the people preserve the country, and that of people's security implies safeguarding security by the whole people. These two postures are closely combined to ensure durable stability and peace for the country. When Vietnam is forced to engage in wars, they will turn into a posture of people's war, or a strong posture where all the people across the whole country will fight the enemies.

In building a posture of people's national defence as well as that of people's security, the first and foremost task is to win people's hearts and minds and to implement a national defence by the people and for the people.

# 18

# VIETNAM TODAY: ITS EMERGING POLITICO-ECONOMIC SYSTEM AND TIES WITH INDIA

PARMANAND

The South-East Asian State of Vietnam—officially called the Socialist Republic of Vietnam (SRV)—occupies a place of great significance in the global and regional politics today.

In the global politics, the SRV is known as a state which kept the present-day's world's sole superpower—the United States of America engaged in a war between 1964 and 1973, and eventually the latter bit the dust. With a population of 78.2 million, the SRV is the 13th most populated state in the world—a fact which naturally and justifiably underlines its importance in international politics. The SRV—formed in April 1975 following the military reunification—also retains its importance in international affairs because it is among the few states that are still under Communist rule.

On the regional plane, the SRV has not only been a member of the Association of South-East Asian Nation (ASEAN) since 1995, it is also the only Communist member of the Association. In truth, the formation of the ASEAN in 1967, mainly aimed at checking the growth of Communism in this part of the world. By holding the 6th summit of the ASEAN'S heads of state and government in its capital Hanoi on December 15-16, 1998, the SRV has, indeed, immensely increased its importance in the region. Not less significantly, Vietnam increased in making other members agree to the entry of Cambodia (considered very friendly to the SRV)—though its formal entry is to be announced on a future date—into the ASEAN.

Vietnam has a land area of 331,700 sq km. and a coastline of 3,260 km. It contains of 61 provinces and cities. Its metropolitan cities include: Ho Chi Minh City, Hanoi, Haiphong and Danang.

On the linguistic plane, the SRV is a multilingual state. Vietnamese is the official language. English, French, Chinese, Russian, Khmer, and some tribal languages are also spoken.

Vietnam has a very high rate of literacy, i.e., 88%. Many Vietnamese privately practice Buddhism (85%), Christianity (12%), and Confucianism (3%). On the ethnic front the Vietnamese constitute 90% of the population and the Chinese 2%. The Khmers and a variety of highland ethnic groups also constitute minority ethnic groups in the state. In 1975-79, the majority ethnic Chinese left the country, some settling in South West China, others fleeing by sea—the "boat people"—to Hong Kong and elsewhere.

The SRV is situated on the rugged eastern part of the Indo-Chinese peninsula. In its west are Laos and Cambodia—the three together constituting Indo-China. In its north is the People's Republic of China. Vietnam's population is concentrated in 2 rice-growing areas: 1) the Red River delta in the north; 2) the Mekong river delta in the south; and 3) quarters of the population living in rural areas are mainly engaged in agricultural pursuits.

Vietnam today has diplomatic relations at the ambassadorial level with 165 countries. Besides, it has entered into commercial treaties with 103 countries. The SRV is a full member of the UNO, ASEAN, IBRD (WB), IMF, ADB, IFC, ISO, ICAO, UNCSTAD, WCO, ECOSOC, WIPO, UNESCO and the UNIDO.

The political system of Vietnam today is more accommodative and pluralistic than ever in the past. In the end of the 20th century and towards the beginning of the 21st century, it is based on the accommodation of all kinds of interest articulations and interest aggregations, as also of dissents and criticisms.

A political system has been defined as the combination of "those social interactions and institutions through which a society makes decisions considered binding by most members of society most of the time".[1]

The political system of the SRV is very largely based on the constitutional system, which has been operative since April 15, 1992. It is the fourth constitutional scheme—the earlier ones being those of November 9, 1946; December 31, 1959; and December 18, 1980. Adopted by the National Assembly of the SRV in 1992, it contains 12 chapters and 147 Articles. The SRV has been adopting new constitutions taking into account the various politico-economic and social changes that are effected over the years.

As for the political regime, Article 1 of the present Constitution states: "The Socialist Republic of Vietnam is an independent and sovereign country enjoying unity and territorial integrity, including its mainland, islands, territorial waters and air space".

The 1992 Constitution emphasizes the importance of the people in the country's political system by asserting that: "The Socialist Republic of Vietnam is a State of the people, from the people, and for the people. All State power belongs to the people and is based on an alliance between the working class, the peasantry, and the intelligentsia".[2]

The National Assembly of the SRV—elected by the Vietnamese people of all hues—is "the highest representative organ of the people and the highest organ of State power of the Socialist Republic of Vietnam". In fact, it is "the only organ with constitutional and legislative powers". On the other hand, it exercises "supreme control over all activities of the State".[3]

The National Assembly—elected for 5 years' duration—has been given a wide range of powers under the Constitution and they include: the power to make and amend the Constitution; to make and amend laws; to exercise supreme control over conformity to the Constitution, the law and the resolutions of the National Assembly; "to decide the country plan for the socio-economic development"; to decide "the national financial and monetary policies; to decide the draft State budget and budgetary appropriations"; to decide the nationalistic policy of the state; to regulate the organization and activity of the National Assembly, the country's President, the government, the People's Courts, the People's Office of Supervision and Control and the local administration.[4]

More importantly, the National Assembly has the power to elect, release from duty, remove from office the country's President and Vice President, the Chairman of the National Assembly, the Vice-Chairman and members of the Standing Committee of the National Assembly, the Prime Minister, the President of the Supreme

People's Court, to set up or suppress government ministries and government organs of ministerial rank; to establish, merge, divide, or adjust the boundaries of provinces and cities under direct central rule; set up or disband special administrative-economic units; abrogate all formal written documents issued by the country's President, the Standing Committee of the National Assembly; proclaim an amnesty; institute titles and ranks in the people's armed forces, in the diplomatic services and other state titles and ranks; to decide issues of war and peace; proclaim a state of emergency; and to hold a referendum.[5]

Needless to stress, the National Assembly has been given significant constitutional and political powers under the 1992 Constitution of the SRV. Outsiders, acculturated to Western democratic norms, might be tempted to believe that the National Assembly might be functioning as a rubber stamp, especially because of the one-party state of the SRV. However, the legislature has been asserting itself vis-a-vis the party and the government in Vietnam.

For instance, when the "powerful Communist Party central committee approved sweeping, liberal changes in the land law designed to open the economy to large-scale commercial farming, the national assembly put its foot down...The legislature refused to approve changes to the 1993 law that would have increased farm sizes and extended rural leases".[6]

The party system of any political system is indisputably the most obvious indicator of the state of the latter—and the SRV is no exception. The failure of the one-party system in several east European states has shown that competitive political pluralism—no matter howsoever inadequate and defective—can not be democratically and effectively replaced by any one-party system. True, the Constitution of the SRV emphsizes the importance of the Communist Party of Vietnam (CPV) by describing it as "the vanguard of the Vietnamese working class, the faithful representative of the rights and interests of the working class, the toiling people and the whole nation" (Article 4 of the Constitution). But quite significantly, it does not prohibit the formation of other political parties in Vietnam. Indeed, non-Communist candidates have been contesting and winning elections to various representative organs in the state. And this phenomenon is increasing rather than decreasing.

Article 50 of the Constitution of the SRV underlines the importance of human rights by stating that "In the Socialist Republic of Vietnam human rights in the polical, civic, economic, cultural and social fields are respected. They are embodied in the citizens' rights and are determined by the Constitution and the law". Important rights include: equality before the law, participation in the administration of the state and management of society, the discussion of problems of the country and the region, right to vote on attaining the age of 18, the right to contest elections on attaining the age of 21, right to work, freedom of belief and of religion.[7]

Like any other Communist state, however, the Constitution of the SRV stresses the importance of citizens' duties as well, and says that the citizen's "rights are inseparable from his duties." It further says: "The State guarantees the right of citizen; the citizen must fulfil his duties to the State and society" (Article 50). The Constitution says: "The citizen must show loyalty to his motherland. To betray one's motherland is the most serious crime"(Article 76). Likewise, Article 77 says: "It is the sacred duty and noble right of the citizen to defend his motherland. The citizen must fulfil his military obligation and join the all-people national defence".

The judiciary and its functions have also been given a place of pride in the constitutional-political scheme of the SRV. Article 127 says: "The Supreme People's Court, the local People's Courts, the Military Tribunals and other tribunals established by law are the judicial organs of the Socialist Republic of Vietnam." It further says: "Under special circumstances, the National Assembly may decide to set up a Special Tribunal". Not less significantly, it also says: "At the grassroots, appropriate popular organizations shall be set up to deal with minor offences and disputes among the people according to the provisions of the law".

The overall duty of the judiciary has been explained in the following words: "It is the duty of the People's Court and the People's Office of Supervision and Control to, within the bounds of their functions, safeguard the socialist legality, the socialist regime and the people's mastery, the property of the State and the collectives, the lives, property, freedom, honour and dignity of the citizen."[8]

The human rights enshrined in the SRV's constitutions are not mere showpieces. They are taken seriously, even if some dilution might be effected by the mention of and stress on fundamental duties. The relevant courts are said to be giving a good account of themselves by protecting the citizens from any possible and probable whims and caprices of the state. The concepts of equality before law and the rule of law seem to be very well respected by relevant courts in the SRV. Apparently, there are trends towards assertion of human rights by the Vietnamese people on the one hand, and their protection by the judiciary, on the other. It obviously augurs well for competitive pluralism at every level and in every sphere of the SRV.

Aviable political system also needs a viable and free Press to sustain and enrich it. On this front, too, the SRV has given a good account of itself. The number of newspapers—accounting for more than 400 at this juncture—is on the increase rather than decrease. Published in various languages—including Vietnamese, English, French, Russian, Chinese and Spanish—some of them are government-controlled or the mouthpiece of the Communist Party of Vietnam. Most of them, however, are free to criticize the government, and they do avail themselves of the freedom—making the Press competitive and pluralistic in the SRV. No less a person than Prime Minister Nguyen Van Linh has been emphasising that the Press persons should not indulge in flattery to keep politicians and officials in good humour. It is also noteworthy that the Prime Minister has stressed that the press people should be very careful about the facts so that the Vietnamese get the authentic information.

The freedom of, and transparency in the Press is bound to stand Vietnam and Vietnamese in good stead in every possible manner and matter.

Like the country's political system, its economic system, too, has shown a great deal of resilience and strength by facing successfully various and serious problems.

The economic system of the SRV is described in the 1992 Constitution of the Camtsy (Article 15) in the following words: "The State promotes a multi-component commodity economy functioning in accordance with market mechanisms under the management of the State and following the socialist orientation. The multi-component economic structure with various forms of organization of production and trading is based on a system of ownership by the entire people, by collectives, and by private individuals, of which ownership by the entire people and by collectives constitute the foundation."

How Vietnam has compromised with changing times and changing aspirations of its people becomes quite vivid from its stated economic policy. Article 16 of the 1992 SRV Constitution says: "The aim of the State's economic policy is to make the people rich and the country strong, satisfy to an ever greater extent the people's material and spiritual (sic) by releasing all productive potential, developing all latent possibilities of all components of the economy—the State sector, the collective sector, the private individual sector, the private capitalist sector, and the State capitalist sector in various forms—pushing on with the construction of material and technical bases, broadening economic, scientific, technical cooperation and expanding intercourse with world markets."

The SRV's economy is mainly agriculture. Teak and bamboo are the chief products, and fishing is important. Its mining industries include cement, chemicals, engineering, leather, oil, gas and mineral extraction, plastics, pulp and paper and textiles. On the other hand, its major mineral and ores include anthracite coal, bauxite, cromite, gold, titan, graphite, iron ore, maganese, tin, zinc and gold. Vietnam exports: coal, rubber, wood, tea, coffee, rice, iron and apatite.[9]

Vietnam has the oil and gas resources of 4-6 billion barrels. Its annual export of crude oil is to the tune of 10.7 million tones. On the other hand, its annual production of gas oil is equivalent to 6.7 million tones.[10]

As for leading foreign investors in Vietnam today, one can count Japan, Singapore, South Korea and Taiwan. On the other hand, its leading trade partners are, France, Hong Kong, Japan, Singapore, Malaysia, South Korea, Taiwan and the USA. Vietnam receive foreign aids and assistance from various agencies, and they include: the IMF, the World Bank, the Asian Development Bank, Japan, Holland, and Denmark. In 1993, the IMF and the WB resumed loans to Vietnam. Total IMF disbursement to Vietnam between 1993 and 98 amounted to $500 million. Annual financial aid from various other international agencies amount to $2.4 billion.[11]

More and more countries today are vying with one another for investing in the SRV, on the one hand, and in having more and more trade with it, on the other.

The political economy of the SRV has been many ups and downs. It saw more downs at time. There were several reasons for that. In the intra-Communist system scramble and struggle, the SRV decided to be closer to the USSR. Obviously, the downslide in the political economy of the USSR resulted in the slashing of the financial assistance from that country to the SRV. It had to face the strongest power—the United States of America—on earth between 1964 and 1975. Vietnamese's moral strength might have stood them in good stead against such a big enemy, but the continuing war was bound to adversely affect the SRV's economy.

The severity of the SRV's economic problems had, indeed, continued after its reunification. On its part, the Communist Party of Vietnam had perceived that its efforts of strengthening its political economy would be supported by the then USSR, China and the Western block. But circumstances conspired otherwise. The Cambodian crisis—which ultimately led to the Sino-Vietnam War in 1979—saw serious alienation of the SRV from China. Eventually, it led to stoppage of all aids and assistance from the People's Republic of China. Besides, the end of the US-Vietnam war also saw the end of all kinds of aids and assistance from the West. The US embargo not only badly circumscribed the Vietnamese economy, it was left completely dependent on the erstwhile Soviet Union for all kinds of help and assistance.

It was against this background that the socio-economic crisis persisted in the SRV, with the inflation rate reaching 77.4% in 1986.[12] It was under these circumstances that Vietnam decided to go in for the *Doi Moi* (Renovation or Renewal). The programme of *Doi Moi* involved several important steps. The Communist Party of Vietnam had to, foremost, compromise its ideological rigidities. As we saw earlier, the SRV's Constitution talks about a "a multi-component commodity economy functioning in accordance with market mechanisms" and its aim at making "the people rich". Besides, the SRV had to change its priorities. In addition, the programme also realized the importance of improving its relations with various countries, including China, the USA and the ASEAN group—indeed, the SRV became a member of this organisation in 1995.

The *Doi Moi* programme saw the SRV recording very significant achievements in its history. Between 1991 and 1997, the average annual growth rate of the GDP was about 8.5%. It is a different matter that from 1998 onwards, the SRV has seen its economic growth slowing down, its purchasing capacity and export market shrank, and foreign investment decreased. According to Dang Ngoc Hung, Counsellor in the Embassy of the Socialist Republic of

Vietnam, New Delhi, there were "internal as well as external reasons" for this. According to the Communist Party of Vietnam, while implementing renewal measures, "new errors were committed."[13]

Learning from its failure, the SRV has chalked out a concrete economic programme for the future, which includes: (1) focusing on agricultural production and rural economic development; (2) expanding both the domestic and export markets; (3) effectively mobilising and using all sources of investment; and (4) improving and stabilizing the national financial system.

One serious hindrance to the growth of Vietnam's political economy is said to be the incomplete economic integration of the northern part of Vietnam with its southern part. This is said to be an important feature of the post-war Vietnam.[14]

One hopes the SRV is able to overcome this problem, too, and is able to move well on the path of new trends in the world economy.

What is the state of Indo-Vietnamese relations today? One can say with a great deal of certainty that the relations between the two states are moving more and more in positive directions. Vietnam is, indeed, cementing its "special relationship" in state-to-state contacts with India.

On December 14, 1998, Vietnamese Vice Minister of Culture and Information Nguyen Trung Kien and India's Ambassador to Vietnam Altaf Seth signed a bilateral cultural exchange programme for 1998-2000 under the provision of bilateral cultural agreement entered into 1976, after the historic "Vietnam War".[15] The 9th meeting of the Indo-Vietnam Joint Commission will be held this year (1999) in New Delhi, and a series of events are now on the cards.

Altaf Seth said in an interview that India would explore setting up a 20-MW prototype nuclear power plant in Vietnam, and an Indian delegation would be visiting the country soon.[16]

The Indian Ambassador to Vietnam said in Hanoi that defence-related matters were also expected to stay on a high note, with Indian Defence Minister George Fernandes scheduled to visit Hanoi in April 1999. On the other hand, the Vietnamese military personnel were periodically receiving training in India and high level visits were taking place, too. Answering a question about the apparent failure of India to sell defence equipment to Vietnam on any significant scale, Seth said price might be a factor.[17]

As for investment in Vietnam, India was already making its presence felt in sugar production and oil exploration. The upgradation of tea plantation and tea processing industry was another promising area. 1989-90, was the peak year of Indo-Vietnamese trade when it reached $150 million. However, in 1996-97, it dropped to $116 million. During 1997-98, however, it rose to $119.56 million.[18] According to *Vietnam—Primary Data and Important Aspects*[19], however, the current bilateral trade between India and Vietnam is $175 million. According to the same information, Indian exports to Vietnam in 1996 was $124.88 million.

It is worth mentioning that India and Vietnam signed a Trade Protocol in December 1995. During the visit of the Vietnamese Prime Minister to India in March 1997, the following agreements were signed: (1)Cooperation in the environmental and forestry sectors; (2) Economic and Commercial Cooperation; (3) Credit and Financial Cooperation; and (4) Investment—Encouragement and Protection.[20]

While India is able to help Vietnam in the fields of engineering, training and technology, Vietnam supplies oil and coal to India. Indian minister for coal visited Vietnam in November 1998, to examine import of coal from Vietnam. On the other hand, some Indian businessmen visited Vietnam to examine the possibility of importing rice from that country for other countries. In the recent trade fair held in New Delhi Vietnam bought electronic equipment from India worth $10 million. India—particularly private businessmen are taking keen interest in developing sugar factories in the SRV. Today some 50 Indian business enterprises are having their offices in Vietnam. Some Indian restaurants, specializing in Indian foods, have earned good reputation for themselves, and they attract a large number of customers.[21]

True, relations between India and Vietnam deteriorated in the aftermath of the 1962, Sino-Indian border war owing to misunderstandings between them. But there was always a large number of admirers of Ho Chi Minh (1890-1969), the paramount leader of Vietnam during his lifetime. Indeed, he had become the symbol of all that was good in Vietnam—because of his charisma, will power and perseverance. His visit to India in February 1958, brought the two countries very close. On the other hand, the October 1954, visit of the then Indian Prime Minister, Jawaharlal Nehru (1889-1964), to the SRV had also created a very positive impact on the front of bilateral relations. The Indo-Vietnamese relations, even during worse days—did not deteriorate beyond a point. There was no cold war like situation between them.

At the crossroads to the 20th and 21st centuries, Indo-Vietnamese ties are becoming more concrete and mutually beneficial. There is a strong and palpable urge among many Indians and Vietnamese of consequence that the two countries should come more and more close economically and technologically. They feel that there should be more interaction between them on the cultural and educational planes. They do not wish to lose time. This itself should stand the two countries in good stead in various ways.

## References


1. (See David Easton, 1984, "political system", in Vernon Bogdanor, ed., *The Blackwell Encyclopaedia of Political Institutions.* Oxford: Blackwell Reference, 478).
2. (See Article 2 of the *Constitution of the Socialist Republic of Vietnam* 1992.)
3. See Article 83 of the Constitution.
4. (See Article 84 of the Constitution.)
5. See article 84 of the Constitution.
6. (See Faith Kcenan, 1998, "No Rubber Stamp: Legislature reverses party bid for land reform", *Far Eastern Economic Review,* Hong Kong, December 10, 26).
7. (See Chapter V of the Constitution of the SRV.)
8. (Article 126 of the Constitution).
9. (For these details see Alan Isaacs, ed., 1989, *The Pan/Mac Millan Encyclopedia,* London: Pan Books, 566; *The Hutchinson Paperback Encyclopedia,* 1990, *op. cit.,* 864; and *Vietnam-Primary Data and Important Aspects,* 1998, *op. cit.*).
10. (See *Vietnam—Primary Data and Important Aspects,* 1998, *op. cit*).
11. *(Ibid.)*
12. (See Communist Party of Vietnam, 1996, *8th National Congress Documents,* Hanoi: The GIOI Publishers, 11th).
13. *(Ibid.)*
14. (See Carlyle A. Thayer, *op. cit.*).
15. (See P.S. Suryanarayana, 1998, "Indo-Vietnam pact on cultural exchanges", *The Hindu,* New Delhi, December 15,8).
16. *(Ibid.)*
17. *(Ibid.)*
18. *(Ibid.)*
19. *(Ibid.)*

20. *(Ibid.)*
21. (Information gathered from various member of the staff of the Embassy of the Socialist Republic of Vietnam in New Delhi.)

## Bibliography

Vernon Bogdanor, ed., 1987, *The Backwell Encyclopaedia of Political Institutions,* Oxford: Blackwell Reference.

Communist Party of Vietnam, 1996, *8th National Congress Documents,* Hanoi: the GIOI Publishers.

David Easton, 1987, "political system", in Vernon Bogdanor, ed., *op.cit.*

Alan Isaacs, ed., 1989, *The Pan/Mac Millan Encyclopedia,* London: Pan Books.

Faith Keenam, 1998, "No Rubber Stamp: Legislature reverses party bid for land reforms", *Far Eastem Economic Review,* Hong Kong, December 10,26.

Joel Krieger, ed., 1993, *The Oxford Companion to Politics of the World,* Oxford: Oxford University Press.

P.S. Suryanarayana, 1998, "Indo-Vietnam pact on cultural exchanges", *The Hindu,* New Delhi, December 15, 8.

Carlyle A. Thayer, 1989, *War by Other Means: National Liberation and Revolution in Vietnam,* Boston.

Carlyle A. Thayer, 1993, "Vietnam", in Joel Krieger, ed., *op. cit.,* 955-56.

*The Constitution of Vietnam,* 1995, Hanoi: The GIOI Publishers; *The Hutchinson Paperback Encyclopaedia,* 1990, London: Arrow Books.

*Vietnam—Primary Data and Important Aspects,* 1998, issued by the Embassy Socialist Republic of Vietnam in New Delhi.

# 19

# EMANCIPATION OF WOMEN

PUJA KHATTAR

No social change can be imposed from above, particularly in backward and agrarian societies. However, Vietnam has thrown up a new model for emancipation of women. This model has some relevance for India and that too when a political debate is going on the crucial question of giving one-third representation to women in Parliament and state legislatures. In India, due to certain historical reason women are put on high pedestal of a "Goddess" and on the other, they are the most oppressed sections of our population in every sphere of life, irrespective of caste, creed, religion and ideologies. This contradiction cannot be resolved through high sounding jargons. In this sense Vietnam's experience has some lessons for our ancient nation.

One noteworthy feature of transformation in Vietnam is the change in the status of women. In the primitive society, the woman played a dominant role and the matriarchal system prevailed. But, during the feudal regime women were regarded as inferior to men. There was a reversal of their status with the patriarchal system that began to prevail in society. They had to do domestic work. School education was denied to them according to Confucian percepts. After the overthrow of the colonial rule and establishments of the Democratic Republic of Vietnam, the state promulgated laws of equality of state between men and women in all fields, cultural, political, social, scientific and technical.

Under the Chinese influence women were regarded as inferior to men. There was no equality between the two sexes even in matters of education and title to property. But, fortunately, during the 15th century this position was changed by the Hung Duc Code which granted women the right of ownership of property on the same basis as men, and women were given even the legal power to bring a regional mandarin before a courty.[1]

Thus, the status of women was improved in spite of the teachings of Confucianism, although, it was taught in schools and popularised in Vietnam from the Ly dynasty in the 11th century to the Nguyen dynasty in the 19th century. The Confucian theory that "men live outside, women inside the family" was applied only to the ruling aristocratic and feudalistic class which was cut off from the productive forces. In reality, in the formative years of the Vietnamese society, men had to fight against the invading enemies against natural calamities to increase production. Historical necessity required them to mobilise their labour for building dams, dykes, and irrigation works to tame the rivers. They were also required to undergo military training and be ready "under arms" to fight the invasions. Thus, when men were obliged to leave their homes and villages to take up arms or take part in civil construction works, women shouldered the responsibilities at home and in the fields. Thus, in spite of the influence of Confucianism, its principles were not or could not be totally followed in practice in certain respects for reasons of historical necessity.

In whatever position—wife, mother, leader or combatant—they are all followers of glistening colour. They are precisely those traditional Vietnamese women who are extremely assiduous in both public affairs and housewifery. In spite of any circumstance, social condition or age, they all share the common feature of living at a time when the country has embarked on renovation and equality.

No word can describe the courage and firm will of the Vietnamese women in overcoming difficulties to improve their professional qualifications. They shoulder the burden of housework, and contribute to the common cause of national defence and construction. So far, the State has conferred the title "Hero Mother" on more than 30,000 women in recognition of their contributions to the national liberation struggle.

Vietnamese women make up 52 per cent of the national workforce working in all branches and occupations, especially in health care and education. There are more and more career women. Women account for 26 per cent of all deputies to National Assembly, tenth legislature (1997-2002), upto 8.5 per cent over the ninth legislature.

According to the International Parliamentary Union, this percentage has placed Vietnam at 13th among 170 countries in the number of female parliamentarians. Of those women deputies to the current National Assembly, seven are holders of Ph.D. degrees and eight MA degrees.

Women make up 10-15 per cent of Central Committee of the Communist Party of Vietnam and 15-20 per cent of the People's Council members at all levels.

Vietnamese women have also proved their adaptability to the market economy. Between 1992 and 1997, the number of women directors of private enterprises nation-wide increased five-fold.

Ho Chi Minh City alone has 1,842 women directors of companies providing employment for 44,700 workhands. The private enterprises directed by women enterpreneurs in Ho Chi Minh City have a total investment capital of Vietnamese Dong 1,265 billion and a prescribed capital of Vietnamese Dong 565 billion dollars.

Now, the state and social organisations have created more favourable conditions for women to study and improved their qualifications so that they can contribute more efficiently to socio-economic development in the country.

The image of Vietnamese girls differed markedly: between the period prior to Chinese domination and the period during Chinese domination. A major difference between the two periods was the effect of Confucian thought.

This was a matriarchal period when women played an important role in the society. This was also the time when Confucianism had not been imported into Vietnam; therefore, the relationships between men and women were more equal.

Those concepts survived untill the turn of the 20th century. Many legends from the time of the Hung kings (the protohistory period) show that young women of that time enjoyed greater independence in choosing a husband than those of the feudal time. One example is the legend of princess, Tien Dung, bathing on the bank of the Red River. Chu Dong Tu, who was such a poor fisherman that he did not even have any clothing. When the princess was approaching his village, the man had to hide by burying himself in the sand.

Unfortunately, his hiding place was the same spot where the princes took bath. The man soon exposed himself under her scoops of water. Thinking it was predestined, the royal teenager decided to marry the poor ordinary man, despite her father, the king's protest.

Women in this period, even teenagers, played as important a role in society as did men. Legend has it that, Fairy Au Co, ancestor of the Vietnamese, taught people to grow mulberry trees, raise silkworms and weave cloth. Young women also participated in military affairs, such as the female general Trung Trac and her sister, Trung Nhi, together known as the Hai Ba Trung sisters, who led an army to defeat the Chinese invaders in the 1st century A.D.

From the end of the first millennium B.C. to the 10th century A.D., China directly controlled Vietnam, which at the time consisted of only the northern part of what is today's Vietnam. During this time Confucianism became well-established as an ideology, resulting in a significant change in the life of Vietnamese women. However, women and sexual relations continued to play an importnat role in rural villages, which was strongly affected by Confucianism, regularly met with resistance from traditional beliefs.

Confucianism was not a religion, but a code of ethics, which established a hierarchy to govern the relationship between the people in an agricultural society. The hierarchy of the social relationships were the king and his subjects, father and son, husband and wife. The family was the basic social unit. The father headed the country. Men dominated, because only men could properly commune with the ancestors and thus continue "the cult of the ancestors" and carry on the line of descent.

Because women had no social importance, they were not educated and frequently illiterate. Even at the turn of the 20th century, under the French colonial education system, very few girls finished primary school in rural areas and even fewer completed secondary school. The number of girls entering universities could be counted on one's fingers.

Women were taught the three obediences and the four virtues. The three obediences were; to her father before marriage, to her husband after marriage and to her son after the husband's death. A woman was merely the shadow of her parents, husband and son. The four virtues were: good work (sewing, cooking, weaving, etc.), good countenance (having a happy and gentle face), good speech (speaking courteously) and good nature (being well-mannered and faithfull). In addition, girls were not allowed to play with boys or even to touch them.

In these times young women were given no choice in their marriage. Everything, including the husband, was arranged by their parents. Girls usually got married at the age of 15 or 16, while marriage at the age of 19 or 20 was considered late for girls. If a woman reached 25 or 26 years of age without having a husband, she was considered to be merchandise that nobody wanted to buy. Some families married their daughters off as early as age 12 or 13. It was not uncommon for a 60 or 70 year-old man to spend money to acquire a teenage bride. Some parents even promised to marry their unborn daughters to the sons of other families.

The belief in predestined fate also governed the treatment of a woman as a wife. By consulting a fortune teller, a man could see how many wives he would have. In some cases, a man was told he must have more than one wife, or he would have no son. In other cases, a girl was forced to accept the status of a second or third wife, simply because destiny dictated that she could be abandoned by her husband if she is married as the first wife.

After marriage the wife's job was to serve the husband, which, in many cases, meant the mother-in-law and to produce sons. She had many duties to fulfill but few rights. It was said that one son was more valuable than ten daughters. If a wife had no sons three years after marriage, she might be mistreated by her husband's family, replaced by a concubine or even abandoned. There were seven reasons, which could cause a wife to be driven from her husband's house. The most serious of which was not bearing a child, in particular, a son. The others were: lustfulness, showing disrespect to her parents-in-law, being talkative, stealing, jealousy and cruelty. Being driven away from the husband's house was the wife's greatest humiliation, since it meant the woman would then be cast off by the entire community.

Virginity was especially important, because no family wanted to raise another family's offspring. Therefore, all sexual relations before or outside marriage were regarded as crimes for both men and women. Boys and girls were separated from the age of 5 or 6.

If a girl lost her virginity before marriage, after the wedding, the husband's family cut off a pigs ears and delivered these together with the girl to her parents' house. Her life essentially ended.

The Vietnamese wife is subjected to the power of the head of family, the master of the conjugal association. Formerly, the husband's authority over the wife was absolute. He even had the right to hire out or to sell his wife to another person.

The husband was entitled to repudiate her in seven cases:

1. She is sterile: having no child is a lack of filial piety vis-a-vis one's parents, that is why a husband can repudiate his wife if she does not bear children.
2. She talks too much, is excessively jealous, and speaks ill of others.
3. She suffers from a horrible disease: i.e. leprosy; she may pollute the sacrifices offered to the spirits.
4. She behaves badly.
5. She steals, to the detriment of her husband or her parents-in-law;
6. She shows disrespect towards her parents-in-law.
7. She does violence on the person of her husband.

This shows how a woman was more than server to a man. It was not merely a man dominated society. But something more than that.

However, distinction must be made between two categories of married women: the spouse or first-rank wife and second-rank wives. There is also a category of women, not married but are members of the family: the woman servants or concubines, who are bought but not married. They can become second-rank wives by a regular marriage, and are only found in very rich families, especially in those of high-ranking mandarins.

Polygamy was lawfully practiced in Vietnam primarily to fulfill the ideal happiness of having many children. It was aimed at contunuing the lineage. When the wife was sterile, the husband took a second-rank wife to have children. Often, it was the sterile wife who invited him to do so. Secondly, polygamy responded to a useful economic idea, particularly in the countryside. Second-rank wives were sure and convenient assistants to the husband. Some land owners had as many second-rank wives as they had farms to be exploited. Thirdly, polygamy satisfied a certain sense of vanity; mandarins, influential notables were proud to have several wives who contributed to enhancing their importance while their aged spouse was also proud, to be the first of all the wives.

Polygamy is primarily practised in the countryside, but contrary ideas coming from the city are becoming more prevalent.

In the cities, amongst the upper and middle classes and even among the masses, polygamy has been seriously weakened under the influence of modern ideas, the Christian religion, education, economic necessities, and new conceptions of the position of women. The reading of books and the cinema have also contributed much to modifying the sentiments and ideals of a husband and wife about marriage and tends to give marriage a character of a more personal than a family union. This evolution is very profound and rapid.

It was not until the turn of the 20th century, with more and more elements of modern culture filtering into Vietnam and the August Revolution of 1945, that old concepts were gradually eliminated. The concepts of individuality and equality upset Confucian thought and society, which helped women to gain importance in marriage, family and society.

Political, economic and cultural reforms in Vietnam have, therefore, eliminated unequal relations between man and woman to some degree, though, the process has yet to be completed. This is providing women an equal status in society and thus creating the objective conditions for full liberation of women. This is an achievement of historical dimension in a backward country— which by itself proves that the path chosen by Vietnam is superior to that of any other developing country.

In this connection, it is pertinent to emphasise that Ho Chi Minh, like Gandhiji and Jawaharlal Nehru was a revolutionary, an unassuming and modest man who electrified and activated the masses of his country. He in his speeches, and writings untiringly stood up against the ruling ideology of the "natural servitude of women". What he was concerned with, however, was not just ideology alone but at the same time, the concrete struggle against the exploitation of women, "Women in the past, present and the future."

The political leadership of Vietnam considered struggle of equality of women as part and parcel of the theory of modernisation of their country from the very beginning. The reason for this is too obvious. No country can modernise and renovate its socio-economic and political structures without liberating women from the bondage of man dominated society. Women not only constitute nearly 50 per cent of population but in every sense of the term a pivot of the family, future generation and thus of the society as a whole. They are the axle around which the society revolved.

The specifics of the Asian societies today cannot be understood unless the ideological and religious factors are taken into account.

The religious systems of the East—Hinduism, Buddhism, Confucianism, Islam and the teachings of countless different religious sects—are of course, diverse but they do have something in common: not one of these religions, which to this day constitute a major unit linking the entire superstructural sphere has ever experienced a profound reformation like European Christianity has for instance. Not one of them could provide such a powerful spiritual justification for the political and socio-economic activities of society and the individual as European Christianity did at one time and especially Protestantism for modernism. This put the European peasantry and urban population in the foreground of the struggle for a modernism. The religious beliefs of the East, like in the West, too, in the past, do not include just adoration of a diety, but also a "Consecrated" way of life and thinking of both society and the individual. Vietnam has begun a struggle against Confucianism as far as status of women is concerned. This has begun to pay rich dividends in the transformation of its political superstructure. This is the moral of the situation of contemporary Vietnam.

## Reference

1. *Women in Vietnam*, pp. 32-34, cited R.S. Chavan *Vietnam : Trial and Triumph*, New Delhi.

# 20

# ASIA PACIFIC SECURITY AND INDO-VIETNAM RELATIONS

GVC NAIDU

Indo-Vietnam relations have come a long way to emerge as one of the most enduring in the Asia Pacific. The bilateral relationship spans a vast spectrum of shared values, common political understanding, promotion of regional peace and stability, and mutually beneficial strategic goals. It is however, against the backdrop of evolving Pacific Asian security after the end of the Cold War that Indo-Vietnam relations have acquired a larger and important dimension. The current economic crisis in the region and politico-strategic implications of this turmoil has further strengthened the need to coopereate more closely between countries such as India and Vietnam. The following is a brief assessment of Indo-Vietnam relations in the context of unfolding Asia Pacific security. For that, a brief examination of certain broad trends in the realm of security that have become too conspicuous to be ignored is essential.

After the end of the Cold War, it was widely believed that the Asia Pacific security, which had begun to show clear signs of stability, might be seriously disturbed. During the Cold War, notwithstanding the bipolar politics and super power presence, political dust was settling down in Indochina on the one hand and on the other the regional organisation the Association of South-East Asian Nations (ASEAN) was beginning to consolidate and emerge as a major player in the management of regional affairs. After overcoming the initial fears of spillover of the Vietnamese intervention in Cambodia into the rest of South-East Asia, a kind of regional balance of power was established in the region Asia. In North-East Asia, despite growing Soviet military buildup in the Far East as a response to consolidation of trilateral relationship among the U.S., Japan and China obviously aimed at Moscow, there was little chance of any conflict breaking out. Even the Korean Peninsula appeared to be relatively stable as long as North Korea perceived that it could count on political and military support of both Moscow and Beijing.

All these dramatically changed with the end of Cold War. Most importantly, initially with the winding up of Soviet bases in Vietnam, the Americans found it futile to maintain large-scale military presence in the region as the possibly fight a global war. The way the U.S. expressed its readiness to close down the bases in the Philippines in the early 1990s and qualitatively reduce its overall commitment to the region brought about fundamental changes in the regional order. It appeared the end of the Cold War more unnerving than the Cold War itself simply because it threw up a number of uncertainties. Coincidentally, tensions in the South China Sea started flaring up making it a major flashpoint that could seriously threaten peace and regional stability. The second issue that assumed considerable significance was the purported nuclear buildup attempt by North Korea. There were also a number of other issues, especally related to unsettled borders/territorial and maritime issues. Japan too started feeling unease about growing Chinese capabilities (augmented by its swelling economic might). Because of what was considered to be an unpredictable security atmosphere there began a region-wide military modernisation programme.

Parallel to the above a new process began to appear, the so-called multilateral mechanisms both for economic and security purposes. The ASEAN Regional Forum (ARF) was borne out of this quest for a region-wide all-inclusive forum where security related issues could be discussed and eventually resolved. A second track at the academic/research level was also initiated to supplement the ARF official activities and to provide valuable intellectual inputs to the ARF under the aegis Council for Security Cooperation in Asia Pacific (CSCAP). Despite some criticism with regard to its slow progress and lack of bold measures, the ARF since its inception in 1994 has made remarkable progress either in terms of promoting confidence among the member states, or in bringing in China (which was initially reluctant) into this process (whose participation was critical to any arrangement to succeed). As a corollary to the ARF's decision, many countries have started bringing out their Defence

White Papers and are aso participating actively in the UN Arms Register on arms transfers. The ARF's progress should be viewed against the backdrop of extremely complex Asian situation during and after the end of the Cold War. The ARF has already brought about some measure of predictability and transparency as far as regional security is concerned.

All this began to change dramatically once again with the onset of the economic crisis which began in July 1997, firstly as mere turbulence in the currency markets but soon became an inferno spreading to most of the East Asian region.

The security ramifications of the economic crisis appear to be more far-reaching than earlier anticipated. These need to be factored into regional security of the Asia Pacific as well as India's relations especially with South-East Asia where Vietnam is a member of ASEAN and India is a Dialogue Partner of ASEAN and a member of the ARF.

At the regional level, as a consequence of the economic crisis certain political trends have become discernible. Perhaps, the most noteworthy, are the unprecedented changes that began to occur all across the region resulting in regime changes either through democratic means or through public pressure. Japan, South Korea, Thailand, the Philippines, and Indonesia are some examples. The second important development has been the new found clamor of openness, economic transparency and political pluralism. While this is a welcome sign, the abrupt transition from authoritarian and semi-authoritarian rule to genuine democracy can have destabilizing impact on regional security especially if it was not smooth. This is particularly so in the case of ASEAN countries which have complex, delicate, diverse and sensitive ethnic composition as it has been amply illustrated by the Indonesian case where any chance of recovery has become all the more painful and difficult because of socio-political turmoil. The third significant outcome appears to be total helplessness of either the established and newly created multilateral mechanisms, such as ASEAN, the Asia Pacific Economic Cooperation (APEC) and the ARF. As a result, what one sees is the revival of Cold War-created 'alliance system' (mostly led by the United States). A process of re-strengthening of American bilateral alliance arrangements seems to be happening. What was thought to be a gradual phasing out of the alliance politics to be replaced by new multilateral frameworks is being reversed placing a big question mark on the future of regional security order, which had begun to evolve along multilateral lines, leading some to wonder the reliability and viability of continued Cold War kind of arrangements. Because of these reasons, the Asian balance of power appears to undergo radical changes, which meant a realignment of forces. The triangular relationship between the U.S., Japan and China becomes the pivotal aspect in the Asia Pacific, which not necessarily is comfortable for a large number of small states. And finally, the impact of the financial crisis on overall defense preparedness, especially of those medium and small states, has come under severe strain. In most cases, after having overcome the biggest problem of internal security threat, these countries had begun to concentrate on beefing up their external defence requirements. Particularly noteworthy has been the modernization of navies and airforces. It was generally perceived that, despite considerable limitations on the part of these nations to individually deter a major external threat, collectively they could be more effective. This was especially true in South-East Asia where several countries have been embroiled in contest for the disputed islands in the South China Sea along with China.

This is roughly the politico-strategic backdrop that has begun to unfold as a consequence of the economic crisis. Two possible scenarios are likely to emerge: first, the crisis persists and China emerges as the most predominant power which would create considerable consternation both in Japan and South-East Asia. And second, the crisis would peter out soon and the region would bounce back to pre-1997 arrangement leading to strengthening of multilateral efforts and the regional balance is not fundamentally disturbed. Obviously, the second scenario is the most preferred option.

Against this background that the impact of Asian economic crisis on India and its relations with East Asia, including Vietnam, need to be analysed. It is two fold: economic and political/strategic. From an economic point of view, one shoud keep in mind the economic liberalization program India began in 1991 and as a corollary to that the so-called Look East policy. The Indian economy, which faces one of its worst times in the early nineties, was badly in need of a thorough reform and the opening up of it to global competition and greater alignment with the rest of the world was indispensable. Look East policy was borne out of this crisis, the Indian economy faced.

It was perceived that the East Asian economic models, which witnessed unprecedented growth in history, were tried to be emulated by emphasizing export promotion and attracting foreign investments in a big way. By then several of these countries (especially Singapore, South Korea, Taiwan, Hong Kong, Malaysia, etc.,) had become capital surplus with large sums of investible capital and rapid growth of their economies also enabled them to become big trading nations. Politically, India after the end of the Cold War was at a crossroads, even as its earlier Non-Aligned policy had become redundant and felt isolated. Strategically, the South-East Asian region began to emerge as an area of vital interests. Thus, a combination of a number of issues brought about a fundamental review of India's foreign policy leading to greater attention to economic component of foreign policy and target the Asia Pacific for greater economic interaction—both to increase bilateral trade and to attract investments. This policy of India by mid 1990s, started paying enormous dividends: India's trade saw the fastest growth with South-East Asia compared with any other region, steady investments started flowing, and more importantly, India became a Dialogue Partner of ASEAN and a member of the newly created ARF. Simultaneously India also forged defence-related bilateral cooperative arrangements with a number of South-East Asian nations.

This is the Asia Pacific security context in which Indo-Vietnam relations need to be examined afresh. Because of an enlightened leadership that led the Indian Independence movement, the need to support anti-colonial and anti-imperialist struggles in the former colonies was duly recognised in the immediate aftermath of India's foreign policy formulation. India to its credit has the distinction of convening the Asian Relations Conference in April 1947, even before attaining complete independence. India also convened a Special Conference on Indonesia in support of Sukarno-led national liberation stuggle against the Dutch. India's support to Vietnam's liberation struggle was in tune with this policy of expressing India's solidarity with other Asian nations.

As far as Vietnam is concerned, a major milestone was India becoming the Chairman of the International Commission for Control and Supervision of the Geneva Accords signed in August 1954, with the aim of establishing peace in Indochina. It was due recognition to India's policy of positive neutrality and non-aligned policy. It could not be implemented because the United States refused to comply. Since then a series of bilateral high level visits took place between India and Vietnam leading to the establishment of close political relationship: the most important of these were Jawaharlal Nehru's visit to Hanoi in October 1954 and President Ho Chi Minh's visit to India in February 1958.

However, the 1962, Sino-Indian war created some misunderstanding between India and Vietnam because of latter's decision to support China. As Vietnam itself was caught in one of the bloodiest wars with the United States, support extended by China and the former Soviet Union was critical to Vietnamese war effort and hence Vietnam had no option but to support China's stance. India was obviously disappointed.

Till about mid 1970s, India's relations with Vietnam were rather subdued. The victories by Vietnam and other Indochina countries in the mid-seventies soon to be followed by serious differences between Vietnam and China (contributed in part by the Sino-Soviet differences) brought about a qualitative change in the bilateral relationship between Hanoi and New Delhi. The Chinese attempt to teach Vietnam a lesson in February 1979, because of Vietnamese military intervention in Cambodia in late 1978, which resulted in the removal of genocidal regime of Pol Pot, brought in the strategic dimension to India's policy toward Vietnam. India was the only non-communist nation that extended recognition to the Vietnam-supported Heng Samrin regime in Phom Penh. India did that at the cost of its relations with the regional organisation ASEAN which was prepared to extend the dialogue partnership to India and start a new phase in India-ASEAN relationship in mid 1980. It took more than a decade for India to repair its relations with ASEAN. That was the beginning of Indo-Vietnam security relationship.

With the end of the Cold War, like most other countries, Vietnam too started liberalising its economy in a big way. Because of changed political conditions, and once Hanoi decided to withdraw its troops from Cambodia, ASEAN found it more useful to bring Hanoi into fold for a variety of reasons. These developments also paved way for India to qualitatively improve its relations not only with Vietnam, but also with rest of South-East Asia too. Although bilateral economic interaction, both trade and investments, has not been spectacular it has been on the upswing. More important perhaps are the common security concerns that are faced by Vietnam and India that have laid solid foundation for bilateral relationship.

As the end of the Cold War has brought forth categorically, in order to sustain strong bonds of friendship between India and Vietnam, it has to be multi-faceted—political, economic and strategic. There are many number of areas in which India and Vietnam could collaborate provided there is sincere political effort by both sides.

# 21

# INDO-VIETNAM TRADE RELATIONS

R.L. VARSHNEY AND R.K. WADHWA

## Significant Developments in Vietnam

After reunification of Vietnam in 1975, Vietnam's leaders have been searching for appropriate strategies to transform its traditional economy. By December 1986, after trial and error efforts to apply a Soviet-type socialist strategy were declared a failure by the now-famous Sixth Party Congress, Vietnam shifted direction and intensified reform of its political economy. The 'demonstration effect' of rapid East Asian growth led Vietnam to adopt the renovation process doi moi. It accepted the market mechanism to allocate resources. Reforms included deregulation of prices, reducing subsidies to state enterprises, ending the collective agricultural system, enacting new commercial ownership laws to encourage private enterprise, enacting new foreign ivestment laws and creating policies directed towards the stabilisation and convertibility of the Vietnamese currency.

Adoption of doi moi by Vietnam clearly marked her long journey towards internationalisation and economic transformation.

As a member of the Council for Mutual Economic Assistance (CMEA), it received virtually no external financial assistance to initiate market reforms. Yet, after a decade of doi moi, Vietnam has achieved successes in stabilisation and structural change, notably, inflation and fiscal deficit control and the liberalisation of agriculture, foreign investment and trade. As a result, inflation fell from 775 per cent in 1986 to 7 per cent in 1993.

Since 1987, foreign direct investment and foreign trade have been key forces of growth and change in Vietnam. By mid 1996, contracted foreign direct investment (FDI) amounted to US $ 20 billion for 1,460 projects. Not only that, there has been a shift from the traditional sector of agriculture to industry, services and infrastructure. The share of total foreign investment in agriculture declined from 22 per cent in 1988-90 to 2 per cent in mid 1996, and its share in industry has grown from 13 per cent to 48 per cent during the same period. There has been a high growth of foreign investment in infrastructure since 1994.

Though the actual investment inflow declined to US $ 1.4 billion in 1998 from US $ 2.4 billion in 1997, indications are that the investment inflow will increase in the coming few years because of the continued efforts of the Government to implement investor-friendly reforms. The decline in the investment inflow during 1998, was due to the bureaucratic delay and the regional crisis. Some of the reforms include considering permitting large foreign companies to set up investment funds and joint-stock companies that will be allowed to issue shares. Besides, the phasing out of dual pricing system under which foreigners pay more than Vietnamese for air and train travel, electricity and phone services, is under active consideration of the Government.

As regards countries of origin for FDI in Vietnam and South Korea ranks first with a share of 15.7 per cent of the new approvals during 1997, followed by Japan 14.3 per cent, and Singapore 11.7 per cent. The potential exists for countries like India to invest in various areas open for foreign investment in Vietnam.

In July 1995, it became the seventh member of the Association of South East Asian Nations (ASEAN). Vietnam has also been admitted as a member of the ASEAN Free Trade Area (AFTA) and is expected to join the World Trade Organisation (WTO) soon.

Although substantial progress has been made towards trade reforms, Vietnam's trade regime is still restricted. The average tariff on imports is high and provides a strong incentive for smuggling which is extensive. There is a high rate of effective protection. As a result, a number of inefficient import substituting industries have been established. However, some change is expected as Vietnam reduced trade barriers on goods coming from other ASEAN countries.

### Vietnam's Foreign Trade

Vietnam continues to suffer from balance of trade deficit for the past few years. The trade deficit rose substantially from US $ 60 million in 1992, to a peak of US $ 3.2 billion in 1996, but declined by 25 per cent in 1997, over the previous year. The decline in the trade deficit is attributed to the recent devaluation of dong. Further restrictions on imports under consideration include strict limits on imports of new cars and suspension of imports of used cars; a ban on import of cement and clinker for the year 1999, after reaching an estimated 800,000 tonnes in 1998; and no change in the import quota for CKD motorbikes during 1999. Table 1 shows the trend in Foreign Trade of Vietnam.

**Table 1**

**Foreign Trade of Vietnam**

*(Us $ Million)*

| *Year* | *Exports* | *Imports* | *Balance of Trade* |
|---|---|---|---|
| 1992 | 2475 | 2535 | -60 |
| 1993 | 2985 | 4162 | -1177 |
| 1994 | 4054 | 5245 | -1191 |
| 1995 | 5198 | 7543 | -2345 |
| 1996* | 7337 | 10481 | -3144 |
| 1997* | 8850 | 11200 | -2350 |

*EIU and Official Estimates.

*Source:* IMF: Vietnam : Selected Issues and Statistical Annex.

A series of adjustments in the exchange rate, relaxation of quantitative controls on imports and decentralisation of foreign trade, led to a surge in exports—the dollar value of exports grew at an average rate of 29 per cent during 1991-96. Vietnam has emerged as a major rice and coffee exporter. In addition, its rising oil exports and growing access to new markets for its textiles and garments, rubber and sea food, have helped it in its export effort. Vietnam supplies 10 per cent of the footwear imported into the European Union. Exports now represent 30 per cent of GDP.

Since 1992, export growth has been outpaced by an even stronger largely investment related import surge. However, the large $ 3.2 billion trade deficit in 1996, led to a restraint on imports. Import restrictions are being tightened to contain trade deficit. Some of the import restrictions include strict limits on import of new cars, and ban on imports of cement and clinker during 1999. Smuggling, however, remains rampant because import licensing favours state owned companies. Tables 2 show Vietnamese exports and imports.

**Table 2**

**Exports**

*(US$ Million FOB)*

| Item | 1992 | 1993 | 1994 | 1995 | 1996 |
|---|---|---|---|---|---|
| Textiles & Garments | 190 | 239 | 476 | 431 | 1,150 |
| Petroleum | 756 | 844 | 866 | 1,024 | 1,346 |
| Rice | 300 | 363 | 425 | 496 | 855 |
| Marine Products | 302 | 427 | 551 | 431 | 651 |
| Coffee | 86 | 110 | 328 | 565 | 337 |
| Rubber | 54 | 74 | 133 | 159 | 163 |
| Coal | 47 | 70 | 75 | 90 | 115 |
| Cashew nuts | 41 | 44 | 59 | 130 | n.a. |
| Total Including Others | 2,475 | 2,985 | 4,054 | 5,198 | 7,337 |

*Sources:* IMF; Vietnam: Selected Issues and Statistical Annex.

**Table 3**

**Imports**

*(US $ Million - CIF)*

| Item | 1992 | 1993 | 1994 | 1995 | 1996 |
|---|---|---|---|---|---|
| Machinery & Spare Parts | 547 | 922 | 1,721 | 2,097 | 3,800 |
| Petroleum Products | 683 | 614 | 696 | 724 | 1,079 |
| Fertilisers | 356 | 189 | 247 | 554 | 628 |
| Steel | 116 | 210 | 204 | 389 | 529 |
| Wheat | 59 | 51 | 52 | 60 | n.a. |
| Textile Yarn | n.a. | n.a. | n.a. | 114 | 158 |
| Monosodium Glutamate | 53 | 70 | 44 | 32 | n.a. |
| Sugar | 4 | 14 | 39 | 61 | n.a. |
| Total Including Others | 2,817 | 3,924 | 5,827 | 8,381 | 11,644 |

*Sources:* IMF; Vietnam: Selected Issues and Statistical Annex.

Among exports, primary products constituted 64 per cent in 1993, showing a reduction from 82 per cent in 1988. The percentage of manufactured goods improved from 18 per cent in 1988 to 35 per cent in 1993. As regards imports, the percentage of intermediate inputs, viz., textile materials, petroleum and products, organic chemicals, medicine and pharmaceutical products, fertilizers, plastic materials and iron and steel declined from 74 per cent in 1988 to 50 per cent in 1993. The import of capital goods increased their importance from 20 per cent in 1988 to 44 per cent in 1993.

Items of import interest to Vietnam include petroleum, good quality used equipment (not more than 10 years old), steel products, road building equipment, scaffolding, machinery for construction of high-rise buildings, chemicals fertilisers, medicines, raw cotton, bath soap, cosmetics, construction equipment and building materials, medical products and pharmaceuticals, dental equipment, and processed foodstuffs.

Potential items in the export basket of Vietnam include agricultural products, handicraft products, seafood, rubber, wood flooring, coffee, coal, tea and rice.

**India and Vietnam**

India has age old ties with Vietnam, both cultural and commercial. India had trade relations with Vietnam and many Indians especially from South India had permanently settled in Ho Chi Minh City (earlier known as Saigon). Many of them had flourishing money lending business. The existence of four big South Indian temples in Saigon, is a testimony for long Indo-Vietnamese relationship.

After the reunification of Vietnam, India also established cordial relations with Vietnam. Vietnam sought India's help in its development. In 1985, at the request of the Government of Vietnam, the Government of India requested the Indian Institute of Foreign Trade to provide training in the field of export management to Vietnamese officials and businessmen and the Institute organised 2 two-week programmes, one in Hanoi and the other in Ho Chi Minh City.

India helped Vietnam in the development of its railways. CIMMCO, a Birla enterprise, had at that time an extensive network of its offices.

The presence of Indian comapanies in the industrial development of Vietnam reflects the cordial and continued relationship between the two countries. M/s Nagarjuna International is building up a sugar factory and the Gadgil Western Corporation is setting up a solid waste treatment plant in Ho Chi Minh City. It is estimated that Indian projects worth more than US $300 million are under negotiation and at various stages of operation.

Tremendous scope, however, exists in Vietnam for Indian investment. Some of the areas which hold promising returns for Indian investors, include:

- Agro processing industries
- Light and heavy electrical equipment/substation equipment/ transmission lines
- Organic/Inorganic/agro chemicals
- Auto components/accessories
- Textile, cement, printing, medical, sugar, food-processing, leather machinery
- Manufacture of paharmaceutical fomulations/bulk drugs, surgical equipment
- Gas/oil based down-stream products
- Construction Projects
- Railway (civil, mechanical & telecommunications)
- IT products
- White goods
- Consumer electronics

Table 4 gives an idea of India's exports and imports to Vietnam.

**Table 4**

**India's Trade with Vietnam**

(Rs. Crore)

| *Year* | *Exports* | *Imports* |
|---|---|---|
| 1993-94 | 87.87 | 137.50 |
| 1994-95 | 133.90 | 138.37 |
| 1995-96 | 416.02 | 51.82 |
| 1996-97 | 419.16 | 6.02 |
| 1997-98 | 450.94 | 27.32 |

*Source:* Monthly Foreign Trade Statistics of India, DGCI&S, Calcutta.

As is evident from the above table, India's exports to Vietnam have shown an increase upto 1995-96, but have now stabilised at

Rs 400 crores. Imports, on the other hand, show an erratic trend, but have been declining in the recent years. India had a trade deficit in 1993-94, but thereafter, India has been having an export surplus. In spite of the large trade potential available in Vietnam, India's trade with Vietnam is estimated to constitute less than one per cent of Vietnam's overall foreign trade. Out of the 324 products that Vietnam imports from different countries approximately 180 products could be supplied by India against the present supply of approximately 20 commodities/product group constituting nearly 10 per cent of the entire product range imported by Vietnam.

The major items of export have been pharmaceuticals, machinery, instruments, rubber manufactured products, cotton yarn, fabrics and made up, chemicals, primary and semi-finished iron and steel, metals, machine tools, plastic linoleum products etc.

The major items of import were cahewnuts and spices. In 1996-97, there was no import of cashewnuts. Other items, which have been imported from Vietnam, include raw silk, natural rubber, and non-ferrous metals.

**Prospects of Indo-Vietnamese Trade**

At present, India has a trade surplus in her trade with Vietnam. To sustain lasting trade relations between any two countries, it is imperative to have a more or less balanced trade. An attempt is made now to discuss the prospects of Indo-Vietnamese trade from this angle.

**Potential Imports from Vietnam**

To find out the potential items that could be imported from Vietnam, we have to look at the basket of exports from Vietnam. Table 2 shows top exports from Vietnam.

A perusal of the table shows that except crude oil, cashewnuts and rubber all other items are exported by India also. India needs crude oil and cashewnuts. If India could import these items from Vietnam, Vietnam's trade deficit with India can be substantially reduced. There is at present a surplus of rubber in India due to recessionary conditions in the automobile sector. However, according to K.J. Mathew, Chairman, Rubber Board, there will be a shortage of rubber and India might have to import 3,000 tonnes of rubber by 2010. Hence India can also import rubber from Vietnam.

## Items that could be Exported by India to Vietnam

A study of the various items imported by Vietnam would enable us to identify items that could be exported by India to Vietnam. Table 5 gives a detailed breakdown of Vietnam imports.

### Table 5

### Vietnam's Imports by Commodities

*(US Millions)*

| *Commodity* | *1988* | *1993* |
|---|---|---|
| Food and tobacco, of which: | 68 | 268 |
| Tobacco and manufacturers | 1 | 88 |
| Intermediate inputs, of which: | 1,257 | 2,312 |
| Textiles materials | 65 | 416 |
| Petroleum and products | 556 | 716 |
| Organic chemicals | 15 | 110 |
| Medicinal, pharm. products | 27 | 118 |
| Fertilizers, manufacturers | 365 | 130 |
| Plastic material, etc. | 11 | 118 |
| Iron and steel | 118 | 146 |
| Capital goods, of which: | 346 | 2,044 |
| Power generating equipment: | 67 | 111 |
| Industrial Machines | 118 | 473 |
| Telecom, sound equipment | 34 | 280 |
| Electronic machinery n.e.s. | 26 | 226 |
| Road Vehicle, of which: | 57 | 615 |
| Pass, motor vehicles, excel buses | 2 | 231 |
| Road motor vehicles n.e.s. | 4 | 42 |
| Motor vehicle parts n.e.s. | 5 | 14 |
| Cycles, motorized or not | 16 | 271 |
| Others | 20 | 20 |
| Total | 1,691 | 4,644 |

*Sources:* UN Trade Data Base; Vietnam Ministry of Trade (for trade with Russia), reproduced in ASEAN Economic Bulletin, November 1996.

A perusal of the above table reveals that major items of Vietnam's imports are petroleum products, textile materials, industrial machines and road vehicles. India is definitely in a position to export textile materials, many types of industrial machinery and commercial vehicles. The vehicles will have to be modified as the steering wheel will have to be put on the left-hand side as Vietnam has 'Drive on the right' rule. Indian commercial vehicles are popular in many developing countries as they can be driven on comparatively bad roads and can withstand overloading. India is already exporting various types of machines and instruments as also machine tools.

**Joint Ventures and Production Cooperation**

As pointed out earlier, over the last 12 years or so, Vietnam has rapidly expanded its economic, commercial and political relationships increasingly with its Asian neighbours and with the world. Foreign investment is now welcome and India could explore the possibilities of establishing joint ventures in Vietnam. India already had on March 31, 1998, 1392 active joint ventures and wholly owned subsidiaries, out of which 541 were in production. The field, in which Indian entrepreneurs have set up companies abroad and have acquired a certain degree of capabilities to compete in the international technology market are light engineering, textiles and allied products, chemicals and pharmaceuticals, food products (including soft drinks), leather and rubber products, iron and steel, commercial vehicles, oilseed crushing and palm oil refining, glass and glass products, pulp and paper, cement products, etc.

Trade associations and businessmen of the two countries, could identify projects which could be taken up for joint ventures. To begin with joint ventures could be established in the field of consumer goods industries. Cooperation could later be extended from production to marketing and export as well. In fact, in many industries, production could be increased to cater to export markets.

To develop tourism in Vietnam, there is need to establish hotels, India could help Vietnam in building many hotels as India has a lot of expertise in this area.

Thus, there are many areas which provide ample opportunities for fruitful cooperation between India and Vietnam.

# 22

# INDO-VIETNAMESE ECONOMIC CO-OPERATION

SHRI PRAKASH

It is interesting to observe that the end of the Cold War and the political disintegration of the former Soviet Union has not changed the basic framework of Indian Foreign Policy, especially, its relations with the developing countries. The wellspring of Panchsheel and Non-Alignment has been the basis of India's external relations, ever since Jawahar Lal Nehru led the newly independent Third World countries— in formulating these doctrines for the conduct of international relations in the post-colonial epoch. Given a stable framework of its foreign policy, it has been easy for India to adjust to a world in which the politics of building rival military alliances, has been replaced by the politics of building and deepening economic and strategic interdependence of promoting mutual development and preserving regional as well as global peace.

On January 2, 1976, both North and South Vietnam were reunited and on 2 July, 1976, the Socialist Republic of Vietnam came into being. India was among the first few countries to recognise the new Government in Hanoi immediately. Since then it has continued to broaden its already ongoing cooperation first started with North Vietnam.

A Vietnamese Economic Delegation led by Vice Minister of Foreign Trade Nguyen Chanh visited India from 26 August-9th September, 1977. The Government of India agreed to cooperate with Vietnam to set up a Rice Research Institute in the Mekong Delta and a Buffalo Breeding Centre near the Ho Chi Minh City on an aid basis at a cost of Rs. 2 crores. In another agreement, signed on 9th, September 1977, the Government of India also agreed to an interest free loan of one lakh tonnes of wheat to Vietnam. The two Institutes were subsequently started towards the end of 1979.

In order to give systematic shape to the economic cooperation between Vietnam and India a high powered Inter-Ministerial Economic Delegation led by Samarendra Kundu, Minister of State for External Affairs, visited Vietnam from 1-7 February 1978. During their visit, they agreed with the Government of Vietnam to give the highest priority to the rehabilitation of their transport network, particularly the railways and the development of agriculture and livestock, both in which India agreed to cooperate. To reciprocate this visit, the Prime Minister of Vietnam, Pham Van Dong paid a 7 day visit to India in late Feb. 1978. During his visit India and Vietnam signed four agreements on economic cooperation. Vietnam was provided a credit of Rs. 100 million to buy railway equipment, livestock and other goods from India at 5% rate of interest. In the field of agriculture, science and technology exchanges were agreed to as well as training programmes for Vietnamese scientists. Both countries agreed to accord 'Most Favoured Nation' treatment to each other and pay for trade in freely convertible currency.

As an indication of a step up in the level of trade relations, a trade protocol was signed between India and Vietnam envisaging a trade turnover of $ 10 million by the end of 1979. It was agreed in the protocol that the items of export from India would be cotton yarn, textile, machinery spare parts, cycle inner tube valves, chemicals for industrial purposes and insecticides. The items identified for import from Vietnam include timber and edible oils. At this time because of its conflict with China, the latter withdrew many times midway from joint projects. India agreed to pick up all these 21 projects.

The momentum of Indian economic aid to Vietnam was kept up in 1979. Between 1978-80, India provided credits of Rs. 40 crore to Vietnam. In 1980-81, it provided another credit of Rs. 40 crores to finance purchase of railway rolling stock, cotton yarn and buffaloes. Later, during the same year an additional loan of Rs. 100 million was given by the Government of India to Vietnam to import Indian textile fabrics for garments. Subsequently, at the end of his four day visit to Vietnam in Feb. 1982, India's External Affairs Minister P.V. Narasimha Rao announced India's decision to give a loan of Rs. 100 million to Vietnam to help reschedule recovery of earlier debts. In December 1982, Nguyen Co Thach, Foreign Minster of Vietnam visited India and signed an agreement to set up a 'Joint Economic, Scientific and Technical Commission'. Vietnam was the first nation in the South-East Asian region with which India established a 'Joint Commission', in order to enhance cooperation in the fields of transport and communications, textile industry and others, geology, mineral exploration and exploration, agriculture, including animal breeding and industrial crops inclusive of processing, science and technology, commerce and trade and other fields of mutual interest. This development gave a planned character to the growth of Indo-Vietnamese Cooperation and provided a model exchanges between countries of the South.

Rajiv Gandhi pursued the policy of friendship with Vietnam and reaffirmed that New Delhi would continue to trade with Hanoi on the basis of 'Most Favoured Nation status'. During his tenure as Prime Minister in July 1985, India agreed to export 50,000 tonnes of wheat in the form of a commodity loan, and start the construction of a jute mill name after Indira Gandhi, which started functioning on 30th January, 1988. Rajiv Gandhi visited Vietnam in November 1985, signed for a credit of Rs. 15 crore and extended a commodity loan of one lakh tonnes of wheat for 1986 and 1987, as Vietnam's food crops were seriously damaged by floods and cyclones around this time. ONGC agreed to prospect for oil off-shore in South Vietnam. During the 1980s, Indian aid to Vietnam totalled US Dollar 8.75 million between 1978-1985. This was less than the 1 billion dollar being given by the Soviet Union, but it still put India among Vietnam's major non Communist suppliers of economic assistance.

On August 15, 1988, India and Vietnam signed an agreement on the peaceful use of atomic energy. This included two elements training in India for Vietnamese scientists and help to bring the Da Lat nuclear research reactor back into operation. Interestingly, the Da Lat nuclear research reactor was built by the US in 1963 and in March 1975, before withdrawing from South Vietnam, the US dismantled its main parts, making it completely inoperative. From March 1982, with Soviet assistance restoration and expansion of this nuclear reactor had begun. It will help to train reactor personnel for Vietnam's future nuclear power generation programme analysing mineral or biological samples and producing necessary isotopes for medical and agricultural research institutions.

Non Congress governments in the 1990s, have continued the tradition of building Indo-Vietnamese cooperation. In April 1990, I.K. Gujral then India's External Affairs Minister visited Hanoi. During this visit the fourth meeting of the Indo-Vietnam Joint Economic, Scientific and Technical Commission was held and New Delhi extended a credit of Rs. 100. million to Vietnam for import of capital and manufactured goods.

Following I.K. Gujral's visit, on Sept. 12, 1990, at Hanoi, Arun Nehru, the then Indian Commerce Minister signed a three year trade treaty with Vietnam in order to achieve a two way trade target of 100 million US Dollars annually, thus giving a major thrust to their economic relations. In the protocol, it was agreed that payments would be made through buyback arrangements in the form of barter trade. India which had an adverse balance of trade with Vietnam expressed keen interest in the export of transport equipment, particularly three wheelers and heavy vehicles, and power generation equipment in mining. Vietnam could depend on India for food, processing textile, leather machinery, chemicals and pharmaceuticals. This trade agreement would remain valid upto December 1993.

The present government has continued the policies of cooperation between India and Vietnam. The Prime Minister of Vietnam Vo Van Kiet made an official visit to India from 7-9 March 1997. He held extensive discussions with the Indian leadership reiterating the continued support of Vietnam on regional and global issues. Another meeting of the Joint Working Group was held in New Delhi, on 16 and 17 January 1997, to review progress on various bilateral cooperation programmes. A work plan for agricultural cooperation was signed bilateral trade increased to Rs. 46,387 lakhs in 1995-96, from Rs. 32,227 lakhs in the previous year. Another credit of Rs. 90 crores on soft terms was extended to Vietnam this year for undertaking capital goods imports from India.[1] Potential in developing small-scale industries was to be explored in Vietnam.

In August 1997, the 8th session of the India-Vietnam Joint Commission was held at Hanoi, with the Indian delegation being led by Saleem Iqbal Shervani, Minister of State for External Affairs accompanied by a small business delegation. Bilateral trade was worth Rs. 418 crores in 1996-97, as compared to Rs. 468 crores in

1995-96. The Joint Commission decided on expansion of cooperation in agriculture, science and technology and small and medium industries. Discussions were also held for promoting cooperation in Civil Aviation and the establishment of a stock exchange in Vietnam. Cooperation in Defence matters also progressed further when Lt. General Soam Chuang, the Director General of the Military Strategic Institute of Vietnam visited India between 7-17 May, 1997. Subsequently, Major General Vu Chunh, Director of Military, Intelligence of Vietnam visited India from 2-9 November, 1997.

It is interesting to note that the 'opening up' of the Vietnamese economy to Foreign Direct Investments and the increase in its volume of trade have also helped to increase the value of trade between India and Vietnam.

**Table 1**

**Indo-Vietnamese Trade** (In Rs. Crore)

| Year | Imports from Vietnam | Exports to Vietnam | Total | %+Over previous Year |
|---|---|---|---|---|
| 1993-94 | 137.50 | 87.87 | 225.37 | |
| 1994-95 | 138.37 | 183.9 | 322.27 | +43% |
| 1995-96 | 51.82 | 416.02 | 467.84 | +45% |
| 1996-97 | 6.02 | 419.16 | 425.18 | +11% |
| 1997-98 | 27.32 | 450.94 | 478.26 | +13% |

At the same time it should be noted that even though India's share of Vietnam's trade which has increased rapidly is less than one per cent. According to UN data the value of Vietnam's aggregate exports was 392.4 million US Dollars in 1993. India's share at 8.1 million USD was just 0.2%. In the same year Vietnam's exports were valued at 298.5 million USD of which only 0.6% were being sent to India. By contrast 58.5 per cent of Vietnam's imports and 67.5 per cent of its exports in 1993, were going to other Asian countries excluding those which were formerly part of Soviet Union. The share of North America too was less than one per cent in the overall value of Vietnam's trade. Clearly, there is much room for trying to increase India's share of Vietnam's trade.

A list of the commodities exported by India to Vietnam and those imported by India as well as its comparison with the commodity composition of Vietnam's aggregate trade will reveal the present nature of their bilateral trade and its potential in the future.

**Table 2**

**Value and List of India's Exports to Vietnam (April 94-March 95)**

(Value in Rs. Lakhs)

| *Name of Commodity* | *Total* | *%Share* |
|---|---|---|
| 1. Aggregate | 18346 | 100% |
| 2. Tobacco unmanufactured | 361.50 | 2% |
| 3. Tobacco manufactured | 156.64 | 0.9% |
| 4. Oil Meals | 659.90 | 3.6% |
| 5. Castor Oil | 141.40 | 0.8% |
| 6. Drugs, Pharmaceuticals and Fine Chemicals | 6870.23 | 37.5% |
| 7. Inorganic/Organic Agro Chemicals | 532.10 | 3% |
| 8. Rubber manufactured products | 2829.59 | 15.4% |
| 9. Plastic and Linoleum Products | 626.42 | 3.41% |
| 10. Machinery and Instruments | 2846.24 | 15.5% |
| 11. Transport equipments | 753.8 | 4.2% |
| 12. Manmade staple fibre | 275.20 | 1.5% |
| 13. Cotton Yarn Fabrics | 612.17 | 3.4% |
| | | (91.2%) |

*Source : Foreign Trade Statistics of India, Commodities and Countries,* March 1995, Pages 506/507.

**Table 3**

**India's Imports from Vietnam**

| *Name of Commodity* | *Aggregate Value in Rs. Lakh* | *% of Total* |
|---|---|---|
| 1. Total imports | 13879.17 | 100% |
| 2. Cashewnuts | 12443.12 | 90% |
| 3. Spices | 28.84 | 0.2% |
| 4. Raw Silk | 622.21 | 4.5% |
| 5. Coal, coke and Briquettes | 193.32 | 1.4% |
| 6. Non Ferrous metals | 111.30 | 0.8% |

*Source : Foreign Trade Statistics of India, Commodities and Countries,* March 1995, p. 138.

A comparison of the commodity composition of India's trade with Vietnam enables us to understand the areas in which the two countries are competitors and those in which they have complementary interest. Tables IV and V tells us about the composition of Vietnam's aggregate exports and imports.

**Table 4**

**Vietnam's Aggregate Exports**

(US Dollar Million FOB)

| *Commodity* | *1992* | *1993* | *1994* | *1995* | *1996* | *1996 as % of Total* |
|---|---|---|---|---|---|---|
| 1. Textiles and Garments | 221 | 336 | 550 | 800 | 1600 | 22% |
| 2. Petroleum | 756 | 844 | 866 | 1024 | 1346 | 18.3% |
| 3. Rice | 86 | 363 | 425 | 549 | 855 | 12% |
| 4. Marine Products | 302 | 427 | 551 | 620 | 651 | 8.9% |
| 5. Coffee | 54 | 74 | 95 | 495 | 337 | 4.6% |
| 6. Rubber | 54 | 74 | 133 | 181 | 163 | 2.2% |
| 7. Coal | 47 | 70 | 71 | 85 | 115 | 1.6% |
| 8. Cashewnuts | 41 | 44 | 59 | 130 | n/a | |
| Total Including Others | 2475 | 2985 | 4054 | 5198 | 7330 | |

*Source : World Bank, Vietnam : Economic Report on Industrialisation and Industrial Policy.*

There are several commodities which Vietnam and India are exporting in common including textiles and garments, rice, marine products, coffee, coal and cashewnuts. The two countries can have joint activities in relation to these commodities— organising trade-fairs, exchanging information about demand, price and quality, coordinating minimum prices— to create a regime of fair competition and fair profits. One can also compare the commodities being imported by India to Vietnam to find out the areas in which there is more potential for India to increase its exports to Vietnam.

**Table 5**

**Aggregate Imports into Vietnam** (in US Dollar Million CIF)

| *Name of Commodity* | *1992* | *1993* | *1994* | *1995* | *1996* | *As % of 1995* |
|---|---|---|---|---|---|---|
| 1. Machinery and Spare parts | 100 | 922 | 1815 | 2761 | n/a | 37% |
| 2. Petroleum Products | 615 | 614 | 696 | 856 | 1079 | 11.3% |
| 3. Fertilizers | 320 | 189 | 247 | 339 | 628 | 8.3% |
| 4. Steel | 104 | 233 | 211 | n/a | 529 | 7% |
| 5. Wheat | 59 | 51 | 52 | 60 | n/a | 0.8% |
| 6. Cotton Textiles | 23 | 54 | 55 | 96 | n/a | 1.3% |
| 7. Monosodium Glutamate | 53 | 70 | 44 | 32 | n/a | 0.43% |
| 8. Sugar | 4 | 14 | 39 | 61 | n/a | 0.8% |

*Source* : Same as for table-4

Amongst the items being imported by Vietnam (fertilizers, salt and sugar) are being exported by India but not to Vietnam. In addition the demand for cotton textiles and machinery will increase with growth in Vietnam. From the point of view of Indian entrepreneurs, Vietnam can provide a friendly point of entry to the ASEAN region and the wider Asia-Pacific beyond. Several Indian industrial houses like the Birlas, Mafatlal and Modi groups have begun operations in Vietnam. Vietnam being a full fledged member of the Asia Pacific Economic Council (APEC) and the ASEAN can support and help to mobilize support for India's full membership or partnership in both these organisations.

Considering that India's share in Vietnam's total trade value and vice-versa is less than one per cent several steps are needed to try and raise the economic relationship between the two countries. Increase in the numbers of Trade Fairs or extent of participation and greater frequency of visits by delegations of officials, business persons, political leaders and exchange of research scholars will help to increase the personal interaction and mutual knowledge about the two countries in India and Vietnam. Similarly, expanding the scope for Media exchange through sales of audio-visual programmes and syndication agreements targeted at businessman, potential tourist groups, students and focussing also on correcting mutual misperceptions will enable a better flow of information leading to greater interest and transparency. Setting a specific target for trade and investments will also provide a benchmark against which to measure actual progress. Initiating joint strategies for developing cooperative security in Asia based on a rational regional balance of power inside the Asian Regional Forum and outside it in the United Nations and in NAM can be another area of mutual cooperation between India and Vietnam. Democratization of the Security Council and inclusion of India as one of the permanent members, further measures of non-discriminatory trade and investment liberalization and disarmament are the other North-South issues which are of common concern to India and Vietnam.

## Reference

1. (1996-97 MEA Annual Report p. 25).

# 23

# FOREIGN ECONOMIC POLICY

**DANG NGOC**

During the past over 10 years of implementation of the Renovation (Doi Moi), the Vietnamese economy has recorded very important achievements, for 7 continuous years, from 1991 to 1997, the average annual growth rate of GDP was about 8.5%. However, from 1998, the economic growth has slowed down, purchasing capacity and export market have shrunk, foreign investment has decreased because of internal as well as external reasons. The total investment of 1998, in the whole society has increased at 3% as estimated and foreign investment reached 61% in comparison with that of 1997. Vietnamese Government have taken a number of measures to overcome these above mentioned difficulties and challenges.

In this spirit we have worked out main tasks and solutions for the socio-economic development for the next period, as following: focusing on agricultural production and rural economic development; expanding both the domestic and export markets; effectively mobilizing and using all sources of investment and improving and stabilizing the national financial system.

As the result of Renovation and open policy of Vietnam's economy, in recent years, FDI have contributed significant part in the transition of our economic mechanism towards industrialization and modernization. As of beginning of 1998, the Government of Vietnam has issued investment licenses to 2,337 projects with the registered investment capital of over US $ 32 billions except for Viet-So oil and gas project. At present, there are 1,948 projects with the amount of over US $ 13 billions making around 40% of total registered capital that have been completed and under construction and are going into operation.

Reviewing the situation of FDI in the past years with regard to the economic crisis in Far East Asia as well as the investment environment in Vietnam has not been attractive, thus leading to the slowdown of FDI into Vietnam.

1. In order to implement the policy of continued improvement of renovation, development of domestic potentiality, increase of the effectiveness of international cooperations, uniform and long term implementations of the policy to attract external potential sources for investment and development purposes, the Government of Vietnam has provided substantial measures to improve the investment environment to FDI projects, fields and locations where investment is encouraged and to achieve the trust of foreign investor community. These new measures help foreign investors in promptly selecting investment opportunitles in Vietnam. New measures have been adopted by Vietnam government as following:

— To issue a list of sectors where investment will not be licensed and the sectors where investment is conditional;

— To issue a list of sectors where investment is encouraged or especially encouraged, and a list of areas where investment is encouraged.

2. In order to encourage investment projects to produce goods for export, projects using high technology as well as projects in the sectors and areas encouraging investment, we have put forward the following regulations:

— The enterprises selling their products to other enterprises for the latter to directly manufacture products for export will be exempted from import duties in raw materials and be exempted from turnover tax of above mentioned products. This is a new preferential treatment of encouraging enterprises in production of goods for export;

— To permit authorized enterprises and enterprises with authorization to carry out export to buy goods and products in Vietnamese market to process for export or to export;

— To exempt import duties to the construction materials to form fixed assets which are not yet produced in the country and raw materials and materials to manufacture equipment and machinery in technological lines;

— To permit projects included in the list of projects where investment is specially encouraged and investment projects in mountainous and remote regions be exempted from import duties of raw materials used for production for a period of 5 years from the commencement of production and to enjoy preferential profit tax rates for the entire duration of their implementation;

— To permit projects included in the list of areas where investment is encouraged and the list of sectors where investment is specially encouraged, to be exempted from profits tax for a duration of four years from the time when their operations start to earn profits and a reduction of 50% for the four subsequent years.

3. In the field of management of the investment activities and improvement of investment procedures, the following concrete measures have been taken:

— All the bodies of state administration must immediately make the reviews and adjustments to keep procedures very simple, prompt, publicly known on the principle of "one door" and "one focal body", especially with regards to procedure after investment licenses;

— Totally eliminate the mechanism whereby a foreign investment enterprise which has been issued with an investment license has to apply for a business license or practicing license for activities which have been permitted in the investment license. This is a substantial in improving post licensing procedures which will create conditions and bases for enterprises to promptly proceed with their business operations in accordance with the investment licenses;

— To further simplify investment procedures and the issue of investment licenses of the projects which export 80% or more. This measure stipulates only 15 days as needed from the receipt of application forms to register and to consider the issuance of invetment licenses.

The cultural and economic interactions between Vietnam and India have gone back to centuries. The cordial and friendly relations between the two countries have been built on the solid foundations of shared political values and strategic perceptions.

There have been significant advances in economic, trade, cultural, scientific and technological cooperation but those progresses remain far from potential and desire of both sides. In the past few years, there were a number of Indian companies that have shown greater interest in investment in many economic areas in Vietnam. As of now the statistics show that there are six joint ventures and four plants with 100% Indian investment of a total over US$160 millions, ranking India 38th among countries as economies investing in Vietnam. This includes ONGC, the Nagarjuna group, KCP Limited, KEC International Limited, SOL Pharmaceutical Limited, SUNITA, Dhampur Sugars.

The bilateral trade of Vietnam and India in 8 months of this year (1998) is approximately about US$ 92 millions. Vietnam imports different products from India such as transport equipment, machinery equipment for sugar plants, steel and metals, pharmaceuticals, rubber products, oil meals with amount of US$ 86 millions, Our Vietnam exports to India organic chemical, spices, raw silks and wood products with amount of US$ 5.5 millions.

# APPENDIX

# MAIN DATA OF FOREIGN INVESTMENT IN VIETNAM

## Foreign Investments in Vietnam

Due to economic reform policies in general and efforts to encourage foreign investment in particular, Vietnam has achieved initially encouraging results in the field of foreign investment. As of May 1997, just 9 years since the approval of the first Law on Foreign Investment, 2,175 projects with registered capital topping US$ 32.5 billions were licenced, of which 342 projects with registered capital of US$ 2.7 billions had their licences withdrawn and 23 projects with registered capital of US$ 121 millions terminated their operations. Actually disbursed capital was US$ 11.5 billion accounting for 35% of licenced capital. So far over 58 countries and territories have invested in Vietnam and all 61 cities/provinces of Vietnam have had foreign investment projects established. There are currently 150,000 people working in businesses with foreign invested capital.

**Foreign Investment by Country and Territory**

| | *Country & Territory* | *Number of Projects* | *Total Capital (US $ billions)* |
|---|---|---|---|
| 1. | Singapore | 166 | 5.2 |
| 2. | Taiwan | 298 | 4.0 |
| 3. | HongKong | 195 | 3.6 |
| 4. | Japan | 208 | 3.1 |
| 5. | South Korea | 190 | 2.5 |
| 6. | United States | 70 | 1.2 |
| 7. | Thailand | 77 | 1.1 |
| 8. | Malaysia | 56 | 1.1 |

| | | |
|---|---|---|
| 9. British Virgin Islands | 49 | 1.0 |
| 10. France | 86 | 0.8 |
| 11. Switzerland | 18 | 0.7 |
| 2. Australia | 53 | 0.7 |
| 13. Britain | 19 | 0.5 |
| 14. Netherlands | 26 | 0.4 |
| 15. Germany | 18 | 0.4 |
| 16. Sweden | 9 | 0.4 |
| 17. Indonesia | 13 | 0.2 |
| 18. Philippines | 16 | 0.2 |
| 19. Russia | 31 | 0.1 |
| 20. Denmark | 2 | 0.1 |
| 21. China | 43 | 0.1 |
| 22. New Zealand | 8 | 0.1 |
| 23. Canada | 13 | 0.1 |
| 24. Remaining Territories | 146 | 2.1 |
| Total | 1,810 | US $ 29.7 billion |

*Source : MPI*

**Total Foreign Investment by Sector**

| *Sector* | *Number of Projects* | *Investment (US $ billions)* |
|---|---|---|
| General Industry | 1,147 | 14.5 |
| Hotels and Zones | 267 | 7.5 |
| Industrial Zones | 16 | 4.0 |
| Oil and Gas | 23 | 1.2 |
| Transport, Communication and Post | 55 | 1.1 |
| Agricultural and Forestry | 57 | 0.4 |
| Finance and Banking | 19 | 0.3 |
| Export Processing Zones | 60 | 0.2 |
| Services | 85 | 0.1 |
| Housing Development | 34 | 0.1 |
| Fisheries | 20 | 0.1 |
| Others | 27 | 0.2 |
| Total | 1,810 | US $ 29.7 billion |

The volume of foreign investment has increased rapidly over the years, from US$ 366 million in 1988, which was the first year of implementing the Law on Foreign Investment, up to US$ 7 billion in 1995 and US$ 8.6 billion in 1996. During the early years of encouraging foreign investment, capital was mainly concentrated in the fields of oil and gas, hotels, and services. In more recent years, foreign investment has extended to industry, including heavy industry, infrastructure development, construction and operation of export processing zones and industrial zones infrastructure. Many reputable investors and multinational corporations have established investment projects in Vietnam.

The form of investment has also changed. During the early years, the joint venture form accounted for more than 80% of all projects, while 100% (wholly) foreign owned businesses accounted for only 6%. Now 100% foreign owned businesses account for 28%, while joint ventures account for 63.5% of all projects.

The recent "crisis" in Asia has brought new challenges but the long-term opportunities remain.

## Appendix I

### Commodity Composition of India's Exports to Vietnam 1991-92 and 1997-98

| | *Rs. Lakhs* | | *% share in total exports* | |
|---|---|---|---|---|
| | *1991-92* | *1997-98* | *1991-92* | *1997-98* |
| Oil Mills | - | 10666 | - | 23.7 |
| Drugs and pharmaceuticals | 242 | 10112 | 7.6 | 22.4 |
| Machinery and instruments | 402 | 9891 | 12.6 | 21.9 |
| Rubber manufactured products | 30 | 3591 | 0.9 | 8.0 |
| Cotton yarn fab. madeups | 51 | 2133 | 1.6 | 4.7 |
| Inorg./org./agro chemicals | 14 | 1940 | 0.4 | 4.3 |
| Transport equipment | 11 | 952 | 0.3 | 2.1 |
| Manufactures of metals | - | 873 | - | 1.9 |
| Marine products | - | 595 | - | 1.3 |
| Plastic and Linoleum products | 2 | 536 | 0.1 | 1.2 |
| Primary and semi-finished I & S | - | 355 | - | 0.8 |
| Paints / enamels / varnishes | - | 267 | - | 0.6 |
| Residual chemicals | 2 | 229 | 0.1 | 0.5 |
| Project goods | 70 | 205 | 2.2 | 0.5 |
| Electronic goods | 295 | 200 | 9.3 | 0.4 |
| Non-ferrous metals | - | 183 | - | 0.4 |
| Aluminium excl. products | - | 178 | - | 0.4 |
| Cotton raw including waste | 1358 | 156 | 42.7 | 0.4 |

| | | | | |
|---|---|---|---|---|
| Finished leather | - | 134 | - | 0.3 |
| Iron and Steel bar / rods | - | 134 | - | - |
| Glas / glassware / ceramics, etc. | 3 | 115 | - | - |
| Dyes and intermediates | 25 | 98 | - | - |
| Spices | - | 98 | - | - |
| Tobacco unmanufactured | 155 | 96 | - | - |
| Paper / wood products | - | 47 | - | - |
| Other cereals | - | 47 | - | - |
| Processed minerals | - | 45 | - | - |
| Manmade yarn fab. madeups | 378 | 43 | - | - |
| Machine tools | 9 | 40 | - | - |
| Total | 3183 | 45094 | 100.0 | 100.0 |
| **Commodity Group-Wise** | | | | |
| (A) Agricultural and allied products | 1513 | 11682 | 47.5 | 25.9 |
| (B) Ores and minerals | - | 66 | - | 0.2 |
| (C) Manufactured goods (1 to 6) | 1549 | 32386 | 48.7 | 71.8 |
| 1. Leather and leather manufactures | 1 | 147 | - | 0.3 |
| 2. Chemicals and related products | 283 | 12679 | 8.9 | 28.1 |
| 3. Engineering goods | 787 | 12854 | 24.7 | 28.5 |
| 4. Textiles (excluding readymade garments) | 429 | 2190 | 13.5 | 4.9 |
| 5. Readymade garments | 15 | 36 | 0.5 | 0.1 |
| 6. Other manufactured goods | 35 | 4481 | 1.1 | 9.9 |
| (D) Other commodities | 120 | 960 | 3.8 | 2.1 |
| Total (A+B+C+D) | 3183 | 45094 | 100.0 | 100.0 |

## Appendix II

### *Commodity Composition of India's Imports from Vietnam 1991-92 and 1997-98*

| | *Rs. Lakhs* | | *% share in total exports* | |
|---|---|---|---|---|
| | *1991-92* | *1997-98* | *1991-92* | *1997-98* |
| Cashewnuts | 6223 | 828 | 66.0 | 30.3 |
| Sprices | - | 64 | - | 2.4 |
| Silk raw | 111 | 62 | 1.2 | 2.3 |
| Non-ferrous metals | - | 43 | - | 1.6 |
| Organic chemicals | - | 40 | - | 1.5 |
| Natural rubber | - | 35 | - | 1.3 |

| | | | | |
|---|---|---|---|---|
| Wood and wood products | 1722 | 31 | 18.3 | 1.1 |
| Medicinal and pharma. | - | 29 | - | 1.1 |
| Chemical material and products | - | 24 | - | 0.9 |
| Essential oil and cosmetic prepn. | 10 | 24 | 0.1 | 0.9 |
| Textile yarn fabrics and madeup | - | 23 | - | 0.8 |
| Professional inst. | - | 21 | - | 0.8 |
| Non-electrical machinery | - | 19 | - | 0.7 |
| Electronic goods | - | 14 | - | 0.5 |
| Artfcl. resins and plastic matrls. | - | 13 | - | 0.5 |
| Coal and coke and briquettes | - | 2 | - | 0.1 |
| Printed books and newspapers, etc. | 1 | - | - | - |
| Manufactures of metals | - | 1 | - | - |
| Metaliferrous ores and scrap | 35 | 1 | 0.4 | - |
| Paper board and manufactures | - | - | - | - |
| Dyeing tanning and colouring matrls. | 1 | - | - | - |
| Total | 9431 | 2732 | 100.0 | 100.0 |

## Commodity Group-wise

| | | | | |
|---|---|---|---|---|
| Food and related items | 8 | 64 | 0.1 | 2.4 |
| Export related items | 6223 | 891 | 66.0 | 32.6 |
| Capital goods | - | 39 | - | 1.4 |
| Raw materials and intermediates | 412 | 160 | 4.4 | 5.9 |
| Manufactured goods | 1722 | 118 | 18.3 | 4.3 |
| Other commodities | 65 | 1459 | 0.7 | 53.4 |
| Total | 9431 | 2732 | 100.0 | 100.0 |

# Appendix III

## *India-Vietnam Trade* ( $ Million)

| *Year* | *India's Exports to Vietnam* | *India's Imports from Vietnam* | *Total Trade* | *Balance of Trade* |
|---|---|---|---|---|
| 1988-89 | 17.1 | 8.0 | 25.1 | 9.1 |
| 1989-90 | 8.1 | 141.4 | 149.5 | -133.3 |
| 1990-91 | 17.2 | 57.7 | 74.9 | -40.5 |
| 1991-92 | 12.9 | 38.3 | 51.2 | -25.4 |
| 1992-93 | 18.6 | 66.0 | 83.6 | -47.4 |
| 1993-94 | 27.8 | 43.8 | 71.6 | -16.0 |
| 1994-95 | 58.0 | 44.0 | 102.0 | 14.0 |
| 1995-96 | 124.4 | 15.5 | 139.9 | 108.9 |
| 1996-97 | 118.2 | 1.7 | 119.9 | 116.5 |

| | | | | |
|---|---|---|---|---|
| 1997-98 | 121.5 | 7.4 | 128.9 | 114.1 |
| April - June | | | | |
| 1997 | 29.2 | 1.1 | 30.3 | 28.1 |
| 1998 | 30.3 | 1.8 | 32.1 | 28.5 |

## Appendix IV

## List of Offices of Indian Companies in Vietnam

Concept Pharmaceuticals
16A/A 1 Le Hong Phong Ṇoi Dai Street,
District 10, HCMC
Mr. G.N. Tiwari
Country Manager
Tel. 8359387
Fax : 848-8334117

*Source: Embassy of India,* Hanoi

### Other Provinces

1. ONGC Videsh Ltd.
   No. 3 Troung Vinh Ky Street,
   Vung Tau
   Ba Ria Vung Tau Province
   Mr. G.S. Pundeer
   Chief Representative
   Tel. 859869
   Fax. 84-64-853293

2. KEC Campha Ltd.
   No. 2 Tran Phu Road,
   Cam Pha Town
   Quang Ninh Province
   Mr. B.N. Pal
   Managing Director
   Tel. 83-33-863756
   Fax. 84-33-862034

*Source: Embassy of India,* Hanoi

### Other Important Address

1. John Dodsworth
   Senior Resident Representative
   International Monetary Fund
   7, Jorbagh, New Delhi
   110003, India
   Tel. (Off.) 4634223/4
   Tel. (Res.) 3014375
   Mobile : 9810019016
   Fax. 4635231 / 3792739
   E-mail : 592-9348@MCIMAIL.COM

2. Asha Qureshi
   Secretary General
   Intnl. Council for Business Promotion
   J-14, Jangpura Ext.
   New Delhi - 110014
   Phone : 4615172
   Fax : 4691564, 4601462.

3. Mr.
   Ambassador
   Embassy of Vietnam
   17, Kautilya Marg,

Chanakyapuri,
New Delhi - 110021
Phone : 3018059
Fax : 3017714

4. Jitendra Sanghvi
Executive Secretary
Indo-Vietnam Chamber of Commerce
Indian Merchant's Chamber
IMC Marg, Churchgate
Mumbai - 400020
Phone : 2046633
Fax : 91-22-2048508
E-Mail : imcindia @giasbmol.vsnl.net .in
Website:
http: //imc.indiaworld.com

5. Jyoti Kapur
Chairman
Vietrade Group
D-161, Defence Colony
New Delhi - 110024
Phone : 4698326, 4634771
Fax : 4622108
Telex : 031-74055

6. Multilateral Trading Pvt. Ltd.
126 B, Tran Quoe Thao, District, 3, HCMC
Tel. 444388
Fax. 298540
Mr. R. Ravikumar,
Managing Director.

JF Trading
181, Nam Ky Khoi Nghia Street,
District 1, HCMC
Mr. Manish Dane
Resident Manager,
Tel. 8294594, 8231791
Fax. (848) 8294590

G. Doulatram & Sons (HK) Ltd.
No. 2 Thi Sach Street,
District 1, HCMC
Mr. Amit Saxena
General Manager
Tel. 8251002, 8244990
Fax. (848) 8251001

7. Zenaust Imports
165A, Ho Van Hue Street,
Phu Nhuan District, HCMC
Mr. Krishnan R.
Manager
Tel. 848-8452443, 8449328
Fax. 848-8452443

8. Namita Industrial & Trading Concepts Pvt. Ltd.
10 Nguyen Hue Street,
District 1, HCMC
Mr. Shantanu Srivastava
Tel. 8290291, 8230521
Fax. 848-8292451

9. Pritsons S.A.
Cho Lon Business Center - Room No. 14
631 Nguyen Hue Street,
District 1, HCMC
Mr. Ramesh Anand
Chief Resident Executive
Tel. 8574421/422, 8579362/363, 8578054
Fax. 848-8574420

10. Thakral Brothers
81, Dong Khoi Street,
District 1, HCMC
Mr. Raj Ahluwalia
Country Manager (Vietnam)

Tel. 8251497
Fax. 848-8225362

11. Indu Worldwide Trades
Room 107/108, 30 Le Thanh Ton Street,
District 1, HCMC
Mr. Arun V. Bahirwani
Manager
Tel. 8295892 Extn. 107
Fax. 848-8296078

12. Evergreen Global Ltd.
290A, Nam Ky Khoi Nghia Street,
District 1, HCMC
Mr. Amal Vakil
Resident Manager
Tel. 8439502, 8900650
Fax. 848-8436630

13. AUM International
6D2 Phan Ke Binh Street,
District 1, HCMC
Mr. Atul Kumar
Tel. 8299577
Fax. 848-8290919

14. Visna Trading Pvt. Ltd.
No. 2 Phung Khac Khoan Street,
District 1, HCMC
Mr. M.S. Rao
Tel. 8220178
Fax. 848-8220179

15. Sarmon Pvt. Ltd.
29, Nguyen Van Mai Street,
District 3, HCMC
Mr. Rishi Raj
Tel. 8202774, 8202776
Fax. 848-8202778

16. Mega Products Ltd.
6-68 Ba Thang Hai Street,
District 10, HCMC
Mr. Paramjit Singh
Tel. 8658801, 8658538
Fax. 848-8658800

17. Dee Pharma Ltd.
4 Dong Khoi Street,
District 1, HCMC
Mr. R.R. Manohar
Tel. 8230685, 8298875
Fax. 848-8291835

18. Lykalab Ltd.
15, Nguyen Van Dau Street,
District Binh Thanh, HCMC
Mr. Sam Devanand
Tel. 8413310
Fax. 848-8442761

19. Ranbaxy Laboratories Ltd.
Harbour View Tower,
35, Nguyen Hue Street.,
District 1, HCMC
Mr. Arun Nayyar
Country Manager
Tel. 8214774
Fax. 848-8214776

20. Raptakos, Brett & Co. Ltd.
18B/36 Ba Thang Haj Street,
District 10, HCMC
Mr. Ajay Panot
Tel. 8650140
Fax. 848-8625946

21. Unicorp Industries (S) Pvt. Ltd.
285B Dien Bien Phu Street
District 3, HCMC
Mr. Lalit Malik

Tel. 8235712, 8235713
Fax. 848-8291413

22. Torrent Exports Ltd.
FTDC Business Center
30, Le Thanh Ton Street,
District 1, HCMC
Mr. Ujjal De
General Manager
Tel. 8298626, 8295892
Fax. 848-8296078,
8222237

23. Amoli Enterprises
133, Ngo Quyen Street,
District, 1, HCMC
Mr. R.K. Dinkar
Tel/Fax. 848-8562908

24. Swiss Singapore Overseas
Ent. Pvt. Ltd.
115/5A Tran Quoc Thao
Street,
District 3, HCMC
Mr. J.D. Jajoo
Chief Representative
Tel. 8202950

25. Dr. Reddy's Laboratories
Ltd.
75/16-18 Su Van Hanh (Noi
Dai) Street,
Ward 12, District 10, HCMC
Mr. P.A. Narayan
Tel. 8650086
Fax. 846-8642276

26. Cadila Healthcare Pvt. Ltd.
226/5 Le Van Sy Street,
HCMC
Mr. D.M. Singh
Export Promotion Manager
Tel. 8448582

27. Indian Dyestuff Ltd. and
Mangalya Trading and
Investment Ltd.
No. 1, Tran Khanh Du
Street, District 1, HCMC
Mrs. Nguyen Thi Kim
Phoung
Deputy Chief
Tel. 8466100
Fax. 848-8466101

28. Microlabs Ltd.
155-A Su Van Hanh Street,
Dist. 10, HCMC
Mr. Ramani Ravi
Tel. 8625489
Fax. 848-8626140

29. Nagarjuna Inernational
50/19 Truong Son Street,
Tan Binh District
HCMC
Mr. A. Nanda Kumar
Managing Director
Tel. 8448972
Fax. 848-8444965

**Indian Companies in Vietnam**

1. Hanoi Cimmco
International
45B, Ly Thuong Kiet. Hanoi
Tel. (Off.) 8264609,
8254037
Tel. (Res.) 8452157
Telex. (84)411316 Cimmco
VT
Fax. (84) (4) 8269471
Sh. Arvind Johar
Chief Resident Manager

2. Project & Equipments Corporation Ltd. (PEC)
   121-122, B-17, Kimlien, Hanoi
   Tel : 8523475
   Fax : 844-8523914
   Sh. P.K. Jain
   Resident Manager
3. Matcon Exp. Ent. Ltd.
   5 Khu, B3b, Giang Vo, Hanoi.
   Tel. (off) 256558
   Contact : Export Manager
4. Namita Industrial & Trading Concepts Pvt. Ltd.
   Pno Ba Trieu, Hanoi
   Tel. 264724
   Fax. 257317
   Mr. Nguyen Thi Phueag Mai,
   Manager.
5. Metazine (India) Ltd.
   8 Trang Thi Street, Hanoi
   Mr. Rajan Khanna
   Chief of Representative Office
   Tel. 8245852
   Fax. 848-8245851
6. Vietrade
   Binh Minh
   89 Lac Trung Street, Hanoi
   Tel. 84-4-9711189
   Fax. 84-4-9711153
   Mr. Ha Van Tham
   Director

*Source : Embassy of India, Hanoi*

**HO CHI MINH CITY**

1. State Bank of India
   4 Ho Tung Mau Street, District 1, HCMC
   Mr. Anup Banerji
   Representative.
   Tel. 224205
   Fax. 84-4-224202
   Telex. 813109 SBI VT
2. Vietrade
   Binh Minh
   22 Hung Vuong - P 2-Q 10, HCMC
   Tel. 84-8-8356854
   Fax. 84-8-8300351
   Mr. Ha Van Thani
   Director
3. Sungrace Mafatlal
   14B, Thai Van Lung, Q-1., HCMC
   Mr. M.I.Vakil,
   Resident Manager,
   Tel. (Off) 292311
   Tel. (Res.) 292311
   Fax. 225276

# Index